Jan Tschichold and the New Typography

**BARD GRADUATE CENTER
NEW YORK CITY**

**YALE UNIVERSITY PRESS
NEW HAVEN AND LONDON**

Paul Stirton

Jan Tschichold and the New Typography

Graphic Design Between the World Wars

This catalogue is published in conjunction with the exhibition *Jan Tschichold and the New Typography: Graphic Design Between the World Wars* held at Bard Graduate Center Gallery in New York City from February 14–July 7, 2019.

CURATOR OF THE EXHIBITION
Paul Stirton

FOCUS PROJECT TEAM
Director of the Gallery and Executive Editor, Gallery Publications
Nina Stritzler-Levine
Head of Focus Gallery Project
Ivan Gaskell
Acting Head of Focus Gallery Project
Aaron Glass
Chief Curator
Marianne Lamonaca
Associate Curator
Caroline Hannah
Director of Publishing
Daniel Lee
Catalogue Design and Production
Cover and interior designed by Jocelyn Lau with art direction by Kate DeWitt
Director of the Digital Media Lab
Jesse Merandy
Manager of Rights and Reproductions
Alexis Mucha

Published by Bard Graduate Center, NYC in association with Yale University Press
302 Temple Street, P.O. Box 209040
New Haven, CT 06520-9040
47 Bedford Square, London WC1B 3DP
yalebooks.com / yalebooks.co.uk

Back cover: see Fig. 24

ISBN 978-0-300-24395-6
Library of Congress Control Number: 2018958326

10 9 8 7 6 5 4 3 2 1
2022 2021 2020 2019

This book is set in Campton and Mallory.

Printed by SYL Creaciones Gráficas, Barcelona, Spain.

PHOTOGRAPHIC AND TEXT CREDITS
Photographs and texts for primary source materials were taken or supplied by the lending institutions, organizations, or individuals credited in the picture captions and are protected by copyright; many names are not repeated here. Individual photographers are credited below. Permission has been sought for use of all copyrighted illustrations in this volume. In several instances, despite extensive research, it has not been possible to locate the original copyright holder. Copyright owners of these works should contact the Bard Graduate Center, 18 West 86th Street, New York, NY 10024.

© 2018 Albert Renger-Patzsch Archiv / Ann u. Jürgen Wilde, Zülpich / Artists Rights Society (ARS), New York: Fig. 63.
© 2018 Artists Rights Society (ARS), New York: Figs. 4, 12, 13, 33, 37, 43, 47, 48, 75.
© 2018 Artists Rights Society (ARS), New York / ADAGP, Paris: Fig. 82.
© 2018 Artists Rights Society (ARS), New York / c/o Pictoright Amsterdam: Figs. 5, 69.
© 2018 Artists Rights Society (ARS), New York / VG Bild-Kunst, Bonn: Figs. 3, 14, 15, 30, 46, 49–52, 61, 62, 64, 66, 70, 71, 73, 74, 78–81.
© 2018 Estate of Alexander Rodchenko / RAO, Moscow / VAGA at ARS, NY: Figs. 34, 39.
© 2018 Estate of László Moholy-Nagy / Artists Rights Society (ARS), New York: Figs. 14, 16, 45.
Digital Image © The Museum of Modern Art/ Licensed by SCALA / Art Resource, NY: Figs. 3, 4, 10, 12–14, 18, 21, 23, 24, 33, 34, 36, 39, 41, 43, 52, 55–60, 62, 65, 66, 70, 71, 73–81, 86, 93.
Imaging Department © President and Fellows of Harvard College: Figs. 15, 30.
Bruce White: Figs. 1, 28, 29.

FOR ISLA, RORY, AND JAMIE

CONTENTS

ix   Director's Foreword

xii   Foreword

xvi   Acknowledgments

1   Introduction: Jan Tschichold and the "Museum" of Graphic Design

17   Chapter 1: Jan Tschichold: Typographer, Designer, Theorist

87   Chapter 2: The New Typography, 1923–33: Theory and Practice

163   Chapter 3: The Final Years: The Fall and Rise of the New Typography

189   Primary Texts on the New Typography

    1. Filippo Tommaso Marinetti, "Rivoluzione tipografica"

    2. El Lissitzky, "Topographie der Typographie"

    3. László Moholy-Nagy, "Die neue Typographie"

    4. El Lissitzky, "Typographische Tatsachen"

    5. László Moholy-Nagy, "Typophoto"

    6. Kurt Schwitters, "Thesen über Typographie"

    7. Iwan Tschichold, "Elementare Typographie"

    8. Willi Baumeister, "Neue Typographie"

    9. Walter Dexel, "Was ist neue Typographie?"

   10. Franz Roh, "Warum 4 Alphabete"

   11. "Normalisierung der Papierformate"

   12. Max Burchartz, "Gestaltung der Reklame"

   13. Johannes Molzahn, Letterhead statement

   14. Lajos Kassák, "Reklám és modern tipográfia"

   15. Jan Tschichold, "Was ist und was will die neue Typografie?"

   16. Władysław Strzemiński, "Druk funkcjonalny"

233   A Note on the Jan Tschichold Collection in the Museum of Modern Art

236   Exhibition Checklist

246   Bibliography

250   Index

Director's Foreword

For decades, art historians and others have dismissed design as being beyond serious consideration as an intellectual and expressive activity because of its association with practical affairs. In Immanuel Kant's terms, design is a matter of labor, not the free play of the faculties. The German graphic and typographic designer Jan Tschichold, the subject of this book and the exhibition that it accompanies, worked in a manner that fully acknowledged—even celebrated—design as labor in the Kantian sense, publishing his ideas in the context of practical education and training for the development of craft skills rather than as matters of intellect and emotion alone.

Paul Stirton makes this aspect of Tschichold's achievement admirably explicit in *Jan Tschichold and the New Typography*, his masterly examination of Tschichold's endeavors. The author came to Bard Graduate Center from Scotland, where he was senior lecturer in the history of art at the University of Glasgow. Central Europe in the first half of the twentieth century is one of his particular areas of exploration, and he has published significant studies on design, notably in Hungary. He is a scholar of considerable range, which makes him the ideal editor of our own journal, *West 86th*.

Paul Stirton has been intrigued by a little-studied cache of material that Jan Tschichold gathered in the course of his correspondence and visits with like-minded fellow graphic designers while still a young man in the 1920s. He used this material for the composition of his study of typographical innovation, *Die neue Typographie* (1928). Like the author, Tschichold was a tireless networker who brought out the best in his colleagues. His collection was acquired by the architect Philip Johnson, who donated it to the Museum of Modern Art. It includes work by designers whom Tschichold promoted, such as Willi Baumeister, Herbert Bayer, Walter Dexel, Gustav Klutsis, El Lissitsky, Johannes Molzahn, Aleksandr Rodchenko, Zdeněk Rossmann, Kurt Schwitters, and Piet Zwart.

The familiarity of some of these names to students of twentieth-century art history but not others suggests the divide between the study of fine art and the relative neglect of design. Some of those celebrated as fine artists—Kurt Schwitters, for instance—had equally important careers as designers that art historians all but ignore. *Jan Tschichold and the New Typography* redresses the balance and provides a clearer idea of the role of design in graphic production than has hitherto been available. Without typefaces, printed words—and all that they convey—are simply not available. Tschichold and his colleagues held that typography was not a transparent medium; rather, it inevitably directed the reader-cum-viewer, shaping how a text is read, and—as Stirton points out, quoting Tschichold, how it "ought to be read." The resulting texts not only reflect the modern world, as visual components of that modern world, they help constitute its character. Thus, there is a moral urgency to making appropriate and fitting typographic design choices, because those choices have consequences for society far beyond the aesthetic realm.

Like others who have realized Focus projects before him, Stirton tested and elaborated his ideas in graduate seminars in the spring and fall semesters of 2018. The students contributed substantively to the project. Participants include Taryn Clary, Elizabeth Koehn, Laura Streller, and Danielle Weindling.

Director's Foreword

We are especially grateful to the lenders to this exhibition: the Museum of Modern Art, Cornelia Tschichold, Jerry Kelly, and an anonymous collector. We also include items from the Bard Graduate Center Library, so I would like to thank its director, Heather Topcik, and her colleagues.

The Focus Project is a collaboration between the Gallery and the Degree Programs and Research Institute of Bard Graduate Center. The commitment of both the dean, Peter N. Miller, and the director of the Gallery, Nina Stritzler-Levine, enabled the project to proceed smoothly. Ivan Gaskell, professor and head of the Focus Project, and Aaron Glass, associate professor and acting head of the Focus Project, guided the exhibition throughout.

Staff members of the Degree Programs and Research Institute and the Gallery collaborated to realize Stirton's ideas: Kate Dewitt, art director; Eric Edler, Gallery registrar; Caroline Hannah, associate curator; Marianne Lamonaca, associate Gallery director and chief curator; Daniel Lee, director of publishing; Jesse Merandy, director of the Digital Media Lab; and Alexis Mucha, manager of rights and reproductions. Ciné Ostrow created a sensitive display for the exhibition. Stirton also benefited from the help of his student assistants, Jaime Ding and Colleen Terrell. This publication could not have been produced without the care that our copyeditor, Carolyn Brown, and proofreader, Christine Gever, brought to their tasks. Many thanks also go to Mark Eastment, editorial director of arts and architecture at Yale University Press in London. I would like to thank those who have made this undertaking possible, including other members of the faculty and staff of Bard Graduate Center who contribute so much to the institution, thereby allowing us to undertake an ambitious project such as *Jan Tschichold and the New Typography*.

SUSAN WEBER
Director and Founder
Iris Horowitz Professor in
the History of the Decorative Arts
Bard Graduate Center

Foreword

The emergence of graphic design as a profession in the twentieth century followed radical developments in printing technology in the later nineteenth century. These advances had allowed the incorporation of text with images derived from photographs in a single printing matrix. For the first time, typography and photographic images could complement one another without requiring two successive processes.

Such technical innovation took place in circumstances of fast-moving social change. Prominent among them were the development of capital-intensive industry on an unprecedented scale and the twin cataclysms of a world war and a revolution in Russia. Paul Stirton carefully places Jan Tschichold and his work—most significantly his book *Die neue Typographie* (1928)—in this milieu. Tschichold was born in Leipzig and named Johannes. He changed his name to "Iwan," or Ivan, to register his socialist political sympathies, then changed it again to Jan, the Germanic though plebeian version of his original given name. These changes reflect the upheavals of the period. The sheer craziness of the 1910s and 1920s meshed well with the youthfulness of those who played creative roles in Tschichold's world. In the year in which he published *Die neue Typographie*, Tschichold turned twenty-six. His closest associates on whose work he drew (and who are represented in the Focus Project exhibition) were in their thirties and early forties.

The year 1928 saw another major change in typography. In November, five years after the proclamation of the founding of the republic on the ruins of the Ottoman Empire, Turkey adopted the Latin alphabet in place of the Arabic script that had been in use under the Ottomans for centuries. This mandate was a vital aspect of Turkish modernization and secularization, promoted by Mustafa Kemal Atatürk, the first president of the Turkish republic. Choice of script mattered in the modern world, not simply instrumentally for the purposes of communication and government, but as a powerful symbol of identity and cultural alignment.

Turkey's resolve had been encouraged by the example of language reform in the Soviet Union, where in 1926 the Turkic-majority republics had adopted the Latin script. Indeed, an early Bolshevik aim was to promote Latin script not only in place of Arabic and other alphabets in use throughout the Russian Empire and subsequently the Soviet Union, but also of Cyrillic, in which Russian and Ukrainian were written. The Bolsheviks sought thereby to deepen the break with czarism, promote socialist revolution internationally, and isolate Muslims within the Soviet Union from their coreligionists elsewhere. In conformity with the application of Joseph Stalin and Nikolai Bukharin's "socialism in one country" doctrine and the increasingly inward turn of Soviet policy, Stalin ordered a halt to the development of a plan to change from Cyrillic to Latin script for the Russian language in 1930. By the late 1930s, those languages of the many Soviet minorities that had adopted the Latin alphabet in place of Arabic script were all forced to relinquish it in favor of Cyrillic. The alphabet in one chosen form—in this instance, Cyrillic—is an instrument of power.

Letterforms vary not only among entire alphabets, such as Latin, Arabic, and Cyrillic, but among calligraphic conventions or typefaces employed with any single given script. German has always been written in the Latin alphabet, but the letterforms of various alphabets vary considerably. In 1928, when Tschichold published *Die neue Typographie*, long-running disputes concerning the appropriate letterform for the German language continued unabated. The principal contestants in the printing of German were the ornate black-letter script called Fraktur and the Latin script known as Antiqua, derived from the capital letters of Roman inscriptions in combination with Carolingian letterforms. During the nineteenth century, Fraktur became associated with solidly Germanic nationalist values, and its supporters denigrated "international" Antiqua forms. An attempt in the Reichstag to replace Fraktur with Antiqua as the official typeface of the empire was defeated in 1911. The tension continued after World War I, and these are the disputatious circumstances in which Jan Tschichold introduced his ideas promoting a radically simplified, sanserif typeface that resembles neither Fraktur nor Antiqua, as though proclaiming "a plague on both your houses."

The young Tschichold was not alone in promoting a new typography. The German type designer Jakob Erbar (1878–1935) had reportedly sketched a design for a geometric sanserif font before World War I, but the war had prevented its development. The Ludwig & Mayer typefoundry released his definitive design as Erbar in 1926. Other designs in the same mode followed, most prominently Futura by Paul Renner, which the Bauer typefoundry released in 1927. Its name is an expression of the idealism associated with all these sanserif forms: novelty and an orientation toward the future rather than the past. Politically, they signaled an alignment with the left, though far from exclusively, as is attested by typographic designs for a wide range of commercial companies seeking to establish a coherent corporate identity in purely visual terms and by their use in advertising as an at times idealistic endeavor.

Such geometric sanserif typographic forms were rejected under Nazi rule. Tschichold was swiftly arrested after the Nazi rise to power in 1933 but was able to leave for Switzerland within five months. Although Adolf Hitler disliked Fraktur, its use continued for a time because of its nationalistic associations. It was not until 1941 that the use of Fraktur and other black-letter typefaces was forbidden.

Given the unavoidable political ramifications of typefaces, readers might feel a sense of relief that the sanserif forms championed by Jan Tschichold, so thoroughly and clearly explored by Paul Stirton in this book and the exhibition it accompanies, have prevailed, whereas both Fraktur and Antiqua have been consigned in the German-speaking lands to occasional use in product promotion and signage when designers seek to evoke nothing more sinister than quaintness or nostalgia. For now, at least, Jan Tschichold's youthful faith in the "Die neue Typographie" seems justified.

IVAN GASKELL
Professor of Cultural History
and Museum Studies
Head of the Focus Project
Bard Graduate Center

Acknowledgments

This book grew out of a class I taught at Bard Graduate Center. It is a pleasure to acknowledge the stimulating atmosphere created there by colleagues and students. It was not long after I arrived in New York that Juliet Kinchin, curator of modern design in the Museum of Modern Art, drew my attention to the Jan Tschichold collection in the Architecture and Design Department. She has been a constant source of advice and support when investigating the collection and in thinking through the practicalities of making an exhibition out of this trove of modernist graphic design. Other staff in "A&D" have been similarly supportive, and I should like to mention Paul Galloway, Erika Mosier, Pamela Popeson, and Martino Stierli, all of whom helped in the realization of the exhibition.

In 2017, I was granted a library fellowship at the Getty Research Institute in Los Angeles that allowed me to study the extensive correspondence between Jan Tschichold and many of the designers mentioned in this book. I am grateful to The Getty for this opportunity to immerse myself in the design world of Weimar Germany.

Bard Graduate Center is a special place largely due to the collegial atmosphere and the excellent support staff. This project could not have been completed without the assistance of the exhibition department, particularly Nina Stritzler-Levine, Marianne Lamonaca, Caroline Hannah, and Alexis Mucha; the library staff, especially Janis Ekdahl, Chantal Sulkow, and Mike Satalof; Jesse Merandy of the Digital Media Lab; and the design department of Kate DeWitt and Jocelyn Lau. I am also grateful to the dean, Peter Miller, who initiated the Focus Project, and to Ivan Gaskell and Aaron Glass, who oversaw the project. My student assistants, Jaime Ding, Colleen Terrell, and Jessica Boven, helped me overcome many practical problems. I can hardly express the extent of my gratitude to Daniel Lee, head of academic publications at BGC and my colleague on *West 86th*, who has steered this book from its inception and maintained a positive and efficient outlook throughout. Special thanks also go to Ciné Ostrow, who designed the exhibition.

This is my first foray into German modernism, so I am indebted to many people who know the material much better than myself. After the late Ruari McLean, the scholars who have made the most substantial contribution to our knowledge of Jan Tschichold are Robin Kinross and Christopher Burke. I am grateful for their support, especially with regard to the translations in the latter stages of this project. Annika Fisher has been the most helpful and reliable advisor on all translation matters, and my copyeditor, Carolyn Brown, has not only tidied up the prose but saved me from many pitfalls.

Over the years, I have benefited from the work of many historians who have informed my approach to the history of graphic design. In this context, therefore, I would like to acknowledge the scholarship and friendship of Jeremy Aynsley, David Crowley, Pat Kirkham, and Jonathan Woodham. It goes without saying that the views expressed below, and any mistakes, are my own.

PAUL STIRTON
Associate Professor
Bard Graduate Center

Editor in Chief
West 86th: A Journal of Decorative Arts, Design History, and Material Culture

GECOMBINEERDE STERKSTROOM-TELEFOONKABEL

60

Introduction

Jan Tschichold and the "Museum" of Graphic Design

Jan Tschichold, the prolific designer, writer, and theorist, was an influential figure in the development of modernist design aesthetics, equivalent in many respects to such luminaries as Le Corbusier or Marcel Breuer. Even so, he is hardly known outside his own field of typography and graphic design. This is understandable given the prestige that architecture and product design enjoy in the popular press and in histories of modern design and culture. And yet the work of Le Corbusier and Breuer was actually used by only a narrow sector of the population. Whether they could afford to or not, few people in the 1920s chose to live in modernist homes or furnish their apartments in a severely modern style. Such tastes may have been all right in magazines or showrooms, but it was too much to ask even the educated bourgeoisie to change their way of life, the patterns of their social interaction, and the comforts they had become used to. Tschichold, however, stood at the forefront of a revolution in visual culture that penetrated every sector of society and carried the ideals of modern design to the most everyday items of printed matter, from billboard advertisements to business cards, book jackets to invoices—in fact, everything that could be printed and that enables the vast network of business and communication in a modern urban society. If modernist design gained any degree of widespread acceptance

1

at the time, it was probably in the visual world of paper transactions, where design features such as asymmetry, contrast, photographic reproduction, and abstract layout became familiar to everyone who could read—and even some who could not.

Tschichold's most important book, *Die neue Typographie,* was published in Berlin in 1928, whereupon it became a manual for practicing graphic designers in Central Europe, offering guidelines on composition, layout, paper size, typefaces, and the integration of photography with text[1] [Fig. 1]. Unlike most of his contemporaries at the forefront of modernist aesthetics, Tschichold had trained as a calligrapher and typesetter in Leipzig, the center of the German printing and publishing industry, so he was well placed to speak directly to the printers, compositors, designers, and apprentices who were the foot soldiers of the trade. Alongside these practical considerations, however, Tschichold

1

provided a rationale for modern graphic design, tracing its origins to avant-garde art, in particular to international Constructivism—a movement in which he felt that typography and graphic design could play a role equal to that of painting, sculpture, or architecture as an agent of social change. To declare his political and artistic sympathies, in late 1923 he changed his name from Johannes to Iwan (or Ivan), thus aligning his views with his contemporaries in the Soviet avant-garde, some of whom he would come to know personally. It was a clear statement of his view that design was bound up with the birth of a new age, and that the forms and institutions of society were in need of radical reform. He was not alone in this. The Russian Revolution of 1917 had inspired a generation of artists and intellectuals in Central Europe to the extent that it had almost become the norm to look expectantly at the new society developing in the Soviet Union and to follow the new art forms being created there.

Although *The New Typography* became a standard text on the subject, and its author the focus of some hostility from conservative critics, Tschichold was not the originator of many of the ideas presented in his book. In 1925 he published a collection of texts acknowledging the sources of his ideas in earlier art movements, especially those in the Netherlands and Soviet Russia. By 1928, the term "the New Typography" was almost a catch phrase in Germany, similar to "the New Objectivity" and other movements that aimed to transform modern society and culture.[2] In fact, many of the leading artist-designers of Central Europe, notably El Lissitzky, László Moholy-Nagy, and Kurt Schwitters, had already entered into the debate about graphic design and modern life. Tschichold's role was to synthesize the various strands of the discourse and to present them in a manner that was accessible and practical to the working designer. Nevertheless, Tschichold's publications served to elevate him to a position of authority in print and design circles. In the years between 1925 and 1933 he was frequently called on to write further thoughts on design and to contribute to exhibitions, journals, and colloquia [Fig. 2]. In 1927, for example, he was one of the founding members of Der Ring neue Werbegestalter (The Ring of New Advertising Designers), an informal group assembled by Kurt Schwitters, and two years later, in 1929, he was on the selection committee for the landmark exhibition *Film und Foto*. These activities brought him into direct contact with a range of designers across the continent whose work he had encountered in books or exhibitions, or whose views he had heard about. Through meetings and correspondence, he was able to build up a network of artist-designers who shared the same

2

2 Kurt Schwitters. Jan Tschichold, ca. 1928.

values—figures such as Herbert Bayer, Max Burchartz, Lajos Kassák, Karel Teige, and Piet Zwart. In a relatively short space of time, Tschichold became the focal point or hub of an international discourse, channeling and synthesizing the debate on design and society that was still unformed and somewhat fragmented.

During this time, he was assembling a substantial collection of contemporary graphic design, not for any financial gain but to provide a repertoire of examples with which to chart the development of new ideas and illustrate his writings. Time and again one finds Tschichold writing to designers whom he admires, offering to exchange examples of work or soliciting pieces he had seen illustrated in magazines, often asking for two copies of certain items in the knowledge that one might be damaged or destroyed when prepared for reproduction in a book or article.[3] This collection was an unparalleled repository of modern graphic design at a time when the designers themselves were often unaware of the shared interests of colleagues in other countries and cities. Tschichold's active collecting allowed him to refine his own work and to clarify his theories on the ways in which graphic design could meet the challenges of modern life. In fact, Tschichold later referred to his collection as "my museum," and that is precisely what it became—a museum of modern graphic design.[4] Although many items were anonymous and, to other people, almost ephemeral—trade catalogues, advertisements, magazine covers, headed notepaper, and the like—this merely served to confirm that the revolution was making headway across a wide front. While much work was being done by leading figures of the modern movement, a great deal of innovative design was being produced in print workshops, classrooms, and studios by little-known and often anonymous designer-printers.

The bulk of Tschichold's collection came from those designers with whom he had struck up a friendship and a correspondence. Moving outward from his initial circle in Germany, soon he was in contact with "like-minded people" in Austria, Czechoslovakia, Hungary, and Poland, as well as with key figures he had identified in the Netherlands and Soviet Union, the two great centers of Constructivist art.[5] The list of his correspondents reads like a roll call of the leading modernists across Central and Eastern Europe, including Ladislav Sutnar, Lajos Kassák, Gustav Klutsis, Aleksandr Rodchenko, Władysław Strzemiński, and Karel Teige. Three figures were particularly close to Tschichold, and he was able to strike up a personal friendship with them based on shared respect for one another's work. They were El Lissitzky, László Moholy-Nagy, and the Dutch designer and critic Piet Zwart, each of whom made a major contribution to the development of modern design.

Moholy-Nagy seems to have coined the term "Die neue Typographie" as the title of a short essay in the catalogue to the Bauhaus exhibition in 1923 (Primary Text, no. 3). Tschichold visited Weimar to see the exhibition and may have met Moholy-Nagy then. In any case, the Hungarian's views inspired Tschichold's mission to address both the practical issues of print technology and the grander ambitions of confronting new ways of seeing and interpreting information. Tschichold was never as profound nor as wide ranging in outlook as Moholy-Nagy, who always maintained an essentially experimental and exploratory attitude toward all media and art forms. By contrast, Tschichold was an interpreter of the diverse theories that were in circulation and someone who could cast this material into a form that would be of practical use to the mainstream designer and printer. An added feature of their relationship was that their wives, Edith Tschichold and Lucia Moholy, were highly educated writers who, in many respects, were full collaborators in the development and expression of the theories that underpinned the new vision [Fig. 3]. The same was true of El Lissitzky and Sophie Küppers, the latter being a curator in the Kestner Gesellschaft in Hanover when El Lissitzky first met her. These three women undertook much of the writing and editing of the texts that appeared under the names of their partners throughout the 1920s, and this created a richer collaborative environment involving all six in the larger project.[6]

3

Tschichold met Lissitzky at some point in 1925, when the Russian was based in Germany and Switzerland, partly to advance the interests of the State Publishing House in Moscow but also to receive treatment for tuberculosis, which he had developed in 1923.[7] Jan and Edith Tschichold entered into a lively and affectionate correspondence with El Lissitzky and his partner, Sophie Lissitzky-Küppers, sharing stories and greetings, as well as reports on the progress of their respective work. Tschichold had also seen Lissitzky's early text "The Topography of Typography" (Primary Text, no. 2), published in Kurt Schwitters's journal *Merz* in July 1923.[8] But it was probably the Russian's supreme confidence with the forms and media of modern art and design, along with his being a direct conduit to the Soviet avant-garde, that inspired the young German to follow his lead. Lissitzky had begun his career designing books in Yiddish for the Jewish community in Moscow around the time of the Revolution of 1917, but he left this behind when he first became acquainted with the work of Kazimir Malevich and the Suprematist circle at Vitebsk in 1919. Although committed to the utopian and transcendental ideals of this radical group, who adopted the name UNOVIS (Followers of the New Art), Lissitzky's background in book publishing enabled him to play a key role in the application of Suprematist and Constructivist principles to the more popular medium of print. In 1919 he designed the famous abstract propaganda poster "Beat the Whites with the Red Wedge," and the following year he devised *About Two Squares*, a children's book published in Germany in 1922, a copy of which had pride of place in Tschichold's collection[9] [Fig. 4].

The Dutch designer Piet Zwart was someone whose work Tschichold admired when he first came across it in 1925. An architect, furniture and clothes designer, historian, and critic, Zwart appears to have been entirely self-taught in graphic design, yet he displayed a precocious skill in handling text, layout, and photographic illustration. His principal client at this time was the Dutch engineering firm Nederlandsche Kabelfabriek (NKF), the commissioning agent having been a personal acquaintance he met through the architect Hendrik Petrus Berlage. The catalogue designs Zwart undertook for NKF struck an immediate chord with Tschichold, and he wrote to the Dutchman requesting copies to use in his forthcoming publications [Fig. 5]. Thus began a correspondence that continued for many years and that allowed Tschichold to illustrate many of the principles of the New Typography using examples drawn from Zwart's publications. When Kurt Schwitters invited Tschichold to join the Ring neue Werbegestalter, a group of artist-designers that Schwitters was forming in 1927, Moholy-Nagy, Lissitzky, and Zwart were among the names Tschichold put forward as candidates for membership.[10]

4 El Lissitzky.
Pro dva kvadrata
(About Two Squares),
1920. Printed by E.
Haberland, Leipzig,
Germany. Published
by Skythen, Berlin,
1922. Letterpress.
The Museum of
Modern Art. Jan
Tschichold Collec-
tion, Gift of Philip
Johnson. 562.1977.
Cat. 8.

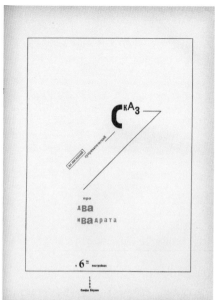

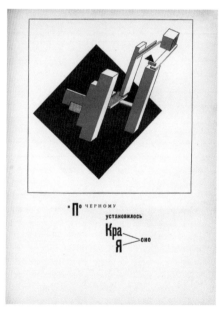

4

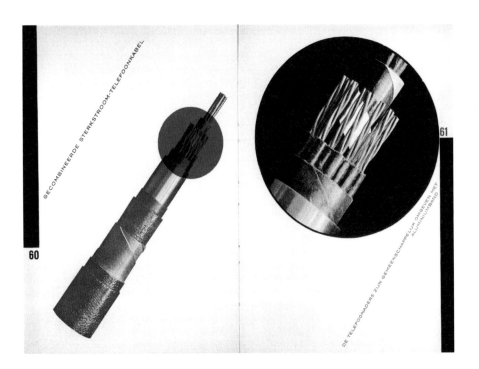

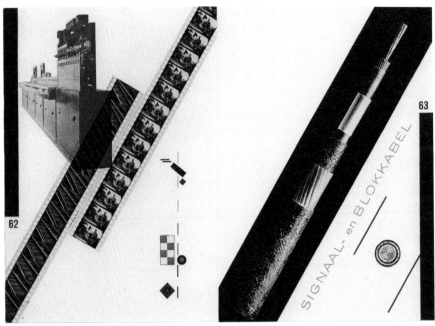

5

Introduction

Kurt Schwitters was another friend and correspondent of Tschichold's, and although they did not always see eye to eye on typographic matters, they remained on good terms until Schwitters's death in England in 1948. Tschichold recognized the role that Futurism and Dada had played in liberating typography from the conventions of traditional book design. In fact, he attributed the fundamental break with traditional typography to these movements.[11] But Tschichold was keen to establish a new order in typographic design rather than remain within the disruptive and absurdist strategies of Dada's "anti-art." Schwitters took typography and print seriously and practiced as a graphic designer for many years, but his work was only partly in step with the New Typography. Nevertheless, he played a key role in organizing and promoting an awareness of modern graphic design through the short-lived Ring. Tschichold designed the phonetic score of Schwitters's sound poem "Ursonate" (primordial sonata), published as a special issue of *Merz* (no. 24) in 1932, and the Tschicholds remained in close contact with Schwitters throughout the war.[12]

Tschichold's collection grew steadily throughout the 1920s and 1930s, serving as a reservoir of examples for his teaching and writing. The collection was particularly useful in the years after his two major publications: "elementare typographie" (1925), a special issue, or *Sonderheft*, of the printing trade journal *Typographische Mitteilungen*, and *Die neue Typographie* (1928), a manual for modern designers. During these years he was teaching typography and calligraphy at the Graphische Berufsschule, a trade school in Munich, and at the Meisterschule für Deutschlands Buchdrucker (Master College for German Book Production), one of the most prestigious higher state colleges, while also assuming the mantle of interpreter and propagandist for the new movement in graphic design. Through his lectures, exhibitions, and publications, Tschichold became one of the primary figures of the New Typography, and his collection was its archive and source material. He expressed the values of the younger generation in March 1933, when he wrote: "We are not concerned with the new for its own sake, rather with what is right, and good. The struggle is not directed against everything old, but against all that is unusable and bad, and not least against the falsely new!"[13] As he was writing these lines, however, Germany was on the threshold of a totalitarian revolution. Shortly after the March 1933 election, the Nazi Party assumed absolute power. As a left-leaning polemicist, a champion of modernist design with a sympathy for Soviet art and values, Tschichold was in danger from the outset. Before the end of the month, he had been arrested and spent several weeks in prison. Released under a general amnesty, in July he and Edith and their young son Peter fled to Switzerland, where he continued to practice as a typographer and graphic designer. The heroic days of the New Typography were coming to an end—in Germany, at least, and increasingly in the Soviet Union as well. Innovative work continued in the Netherlands, Switzerland, Czechoslovakia, and Poland throughout the 1930s, but Tschichold was developing doubts about the ability of the movement to represent the aesthetic or political ideals that he had initially upheld. By 1937 he began to question many of the principles that he had championed in his classic texts, "elementare typographie" and *The New Typography*. With little work to occupy him and considerable financial hardship, he began to dispose of his collection through sales to dealers and museums.

In the postwar period, Tschichold came back into international prominence, but this was mostly for his work at Penguin Books in London, not for a reassertion of militant modernism. While in Switzerland, he had returned to the more conventional forms of traditional book design, reaffirming the use of historic typefaces, symmetrical layout, and careful presswork. In March 1947 Allen Lane appointed him to direct the overall design policy and corporate identity of the world's largest paperback publisher. Tschichold established the Penguin Composition Rules, upholding the classic design reform principles of orderliness, clarity, and uniformity across a vast range of titles. Tschichold did not design the basic Penguin identity—the color schemes and cover designs had been set by Edward Young in the 1930s—but he simplified the designs and established the underlying format or template for each book in their various series to ensure high standards of printing and production.[14] When brought to Penguin, one of the first decisions he made was to introduce the Venetian Renaissance typefaces of Bembo and Aldus to the book texts. This is a far cry from the radical stance of the 1920s, when sanserif was to be the face of the future. Ironically, Tschichold would be criticized by Max Bill, the modernist designer and Bauhaus alumnus, for betraying the movement that he had once represented, thus ensuring that the great debates of the 1920s would be carried into the second half of the twentieth century.[15]

The New Typography and the great modernist project in graphic design was not invented by Jan Tschichold; he did not even coin the term. But he was the chief interpreter of the movement and has come to be regarded as its principal exponent. This role at the center of the movement is slightly misleading, however. In his various writings, Tschichold tried to indicate the range and diversity within the New Typography, as well as giving names to the many designers who produced innovative work within the broader ideology. As he wrote in 1928, it was principally Willi Baumeister, Walter Dexel, Johannes Molzahn, and a few others who had "made the New Typography a reality."[16] Many of these artist-designers also contributed to the theoretical debates that surrounded the movement, selections from which are assembled in the Primary Texts at the end of the volume. By contrast, it is also apparent that the Bauhaus played a relatively modest, not to say marginal, role in the story. Moholy-Nagy may have coined the term "New Typography," and Herbert Bayer became one of its leading exponents, but graphic design was always a minor activity in both the Weimar and Dessau incarnations of the college. In fact, many of the true innovators were resentful of the claims made by Bauhaus masters and alumni in a field where their contribution was modest at best.[17] It is the aim

of this book to look again at the decade 1923–33 and trace the contributions of these designers along with the better-known figures,
such as El Lissitzky and Kurt Schwitters. The first blast may have been
Moholy-Nagy's essay in the Bauhaus catalogue of 1923, but there were
already several other artist-designers experimenting with the same
ideas and trying to work out new principles for graphic design. *Jan
Tschichold and the New Typography* and the exhibition that accompanies it will attempt to shed some light on this broad movement in
Germany and Central Europe in the 1920s, one that set out to revolutionize the way we communicate through print.

1 Jan Tschichold, *Die neue Typographie* (Berlin:
Verlag des Bildungsverbandes der deutschen
Buchdrucker, 1928). Republished as *The New
Typography*, trans. Ruari McLean with an introduction by Robin Kinross (Berkeley: University
of California Press, 1995). All quotations and
page references to the book are taken from the
1995 English edition. Unless otherwise indicated,
material quoted from other primary sources has
been translated by the author.

2 "Neue Sachlichkeit" (New Objectivity) was
a cultural and artistic movement that opposed
the dominant expressionism with an emphasis
on realism and objectivity. Taking its name from
an exhibition at Mannheim in 1923, the curator,
Gustav Hartlaub, described the movement as
"new realism bearing a socialist flavor." The leading artists were Otto Dix and Georg Grosz, but
the values also engaged writers such as Bertolt
Brecht and intellectuals such as Georg Lukács
and Siegfried Kracauer.

3 On January 19, 1925, for example, Tschichold
wrote to El Lissitzky requesting a copy of *Dlia
golosa* (For the Voice). El Lissitzky sent one by
return along with *Pro dva kvadrata* (About Two

Squares). Jan and Edith Tschichold Papers,
Getty Research Institute, Special Collections,
acc. no. 930030, hereafter referred to as the
"Tschichold Papers." The same collection includes
letters from Tschichold to Willi Baumeister,
Max Burchartz, Władysław Strzemiński, Karel
Teige, and Piet Zwart, among others, asking for
examples of their work, indicating how assiduous
Tschichold was in gathering material.

4 In a letter to Friedrich Vordemberge-
Gildewert, May 23, 1933, Tschichold refers to
the collection as his "private museum," which he
hoped might be preserved for history. Tschichold
Papers.

5 Tschichold to Piet Zwart, November 30, 1927,
Tschichold Papers.

6 In 1982, Edith Tschichold wrote to Lucia: "It's
about time your important contribution to the
history of photography was finally shown, and
that for once it was said that you edited all of
Moholy's books and articles, and rewrote them in
proper German. When one heard Moholy speak,
it was of course somehow very charming, but
speech and the written word are two different
things indeed." Quoted in Meghan Forbes, "'What

Could I Lose': The Fate of Lucia Moholy," *Michigan Quarterly Review* 55, no. 1 (Winter 2016): 28.

7 El Lissitzky studied architecture and engineering at the Technische Hochschule in Darmstadt before the First World War. In 1921 he returned to Germany and was based there until 1925, when he took up a position in the Moscow Vkhutemas, the Russian state art and technical school. He was able to make occasional trips back to the West in connection with exhibitions.

8 El Lissitzky, "Topographie der Typographie," *Merz* no. 4 (July 1923): 47.

9 On the history of *About Two Squares*, see El Lissitzky, *About Two Squares: In Six Constructions; A Suprematist Tale* (Cambridge, MA: MIT Press, 1991). The visual character of the design is emphasized in the text. At one point, Lissitzky writes, "Do not read. Take paper, columns, blocks. Fold, color, build."

10 Kees Broos, "Das kurze, aber heftige Leben des Rings 'neue Werbergestalter,'" in *Typographie kann unter Umständen Kunst sein: Ring "neue werbegestalter"; Die Amsterdamer Ausstellung 1931*, ed. Volker Rattemeyer and Dietrich Helms (Wiesbaden: Museum Wiesbaden, 1990), 8–9.

11 "In France Guillaume Apollinaire with his *Calligrammes*, in Italy Marinetti with *Les mots en liberté futuristes* (1919), in Germany the Dadaists all gave impulse to the new development of typography.... In any event, the pamphlets and writings of the Dadaists (which date from the war years) are the earliest documents of New Typography in Germany." Jan Tschichold, "Was ist und was will die neue Typographie?," in *Eine Stunde Druckgestaltung: Grundbegriffe der Neuen Typografie in Bildbeispielen für Setzer, Werbefachleute, Drucksachenverbraucher und Bibliofilen* (Stuttgart: Akademischer Verlag Fritz Wedekind, 1930), 6–7. See Primary Text, no. 15.

12 Edith Tschichold kept Schwitters informed about his family in Germany during the war. In 1946 Schwitters dedicated one of his collages to Edith. Kurt and Ernst Schwitters, eds., *Kurt Schwitters: Catalogue raisonné*, vol. 3: 1937–1948 (Hanover: Sprengel Museum, 2006), no. 3367, illustr. p. 566.

13 *Typographische Mitteilungen* (March 1933): 65.

14 Phil Baines, *Penguin by Design: A Cover Story 1935–2005* (London: Allen Lane, 2005), 19–65.

15 In 1946 Max Bill and Jan Tschichold conducted a bitter debate on the relevance of modern typography in the pages of *Schweizer graphische Mitteilungen*, each accusing the other of being an ally of Nazism. See Christopher Burke and Robin Kinross, eds., "The Dispute between Max Bill and Tschichold of 1946," *Typography Papers*, no. 4 (2000), and Hans Rudolf Brosshard, *Max Bill Kontra Jan Tschichold: Der Typografiestreit der Moderne* (Zurich: Niggli, 2012).

16 Jan Tschichold, *Die neue Typographie* [The new typography] (Berlin: Verlag des Bildungsverbandes der deutschen Buchdrucker, 1928), 56–58.

17 See discussion in chapter 2 on the "Ring." In a letter of October 16, 1924, El Lissitzky criticized the tendency to elevate the Bauhaus over other initiatives: "By the way, I was told that Moholy is also preparing a book on 1914–24, in which everything before 1920 is treated as mere fertilizer for the Bauhaus, which then accomplishes everything and surpasses all that has gone before. Jolly little idea, what? Scurrilous, skullduggery!" Sophie Lissitzky-Küppers, *El Lissitzky: Life, Letters, Texts* (Greenwich, CT: New York Graphic Society, 1968), 53.

Chapter 1

Jan Tschichold: Typographer, Designer, Theorist

For the man of today there exists only the equilibrium between nature and spirit. At every moment of the past all variations of the old were "new"—but they were not "THE" new. We must never forget that we are now at a turning-point of civilization, at the end of everything old. This parting of the ways is absolute and final.
—PIET MONDRIAN, EPIGRAPH TO *DIE NEUE TYPOGRAPHIE* (1928)

Born in Leipzig, the center of the German book printing industry, Johannes "Tzschichhold" followed in his father's footsteps, training as a sign painter and "lettering artist" (*Schriftzeichner*), with the intention of becoming a schoolteacher.[1] His commitment to the craft of lettering became much more serious when in 1919 he entered the Königliche Akademie für graphische Künste und Buchgewerbe (Royal Academy of Graphic Arts and the Book Trade) [Fig. 6]. One of the oldest and most prestigious academies in Wilhelmine Germany, it has retained its reputation to this day. While there, Tschichold refined his calligraphy under Hermann Delitsch (1869–1937), a historian and scholar best known for his writings on early script forms, although he also designed typefaces for the Klinkhardt foundry. Delitsch had been a pupil of Rudolf von Larisch

6

(1856–1934), one of the great figures of German calligraphy, who along with the younger Rudolf Koch (1876–1934) established fine penmanship as a central pursuit of the arts and crafts in the German-speaking world.[2] Taking their lead from the English calligrapher Edward Johnston (1872–1944), and ultimately from William Morris, Larisch and Koch succeeded in imbuing the revival of historic scripts and the discipline of calligraphy with a meaning that was both personally expressive while also being a celebration of German national identity[3] [Fig. 7]. There is every reason to assume that Tschichold subscribed to this view: his early calligraphic work is not only superb in technique, but like that of many of his contemporaries, it appears to express a larger moral and spiritual ideal. Many years later, Tschichold recalled the almost monkish solitude and dedication required for this craft: "This silent work, which demands great concentration, is the real foundation for all my later work."[4]

In addition to these classes in calligraphy, he took lessons in print-making and bookbinding, crafts that offered a more practical training than calligraphy in the skills required for anyone intending to enter the printing industry. By his own admission, Tschichold was not a particularly dedicated student, or at least not a very respectful one, claiming to have learned very little in his time at the college.[5] He must have shown some promise, however, because he was commissioned to design poetry books based on his calligraphy for the Berlin publisher Karl Schnabel,

7

although he was only seventeen[6] [Fig. 8]. The editor at Schnabel then was Heinrich Wieynck (1874–1931), a teacher of calligraphy at the Akademie für Kunstgewerbe (Academy of Applied Arts) in Dresden, which was probably the reason that Tschichold transferred his studies there in 1920. By the time he returned to Leipzig the following year, Tschichold was a master student working under Walter Tiemann (1876–1951) and, although only eighteen years old, directing classes himself. Tiemann was a different type of designer from those Tschichold had previously encountered. Although trained in calligraphy, like most of his generation, Tiemann had quickly moved into the commercial book trade, founding the Janus-Presse, a private press that was a central plank of the Buchkunstbewegung (Book Arts Movement), for which he designed a specific typeface[7] [Fig. 9]. He was also a consultant to other presses, establishing the house style for the Insel Verlag, famous for their literature list and decorative gift books. Tiemann had been an organizer and juror for the massive *Internationale Ausstellung für Buchgewerbe und Graphik* (International Exhibition of Graphics and the Book Trade), or Bugra, held in Leipzig in 1914, and he went on to become the director of the Königlichen Akademie für graphische Künste und Buchgewerbe, placing him at the center of the design reform movement for fine printing in Germany.[8] Tschichold had visited Bugra as a child and treasured the catalogue as a touchstone for his subsequent work.

TSCHICHOLD AND THE AVANT-GARDE

Although his work up to this point was in a broadly historicist manner, especially in the tradition of fine calligraphy and book design that had thrived in Wilhelmine Germany, at some stage in the early 1920s Tschichold became disaffected with the current German arts and crafts tradition and developed an interest in recent trends in avant-garde art. A key to this change of heart may be found in his response to an exhibition devoted to Rudolf Koch in 1922, after which Tschichold visited the calligrapher in Offenbach am Main, reporting later that he could not be

8   Johannes Tschichold.
Page from Friedrich
Schiller, *An die Freude*
(Ode to Joy). Published
by Karl Schnabel, Berlin,
1919. Calligraphy, trans-
ferred by photolithogra-
phy. Collection of Jerry
Kelly. Cat. 94.

9   Walter Tiemann.
Colophon for the
Janus-Presse, 1910.

8

9

a true follower because Koch was too narrowly Germanic and historical
in outlook and consequently out of step with "the complex philosophy of the cultivated person in the present day."[9] This was more than a
change of taste or preference. The young Tschichold was turning his
back on the entire movement of national history and national style that
had looked back to the Gothic world as the fountainhead of German
culture. In the years before the First World War, expressionist artists and
filmmakers had elevated the Gothic as a paradigmatic phase of Germanic
culture, and this movement continued to exert a powerful influence
in the years following the defeat of 1918, when many artists and writers
attempted to pick up the threads of their earlier work.[10] The tide was
beginning to turn, however, and Tschichold was at the forefront of this
shift. It would be a few years before figures such as Bertolt Brecht,

Siegfried Kracauer, and Georg Lukács would launch withering attacks on expressionism and medievalism as symptoms of a delirious escapism from the real conditions of modern life.[11]

Tschichold's interest in avant-garde art was focused particularly on Russian Constructivism and De Stijl, two groups that espoused complete abstraction in art and design and a rigorous application of geometric form and primary colors.[12] It is unclear how or when Tschichold first came into contact with these movements, but there was much interest on the pages of radical journals in 1922–23. De Stijl was fairly well known in progressive art circles soon after its foundation in 1917. Theo van Doesburg, the leading theorist and propagandist for the group, was a frequent visitor to Germany and a tireless campaigner for the avant-garde, wearing alternately his De Stijl and Dada hats depending on the context[13] [Fig. 10]. He was the main instigator of the Congress of the Union of International Progressive Artists in Dusseldorf in May 1922, and in September of that year, the Congress of Constructivists and Dadaists in Weimar [Fig. 11]. These meetings drew together an odd assortment of artists and critics from across Europe, including Hans Arp, Hans Richter, Sophie Taeuber-Arp, and Tristan Tzara, as well as artist-designers such as Max Burchartz, El Lissitzky, László and Lucia Moholy-Nagy, and Kurt Schwitters, each of whom would go on to make important contributions to the New Typography. The following month, the Van Diemen Gallery in Berlin held the *Erste russische Kunstausstellung* (First Russian Art Exhibition), which was the first substantial showing of Russian art in the West since the Revolution of 1917, with a large contemporary section selected by Naum Gabo. With more than seven hundred works on display, including theater designs and architectural models, and a catalogue cover designed by Lissitzky, this event generated great excitement in the art press as well as among those who were able to attend[14] [Fig. 12]. The exhibition was supposed to travel to other European capitals, but in the end the Stedelijk Museum in Amsterdam was the only other venue, which nevertheless helped spread awareness of recent Soviet art even more widely.

10 Theo van Doesburg (possibly with Vilmos Huszár). *De Stijl NB* 73/74, 1926. Letterpress. The Museum of Modern Art. Jan Tschichold Collection, Gift of Philip Johnson. 674.1999. Cat. 4.

11 Congress of Constructivists and Dadaists, Weimar, 1922. *From rear, left to right: first row*, Lucia Moholy, Alfréd Kemény, László Moholy-Nagy; *second row*, Lotte Burchartz, El Lissitzky (with pipe and cap), Cornelis van Eesteren, Bernhard Sturtzkopf; *third row*, Max Burchartz (with child on his shoulders), Harry Scheibe, Theo van Doesburg (with De Stijl NB no. 6 on hat), Hans Vogel, Peter Röhl; *fourth row*, Alexa Röhl (in all black), Nelly van Doesburg, Tristan Tzara, Nini Smit, Hans Arp; *fifth row*, Werner Graeff and Hans Richter (on ground).

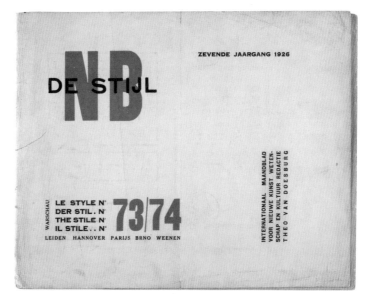

10

11

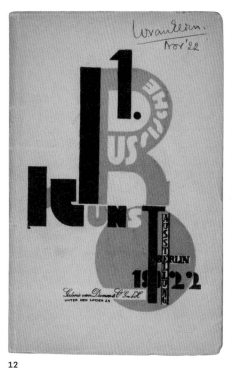

12

13

The Russian avant-garde was enjoying a high profile in the visual art circles of Central Europe. In June 1922, the Hungarian journal *Egység* (Unity) was the first to publish a substantial group of texts from the various Russian Constructivist groups, largely as a result of contacts made by Béla Uitz on his visit to Moscow a year earlier.[15] Soon other journals would follow suit, notably *Veshch/Gegenstand/Objet* (Object), edited by Lissitzky and Ilya Ehrenburg, a double issue of which was published in Berlin that same year[16] [Fig. 13]. In addition, during 1922 Moholy-Nagy's work was featured in exhibitions and on the covers of magazines from Berlin to Belgrade.[17] Anyone in Germany with a passing interest in contemporary art and culture could hardly fail to be aware of the emergence of Constructivism as a force to be reckoned with. Whether Tschichold visited any of these exhibitions is not clear, but this surge of information and images must have offered an alternative to his growing disaffection with the arts and crafts. It is possible that these aesthetic principles crystallized when he visited the Bauhaus exhibition at Weimar in 1923 [Fig. 14].

The Bauhaus Ausstellung was a pivotal moment in the history of the institution and indeed of the modern movement in Central Europe. As is well known, the Staatliche Bauhaus had been set up in 1919 on the embers of the prewar Weimar School of Arts and Crafts, a progressive training college that under its director, Henry van de Velde, had sought to inculcate the values of the English Arts and Crafts movement and the "New Art" in the next generation of artist-craftsmen.[18] To some

12 El Lissitzky. *Erste russische Kunstausstellung* (First Russian Art Exhibition) catalogue cover, 1922. Published by Internationale Arbeiterhilfe, Berlin. Letterpress. The Museum of Modern Art. Gift of the Judith Rothschild Foundation. 304.2001.

13 El Lissitzky. *Veshch/ Gegenstand/Objet*, nos. 1–2, cover, 1922. Letterpress. The Museum of Modern Art. Gift of the Judith Rothschild Foundation, 219.2001.A.

14 Herbert Bayer. *Staatliches Bauhaus in Weimar, 1919–1923* (State Bauhaus in Weimer) cover, 1923. Published by Bauhaus Verlag, Weimar. Letterpress. The Museum of Modern Art. Jan Tschichold Collection, Gift of Philip Johnson, 1999. 570.1999. Cat. 14.

14

extent, the Bauhaus under its first director, Walter Gropius, endorsed many of these prewar values, although Gropius clearly felt there was a new set of challenges facing architecture and design in the postwar economic and cultural landscape. These first four years of the college might be regarded as a period of experiment. Despite the stated aim in the *Manifest und Programm* of April 1919—to instill strict workshop practices—there was no clear aesthetic or pedagogical system. Instead, emphasis was placed on developing the students' individual creative abilities and providing training in materials and techniques[19] [Fig. 15]. The studios for different media operated independently for the most part, under the direction of a form master and a technical leader. The student intake in these first few years was also somewhat diverse. Many of the students were young women of middle-class backgrounds,

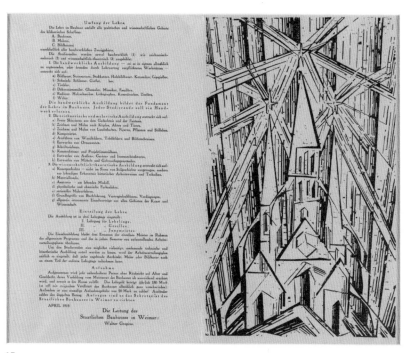

15

while a number of the men were older and battle-hardened, having spent part (or all) of the previous four years in the army. As a microcosm of the challenges facing the Bauhaus, one might look at the ceramics studio. Not only was it based in a medieval castle, some twenty miles from the main college, but the first students had a considerable range in age, experience, and political affiliation. Forced together in an enclosed environment to acquire new skills and discover some sense of their individual creativity, the studio soon became a crucible of sexual and political tension.[20] Visitors to the Bauhaus in this early period were often disappointed by the gap between the grand aims set out in its opening manifesto—to "create the new structure of the future"—and the culture that had developed within the various studios. As van Doesburg wrote, with some understatement, following his visit in 1921: "the results of this institute . . . leave much to be desired."[21]

Many of these contradictions were apparent in the work produced by both staff and students at the Weimar Bauhaus, best seen in the first major exhibition to showcase their work in 1921, when the Sommerfeld House was opened to the public. This neo-vernacular building, constructed for a timber merchant using wood that had been salvaged from a wrecked ship, reveals some of the tendencies then at work in the college, not least a lingering preoccupation with expressionism alongside tentative gropings after a new sensibility. This was not unusual. A conflicted and somewhat confused mixture of values was true of the larger cultural scene in early Weimar Germany, with prewar expressionism still ascendant in film, literature, dance, and the visual arts. Nevertheless, the 1923 exhibition was held to overcome some of these divisive tendencies and to reorient the college, as well as to appease the Weimar authorities, who were anxious to see that their investment in an arts and crafts college would bring some benefits to local industry. Three events in that year indicate the new direction that Gropius would take. First, the exhibition itself showcased a very different type of design from that shown just two years earlier. Haus am Horn, designed by Georg Muche and

Adolf Meyer, exemplified the simple, rectilinear aesthetic that had been debated in architecture and design circles in Germany for more than a decade. The interior of the house, especially the kitchen designed by Benita Koch-Otte, offered a series of clean, hard surfaces, modular storage units, and features that evoked efficiency and practicality rather than tradition or symbolism. Rarely had factory forms and materials been introduced so comprehensively in a domestic setting. Second, at the opening of the exhibition in August 1923, Gropius came up with a new manifesto for the college—"Art and Technology: A New Unity"—that helped to indicate a new direction for the Weimar Bauhaus, focused more directly on design for industry, or at least for the market.[22]

The third event of 1923 was the appointment in March of László Moholy-Nagy, initially to replace the Swiss-born artist and pedagogue Johannes Itten as leader of the *Vorkurs*, or first-year studios, but also to take over running the metal workshop. Not only did Moholy-Nagy have a very different journey to Weimar from most of the other teachers, he was also firmly within the Constructivist camp and committed to an experimental approach to new materials and processes. Moholy-Nagy's principal contribution to the exhibition was the design of the catalogue. The cover was by Herbert Bayer, still a student at the time, but the inner pages, employing bold rules to create a grid within which blocks of text could be organized, was pure Moholy-Nagy [Fig. 16]. He also employed the unusual feature of setting many proper names and titles vertically in the left margin, at right angles to the text. Although largely untrained in typography, this was a style he would use for other Bauhaus publications, and which would be much discussed over the next few years. In addition, Moholy-Nagy provided a short essay, "Die neue Typographie" (Primary Text, no. 3), in which he laid out some of the first principles of modern design. "Typography is an instrument of communication," he begins, stating the obvious, before going on to note: "It must be as clear and effective as possible."[23] For Moholy-Nagy, typography was not a crystal goblet, an invisible medium through which ideas could be com-

16

municated imperceptibly, but an engine that drives the message, shapes its meaning, and does so in a manner that reflects the experience of modern life. Moholy-Nagy believed in "absolute clarity" that should not be compromised by aesthetics. The graphic designer must also use all the resources at his or her disposal: "all typefaces, font sizes, geometric shapes, colors, etc." Above all, typography must come to terms with photography, the most important medium for recording the world and revealing its complexity. Especially now that the technology was widely available, photography must be integrated with text and allowed to fulfill its commanding role in visual communication: "The objectivity of photography liberates the receptive reader from the crutches of the author's personal descriptions and forces him, more than ever, to form his own opinion."

Tschichold may have acquired some furniture at the Bauhaus exhibition. He was certainly trying to purchase a rug after a design by Paul Klee in 1925, which Gropius himself had to explain would be three times the stated price because of the unexpected difficulties of weaving Klee's design.[24] Apart from the impressive declaration of new principles in the catalogue, however, it is difficult to see what Tschichold might have taken from the current activity at the college. At that time, there was no formal training in graphic design or advertising, and the primitive printing facilities were used mostly for printing invitations to college events and Bauhaus portfolios of artists' prints. From the photographs in the catalogue, it is clear that the college was dependent on a set of old hand presses, because the machine presses had been confiscated at the outbreak of war almost a decade earlier.[25] For someone trained in a higher trade college and currently teaching in one of the state schools of printing, this could hardly have impressed an aspiring designer for print. Although there were clearly signs of excellent design in the work of Moholy-Nagy and Bayer, the character of Bauhaus publications and printed material was still dominated by the quirky, individualized work of expressionists like Lyonel Feininger. This was not the way forward to the New Typography, and it was a style that Tschichold came to despise.

MODERNISM IN GRAPHIC DESIGN
In 1924, Tschichold produced what was probably his first full exercise in a modern style—at least the first that went into print for a commercial client—a poster for the Polish bookshop and publisher Philobiblon [Fig. 17]. Printed in black and gold with a bold uppercase *P* set at an angle, with accompanying text ("books by Philobiblon are available in Warsaw") in sanserif organized in perpendicular lines radiating outward, it betrays a debt to recent Soviet work. Although the Slavic language may emphasize the effect, there are unmistakable echoes of El Lissitzky's covers for *About Two Squares* and *Veshch* [see Figs. 4 and 13]. When Tschichold changed his name from Johannes to Iwan, it was a clear statement of

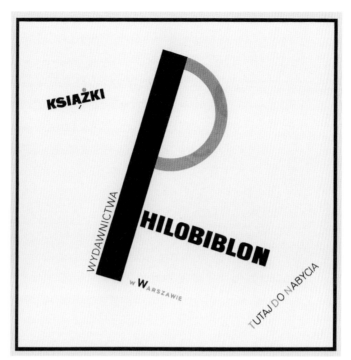

17

his sympathies with Soviet Russia and the ideals of design as a force for
social change as well as a medium of aesthetic innovation. This first
sign of a new approach, however, was a mere indication of Tschichold's
grander plans. Throughout 1924 and into the following year, he began
gathering material for a special issue of *Typographische Mitteilungen*,
the journal of the educational wing of the German printing union
(Bildungsverband der Deutschen Buchdrucker) with a wide readership
in the trade.[26] In fact, Tschichold had already gone into print with a
short manifesto for "Die neue Typographie" in the left-wing literary journal *Kulturschau*.[27] Consisting of sixteen points, delivered in the manner
of a manifesto, it was very much a document of its time. Even before
Moholy-Nagy's essay on the New Typography for the July–September
1923 exhibition, Lissitzky had published "The Topography of Typography"

in the March issue of *Merz*, consisting of eight points culminating in a call for "The Electro-Library" (Primary Text, no. 2), which would transcend the book. This was closely followed by several short texts on the subject by Kurt Schwitters, the most substantial being his "Theses on Typography" (Primary Text, no. 6), which appeared in *Merz* no. 11 (November 1924), partly as a riposte to Lissitzky's statements.[28] Tschichold did not have much space to elaborate on his views in *Kulturschau*, but in the captions to the two illustrations, he made it quite clear that the founders of the new movement, just gathering speed, were Lissitzky and Moholy-Nagy.

The preparations for a special issue of *Typographische Mitteilungen* were undertaken in late 1924 and the early months of 1925. Tschichold reported to a friend that it would be published in July, but it did not appear until October.[29] Unusually for a trade journal with a conventional character, Tschichold's "elementare typographie" (all in lowercase) was a startling expression of the new ideas in both form and content [Fig. 18]. To begin with, it was a self-contained booklet, a *Sonderheft* (special issue), inserted within the main journal, printed on heavier white paper, with a bold title page consisting of a rectilinear arrangement of lines and text in red and black. The list of names in alphabetical order on the lower right gave some indication of what to expect: Natan Altman, Otto Baumberger, Herbert Bayer, Max Burchartz, El Lissitzky, László Moholy-Nagy, Molnar F. Farkas (Farkas Molnár), Johannes Molzahn, Kurt Schwitters, Mart Stam, and finally "Ivan" Tschichold. The main texts inside were passages from Moholy-Nagy's "Typophoto" (Primary Text, no. 5), drawn from his recently published Bauhaus book *Malerei, Photographie, Film* (Painting, Photography, Film), and a short piece on advertising attributed to Lissitzky and the Dutch architect-designer Mart Stam, from the Swiss journal *ABC*.[30] These extracts were interspersed with illustrations, including Bayer's *Notgeld* (emergency money) banknotes, Lissitzky's *About Two Squares*, Moholy-Nagy's Bauhaus publications, and various book covers and typographic designs.

18 Jan Tschichold.
*Typographische Mit-
teilungen, Sonderheft:
Elementare Typo-
graphie* (Typographic
Studies, special
issue: Elemental
Typography), October
1925. Published by
Bildungsverband der
deutschen Buch-
druker, Berlin. Letter-
press. The Museum
of Modern Art. Gift
of Suzanne Slesin.
698.2013. Cat. 2.

18

Tschichold also took this opportunity to present his ten-point plan for "elementare typographie" (Primary Text, no. 7), opening with the simple statement that "the new typography is purposeful." This is simple enough to have appeared in almost any book on typography, but Tschichold goes on to elaborate many of the points already raised by Moholy-Nagy and Lissitzky: the need for clear, urgent expression of the content; the exclusive use of sanserif letterforms, preferably lowercase; standardized paper sizes; the elimination of unnecessary ornament; and the integration of photography into the body of the text. These points were already circulating in the world of printing in Germany, but Tschichold expresses them in a manner that was helpful to the uninitiated. He also goes out of his way to give practical meaning to some aspects of the guidelines, which none of the earlier theorists had attempted. When he writes "by using very different sizes and shapes, without regard to previous aesthetic attitudes, the logical structure of the printed area is made visually perceptible" or "the unprinted parts of the paper are just as much means of the design as are the printed forms," we can begin to recognize the liberation of the page from its earlier rigid format to one in which the open book, the handbill, the magazine advertisement, or the poster should be treated as an abstract field in which the text and imagery can be arranged in ways that create a visually exciting composition while also emphasizing the message.

One unexpected item in "elementare typographie" was the "Programm der Konstruktivisten," Tschichold's translation of the 1922 "Program of the First Working Group of Constructivists" by Aleksandr Rodchenko and Varvara Stepanova.[31] Tschichold had made it quite clear that he saw the roots of the new graphic design in the theories and worldview of recent abstract art movements. "The New Typography, to which this special edition of *Typographische Mitteilungen* is dedicated, builds on the findings of the consistent work of Russian Suprematism, Dutch Neoplasticism, and especially that of Constructivism."[32] The "Programm der Konstruktivisten" and Natan Altman's text "Elementare Gesichtspunkte" (Elementary points of view) may have only a tangential relation to graphic design, but they indicate something of Tschichold's fascination with Soviet Russia at this time. Although he omitted many of the more overt political statements from the manifesto, its inclusion in a trade publication is further evidence of his growing belief in the role of abstract art in the development of a new graphic design vocabulary and of his commitment to the idea that modern design should have a social and political dimension—with radical design as merely one aspect of a program for radical social change.

When "elementare typographie" did appear, it caused some disturbance in the printing world. Tschichold's circle greeted it with rapturous enthusiasm. Moholy-Nagy and Walter Gropius each wrote to congratulate him, despite Tschichold's having played down the role of the Bauhaus in the field of graphic design.[33] El Lissitzky was perhaps the most complimentary, opening his letter as follows:

DEAR TSCHICHOLD,
                    BRAVO,
                              BRAVO,
                                        I most warmly congratulate you on the beautiful piece of printing that is *Elementare Typographie*. It is a physical pleasure for me to hold a work of such quality in my hands, my fingers, my eyes. My nerve antennae stretch, and the whole motor increases its speed. And that is ultimately what it is all about—overcoming inertia. . . . This is all your own doing. It is an achievement that this is a special issue of a professional journal /not an art journal/ and so I hope it will reach the working printer and he will gain self-confidence, and this will stimulate him to inventive uses of his typecase.[34]

The traditionalists were less enthusiastic about both the promotion of this graphic style and the theories that lay behind it. Some suggested that the supposed "new" typography offered nothing new, or else they criticized the rigidity of the new style and its inability to respond to the emotional or intellectual character of the text. The most vociferous complaints, however, were directed at the political content. So great was the response that *Typographische Mitteilungen* devoted four sections to letters on "elementare typographie" between August and December 1926, and two other trade journals carried the same review accusing Tschichold of extreme left-wing views, which they felt had no place in typography.[35] Tschichold was becoming a name in the printing world, but a name as famous for his communist sympathies as for his design work. In an article titled "Ein Verfechter für Konstruktivismus" (A protagonist for constructivism), Albert Giesecke went so far as to call Tschichold a *Kunstbolschewist* (an art Bolshevik), an association that would stick to him throughout his years in Germany.[36]

A different set of complaints emerged from within the modernist camp. When Tschichold reached out to Walter Dexel, possibly to make amends for not including him in "elementare typographie," Dexel replied, complaining that there were too many Russians and Hungarians and not enough Dutch and Germans, whom he felt were the true innovators. He ended on a schoolmasterish note: "I am glad to hear that you would like to inform yourself more extensively in the future."[37] This was not entirely a patronizing jibe. Tschichold had ended "elementare typographie" with an appeal to readers to send him examples of New Typography with a view of including them in future exhibitions, essays, or lectures. There was, in other words, already a campaign in progress to promote the new ideas and to build on the achievements of the previous two years.

THE PROFESSIONAL DESIGNER AND TEACHER
Tschichold's plans evolved in the wake of the *Typographische Mitteilungen* controversy, although the next few months could hardly be

described as a straightforward development of his recent position at the forefront of a design reform movement. In March 1926, he married (Maria Mathilde) Edith Kramer, a young writer training to be a journalist, who shared his political and aesthetic ideals. The couple moved to Berlin, where they felt there would be more opportunities. Leipzig may have been the center of the book printing industry, which was still Tschichold's principal vocation, but the capital was undoubtedly the place where new ideas were given greater prominence. For the Tschicholds, however, Berlin offered very little. The printers and publishers there were more conservative than expected, showing little interest in the debates on design in journals and print workshops across the country. In addition, Tschichold's politics were becoming an impediment to commissions from the main publishing houses. In any case, events far away from the capital would soon guide them in a different direction.

In March 1926, Paul Renner left the main art and design college in Frankfurt, the Städelschule, to take up a new position as director of the Graphische Berufsschule in Munich, a vocational or trade school founded in 1905 to train young men in the various branches of printing. Renner was an accomplished typographer and type designer, whose work for the Bauer Typefoundry in Frankfurt was about to place him at the forefront of the modern movement in graphic design. Futura, the sanserif typeface that Renner designed for Bauer, became the default for modern advertising design almost as soon as it was released in 1927 [Fig. 19]. Renner was not a radical in outlook, however, nor really a theorist of the larger ideals of modern art and design, at least not in the same mold as those whom Tschichold had included in "elementare typographie." A member of the Deutscher Werkbund and an upholder of the highest standards in typographic design, he was more of a moderate reformer than a revolutionary. He was first drawn into the circle of the New Typography, no doubt, by his respect for Tschichold's abilities as a calligrapher, typographer, and designer. Renner always prized

technical skill over the grand and totalizing theories that were a hallmark of modernist discourse in the 1920s. But he had also been implicated in the political radicalism attached to Tschichold during the debates surrounding "elementare typographie," an accusation that he firmly rejected and no doubt found embarrassing. In 1925, Hermann Hoffmann described them both as Bolsheviks, an inflammatory insult more than a description of actual allegiance to Soviet communism, but one with real conse-

19 Paul Renner.
Futura typeface,
Bauer typefoundry
advertisement, 1927.
Letterpress. Private
collection.

20 Jan Tschichold.
Invitation for a lecture
on the New Typog-
raphy, Munich, 1927.
Private collection.

quences, even in Weimar Germany. Having been jointly accused, Renner
may have felt some responsibility toward his younger colleague, defend-
ing him in print and offering him a position teaching calligraphy and
typography at the Berufsschule. Tschichold took up his new position at
the beginning of June 1926, just two weeks after he had given a lecture
in the school more or less declaring his design principles. The title of the
lecture was "The New Typography" [Fig. 20].

This was an exciting time for the Berufsschule because Renner was
making plans to establish the national school of advanced printing alongside the main vocational school. In fact, the proximity of the Berufsschule
helped to confirm Munich as the site of the new Meisterschule für
Deutschlands Buchdrucke, because the two institutions would be able
to share equipment and expertise. Renner and Tschichold taught in
both institutions. Although supportive, Renner was very conscious of the
dangers of political interference in a national college and was therefore

jan tschichold:

lichtbildervortrag **die neue typographie**

am mittwoch, 11. mai 1927, abends 8 uhr, in der aula der graphischen berufsschule,
pranckhstraße 2, am marsfeld, straßenbahnlinien: 3 (haltestelle hackerbrücke),
1, 4 und 11 (haltestelle pappenheimstraße) ● der vortrag wird von über hundert
größtenteils mehrfarbigen lichtbildern begleitet, eine diskussion findet nicht statt

freier eintritt

veranstalter:
bildungsverband
der deutschen
buchdrucker
ortsgruppe
münchen
vorsitzender:
J. lehnacker
münchen
fröttmaninger-
straße 14 c

20

anxious to project a favorable image to the outside world, especially in a city such as Munich, which, despite its short revolutionary outburst in 1919, had a history of conservatism. One achievement was to persuade Tschichold to change his Christian name from Ivan to something less inflammatory. The younger man chose Jan, a simpler version of his baptismal name, Johannes. Despite these concessions and Tschichold's rising reputation in the world of printing and typography, there seems to have been a pervasive sense that Renner did not entirely trust him. Tschichold was never given a full professorship, remaining a lecturer, or *Studienrat*, for the entire period of his employment there. At various stages, Renner also sounded out other lecturers as possible replacements for Tschichold, notably Georg Trump, a gifted designer, who established a reputation in Bielefeld as both a designer and teacher and who joined the staff of the Meisterschule for a short while in 1930. It is not clear whether Tschichold resented Trump's presence, but he clearly admired Trump's work and had already begun collecting examples of his advertising designs.

Tschichold earned his living from teaching, but he also undertook design work as it came available. Much of this was small—letterheads, business cards, and college publications—often for family and friends. His simple red-and-black letterhead for Nina Chmelowa, a Russian dancer whom he had met in Leipzig, was perhaps the first of his designs in the new manner beyond the stationery he prepared for himself and his wife, Edith [Fig. 21]. The integration of names in sanserif with rectangular blocks in red and black framing the letter space is reminiscent of the letterheads on which Lissitzky wrote to him. His most interesting work in these early years in Munich, however, was for the Phoebus-Palast cinema, which when it opened in 1926 was the largest cinema in Germany, seating more than two thousand people.[38] Tschichold was given considerable artistic freedom by Phoebus-Palast and designed a suite of graphic material for this client: promotional posters and also newspaper advertisements and programs that established a strong visual identity

21

for the venue. Part of the challenge of the posters was that they had to be designed quickly; there was little time between the announcement of the film and the screening, so Tschichold often composed the designs at the printshop, working from concepts he had sketched out in advance. Nevertheless, he succeeded in producing a series of original designs for each of the dozens of films, some exclusively typographical and others combining image and text. Posters for *Napoleon* (directed by Abel Gance) and *Die Hose* (The Trousers, directed by Hans Behrendt), both filmed in

1927, are among his most famous, employing bold juxtapositions of crisp geometric elements in red with sanserif text on the diagonal and discreet photomontage of the main character [Figs. 22 and 23]. Within these abstract formal compositions, there is a clear attempt to develop a graphic language appropriate to the medium of film. The linear framework in *Die Frau ohne Namen* (The Woman Without a Name, 1927) describes the conical beam of the cinematic projector and taut flow of the film reel,

22

22 Jan Tschichold. *Napoleon*, Phoebus Palast poster, 1927. Lithograph. Private collection.

23 Jan Tschichold. *Die Hose* (The Trousers), Phoebus Palast poster, 1926. Printed by F. Bruckmann AG. Munich. Offset lithograph. The Museum of Modern Art. Gift of Armin Hofmann. 1284.1968. Cat. 101.

23

while the deep recession emphasizes the sense of movement carried through to the railway engine rushing out toward the spectator [Fig. 24]. The dynamic composition and use of brilliant red heighten the drama and convey a sense of excitement.

A similar effect can be seen in the poster for *Laster der Menschheit* (The Vice of Humanity, 1927), in which the photomontage imitates the projection of a film onto a cinema screen, with the lines of text marking intermediate stages between the projector and the image [Fig. 25].

24

Tschichold had strong views on poster design, believing that posters should use the essential features of the printed surface, exploiting positive and negative space, with contrasts in scale and tone and crisp outline. The poster artist, he argued, should reject sensationalism and individual expression "with the sternest avoidance of 'handwriting effects'" and the "nibbled" lettering that he felt had degenerated into a mannerism.[39] This was particularly relevant to film posters in the 1920s, a time when expressionism was still a vital force in the German film industry.[40] His design for *Laster der Menschheit* is a remarkably restrained representation of the theme, given that the plot involves a mother's alienation from her daughter as the result of cocaine addiction and her attempts to keep the daughter out of the clutches of her evil dealer. An Austrian poster for the same film by Mihály Bíro, for example, is a lurid depiction of a naked woman trapped in the web of an enormous green spider [Fig. 26]. These contrasts gave rise to a lively debate about the most appropriate way to advertise film, preserving the widespread appeal of what was already a mass entertainment but equally attempting to find forms and techniques that represent the medium effectively.

"PURITY, CLARITY, FITNESS FOR PURPOSE": DIE NEUE TYPOGRAPHIE

Before arriving in Munich, Tschichold had begun gathering material for a more ambitious publication than his previous efforts. His "elementary typography" was a striking contribution to the debate, but it was something of a patchwork of different statements and images. Tschichold was planning a more comprehensive and singular exposition of the new ideas on graphic design. It was during this time that he began to correspond with many of the designers throughout Europe whose work he admired. Kurt Schwitters was an early correspondent, as were László Moholy-Nagy and professional designers such as Max Burchartz, Walter Dexel, and Johannes Molzahn. His closest personal friend and counselor,

25

26

however, was El Lissitzky, who lived in Central Europe for several years in the 1920s. Tschichold also began to reach out to designers in other countries. Soon he was in touch with Piet Zwart and Paul Schuitema in the Netherlands, Lajos Kassák in Vienna and Budapest, Władysław Strzemiński in Poland, and Karel Teige, Zdeněk Rossmann, and Ladislav Sutnar in Czechoslovakia. This correspondence not only enabled these designers to participate in the networks already being created and to share their views on design and society, it also allowed them to gather examples of one another's work. Tschichold was, in effect, assembling a comprehensive collection of modernist graphic design as it was appearing in print. In the absence of exhibition venues or collecting circles, much innovative printed matter remained with individual designers and their clients, with few opportunities for outsiders to see this work. The main print and design magazines, such as *Gebrauchsgraphik* and *Reklame*, were slow to pick up on new developments, largely because they had a broader audience and thus tended to reflect many of the conventions in everyday use by their professional readers.

It was precisely to help overcome these barriers and to publicize this type of work that Kurt Schwitters set up the Ring neuer Werbegestalter in 1927. The founding members were Willi Baumeister, Max Burchartz, Walter Dexel, César Domela, Robert Michel, Schwitters himself, Georg Trump, and Friedrich Vordemberge-Gildewart, all practicing graphic designers, although several of them were also active as painters and designers in other media. Tschichold was an obvious choice to join this group, and he played an active part, designing their notepaper and contributing to the two exhibitions that toured a series of venues during the following three years. He also proposed several new members (Lajos Kassák, El Lissitzky, Karel Teige, and Piet Zwart) to extend the range of the group.[41] There was clearly a need for such an organization. Although graphic design was not yet an identifiable profession—the term was only coined in 1923 in the United States—

there was a rising demand for high-quality design for print, especially for the expanding industrial and commercial sector in the German economy. Designers who understood the potential as well as the processes of print technology were in demand, but the group was also aiming to revolutionize the formal vocabulary of commercial graphics and to move on to a fundamental reform of the ways that information was presented, read, and understood. In this, the Ring, like many of the preceding theorists and critics, was embarking on a new mode of visual literacy in which text, imagery, positioning, and sequence could all become integrated within a larger design philosophy.

Tschichold was responding to the same demand when he published *Die neue Typographie* in 1928, a few months after the inauguration of the Ring.[42] He also had considerable support from within the printing trade. The book was published by the Bildungsverband der Deutschen Buchdrucker, the educational branch of the printing trade union, which was undergoing something of a boom under its current chairman, Joseph Seitz. Union membership had increased dramatically over the previous few years, to the extent that by 1930 there were more than ninety thousand members of the association (*Verband*) in some 670 local branches spread across the entire country.[43] In 1924, imbued with a spirit of confidence about their role in contemporary culture and society, the Bildungsverband commissioned the architect Max Taut to design new offices in Berlin's Kreuzberg district in a severe modern style. To mark the opening of their new building in 1926, the association published a book of photographs titled *Max Taut: Buildings and Plans* with text by Adolf Behne.[44] The book, designed by Johannes Molzahn, is a classic example of the New Typography, employing a rectilinear grid to break up the page, creating an assertive interrelationship between text and photography [Fig. 27]. Given these initiatives in architecture and graphic design, one can see the extent to which Tschichold's aims to promote the New Typography sit comfortably within the larger ideals of the union.

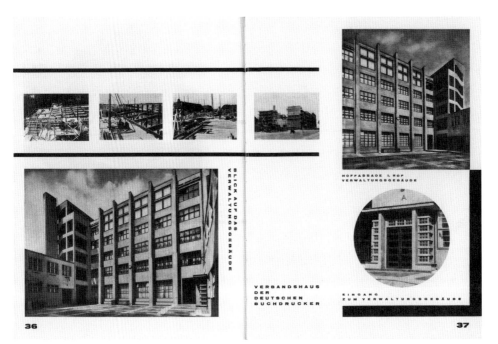

27

Aimed at practicing designers and people who had come through the trade schools and the printing industry rather than academies of art, Tschichold's book had a simple, utilitarian look, small in format and without a jacket [Fig. 28]. It declared itself a "manual," giving practical advice and guidance on issues such as paper size, photography, and the various types of work graphic designers undertake: trademarks, letterheads, envelopes, postcards, business cards, advertisements, newspapers, magazines, graphs, and tables. Only at the end does Tschichold include a chapter on "The New Book," which was, after all, his own discipline and still the most recognizable pursuit within the entire field. This range and sequence indicate the extent to which Tschichold—and the New Typography as a movement—was attempting to map out a new field of professional design. Given the sources of his views, Tschichold could not leave out the theories that underpinned his approach to the subject. The book

27 Adolf Behne. *Max Taut: Bauten und Pläne*, pages 36–37, 1927. Published by Fredrich Ernst Hubsch Verlag, Berlin/Leipzig. Private collection.

28 Jan Tschichold. *Die neue Typographie*, 1928. Published by Bildungsverband der deutschen Buch-drucker, Berlin. Bard Graduate Center Library. Cat. 1.

is therefore divided into two parts. In the first, "Growth and Nature of the New Typography," Tschichold prepares the ground for the more practical matters in the second part, "Principal Typographic Categories."

Opening his discussion with a chapter on "The New World View," Tschichold reminds the reader that we are living through a period of great technological and social change, and that if we are to take full advantage of this, we must abandon many of our conventional notions of art and culture. Listing the features that epitomize the modern world—"Car Airplane Telephone Wireless Factory Neon-advertising New York!"—Tschichold goes on: "These objects, designed without reference to the aesthetics of the past, have been created by a new kind of man: **the engineer!**"[45] This is not exactly new. Such messianic statements on the need for new values, new solutions, and the "new man" to confront the challenges of the modern world were common at the time in manifestos on contemporary architecture, music, literature, and politics. Indeed, these claims were already a feature of the articles on modern typography that had been appearing sporadically during the previous five years. Such statements, however, had rarely been made in a practical handbook for emerg-

28

ing printers and graphic designers. Tschichold goes on to emphasize that modern design is not a self-contained activity but part of a larger movement. In a section of the chapter titled "Unity of Life!," he comes closest to advocating a form of social engineering through design, emphasizing the role that typography, along with architecture, will play in bringing about the new age. He juxtaposes the "old" typography with the new, and while stating that they cannot exist together, he is in no doubt that "the future will belong to the new typography."[46] This contrast in design styles—the old and the new—provides a stark indication of the formal characteristics of the new style. In a chapter on "The Old Typography (1440–1914)," Tschichold describes and illustrates the type of fine printing that most printers and designers would have been familiar with, from Johannes Gutenberg's forty-two-line Bible to the various "tendencies" that he identifies in the modern world. Throughout, Tschichold emphasizes the ways in which design relates to the *Weltanschauung*, or worldview, of its period. So the Arts and Crafts style and the "industrial" and imperial styles all led in different—and always "wrong"—directions. "It is essential to realize today that the 'forms' we need to express our modern world can never be found in the work of a single personality and its 'private' language. . . . The domination of a culture by the private design-concepts of a few 'prominent' individuals, in other words an artistic dictatorship, cannot be accepted."[47] One can sense Tschichold's contempt for earlier design principles, and the rising confidence of the young zealot as he consigns these sacred cows to the dustbin of history.

Another feature running through *Die neue Typographie* is not only his belief in the logic of history and modern life but his contempt for individualism and "artistic printing," which he sees as more than an irrelevance; it is a betrayal of the challenges facing the New Typography. Given this disdain, it is interesting to follow Tschichold's reasoning as he locates the sources of a modern sensibility in "the New Art." After a fairly routine reading of the major landmarks in the history of art, he traces the beginnings of modernity to the French Revolution—after which the bourgeoisie attained "a form of expression of its own"—and to the invention of photography, which liberated painters from the burden of representation.[48] There follows a short survey of modern painting from Édouard Manet to the First World War, taking in all the "isms," after which he can turn to the "generation which followed on after the war" that has a direct bearing on graphic design and modern life. Following some discussion of Dada and Cubism, he quickly turns to Suprematism, Constructivism, and De Stijl, the movements he had highlighted in "elementare typographie" as the true sources of the new collective art and design, illustrating it with work by Lajos Kassák, El Lissitzky, Kazimir Malevich, Piet Mondrian, Aleksandr Rodchenko, and Vladimir Tatlin. Tschichold proceeds to examine works in new media, such as Man Ray's photograms, photographic images made directly onto light-sensitive paper, without the use of a camera. As a piece of art history, this sequence seems fairly conventional nowadays, but it was radical then, well informed, and couched in a language that expresses the author's commitment to the underlying ideas. Tschichold repeatedly turns aside to make sweeping statements on art, culture, and modernity: "art does not consist in superficially copying nature, but in the creation of form that takes its laws not from the external appearance of nature but from its internal structure"; "modern painting shows that it has developed out of the collective spirit of the time."[49]

The discussion of "the New Art" is a preamble to "The History of the New Typography," in which Tschichold describes some of the reforms in printing and type design of the late nineteenth and early twentieth centuries, before turning to a "non-technician," the Italian poet and Futurist Filippo Tommaso Marinetti, whose book *Les mots en liberté futuristes* (Futurist Words in Freedom, 1919) is described as the "curtain-raiser for the change-over from ornamental to functional typography."[50] Tschichold then outlines or illustrates work by El Lissitzky, László Moholy-Nagy, Kurt Schwitters, Tristan Tzara, and Theo van Doesburg before describing the work of some of his German colleagues. An important feature of this section, as it had been in "elementare typographie" three years earlier, was the republication of various manifestos. Marinetti's "Typographic Revolution" of May 1913 (Primary Text, no. 1) is printed in translation, as is Lissitzky's "Topography of Typography" (Primary Text, no. 2), which first appeared in the Dadaist journal *Merz* no. 4 in July 1923. Kurt Schwitters's work is mentioned, as is Moholy-Nagy's pioneering short essay from the Bauhaus exhibition catalogue of 1923, in which the term *Die neue Typographie* was first used, but their texts are not reprinted. The main theoretical exposition of the New Typography follows, emphasizing "clarity" and the first objective of the movement, which is "to develop its visible form out of the functions of the text."[51] Tschichold is at pains to emphasize the coherence and almost scientific logic of the new approach, as if a text might naturally assume or evolve into the form that its content and function dictate. At the same time, Tschichold sees the New Typography as a directing medium, shaping how a text is read and how it "ought to be read": "it is true that we usually read from top left to bottom right—but this is not a law."[52]

One of the first things that Tschichold felt had to be abandoned was "symmetry," in book design as in all other forms of graphic design. This allows for a new "rhythm," and not only is asymmetry "more optically effective than symmetry," it is "also an expression of our own movement, and that of modern life" [Fig. 29]. Indeed, asymmetry is almost the key to the new style; it is lively, it has greater diversity, and "it is the only way to make a better, more natural order possible." It goes without saying that ornament for its own sake is discouraged.[53] In this, Tschichold repeats the views of Adolf Loos from his 1910 essay "Ornament and Crime."[54] "The use of ornament, in whatever style or quality, comes from an attitude of childish naivety. It shows a reluctance to use 'pure design,' a giving-in to a primitive instinct to decorate."[55] Thereafter, Tschichold goes through various elements of graphic design, touching on form, color, contrast, type, and expression, before turning to orthography, or the conventions of written language.

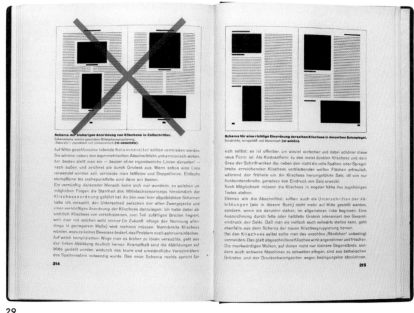

29 Jan Tschichold. *Die neue Typographie*, pages 214–215, 1928. Published by Bildungsverband der deutschen Buchdrucker, Berlin. Bard Graduate Center Library. Cat. 1.

29

Spelling, letterforms, and the representation of the spoken word through symbols are fundamental to all written languages, but they have a particular significance in German because all nouns are capitalized. This creates a different rhythm and emphasis within the sentence compared to its equivalent in English or French. As Adolf Loos pointed out, "when a German takes a pen to write something, he no longer is able to write as he thinks or speaks."[56] Heavy capitalization also poses problems when teaching the language to children, quite apart from any additional burdens it creates in typesetting and legibility. In seeking to roll back this tradition, Tschichold emphasizes that it is a relatively recent development, from the seventeenth century in fact, and that it bears little or no relationship to the origins of the language. Tschichold's solution is simple but radical: the exclusive use of lowercase for text and the possible use of uppercase letters in headings. Tschichold was not the first to propose this. Jacob Grimm had suggested it in the early nineteenth century, and many writers, philologists, and designers had advocated similar reforms in recent years, not least Herbert Bayer, who developed his "universal" lettering designs at the Bauhaus between 1925 and 1927 [Fig. 30]. The strongest advocate for reform of orthography, however, was Walter Porstmann (1886–1959), engineer, mathematician, and champion of standardization in all spheres of life. He above all provided the clearest arguments for adopting lowercase lettering on the grounds of efficiency and economy.[57] To the modernists, lowercase had a certain pared-down, essentialist beauty, but this proposal could be bolstered by the argument of efficiency in terms of both monetary costs and human effort. "A completely one-type system, using lower case only, would be of great advantage to the national economy: it would entail savings and simplification in many areas; and would also result in great savings of spiritual and intellectual energy at present wasted: we can mention here the teaching of writing and orthography, a great simplification in typewriters and typing technique, a relief for memory, type design, type-cutting, type-casting,

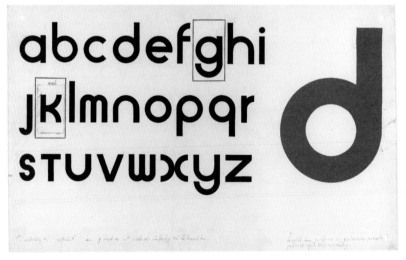

30

and all composition methods—and so on."[58] Interestingly, Walter Gropius had praised "elementare typographie" on the grounds that it lent support to his attempts to introduce exclusively lowercase lettering in Bauhaus publications and publicity.[59] Franz Roh, an art historian and close friend of Tschichold, also chose to hammer home this point with a simple diagram asking "Why 4 Alphabets?" (Primary Text, no. 10).

As regards the selection of letterforms and typefaces, again Tschichold was unequivocal: "Among all the types that are available, the so-called 'Grotesque' (sanserif) or 'block letter' ('skeleton letters' would be a better name) is the only one in spiritual accordance with our time."[60] This also was not new, but again, it had particular resonance in Germany, where Gothic typefaces had been in use for reading, not just display, at all levels of society. There was a long history of allegiance to Gothic script as something that bound German-speaking peoples together before there was any real movement to establish a German nation. Gutenberg's books were printed using Gothic, or "black letter"; Martin Luther's writings appeared in black letter; and most German schoolchildren up to the First World War learned to read in black letter. To some, allegiance to Gothic script was an assertion of German cultural identity, and Otto von Bismarck, the architect of German unification, is reported to have returned gifts of books set in Antiqua with the curt statement, "Deutsche Bücher in lateinischen Buchstaben lese ich nicht" (I do not read German books in Latin letters).[61] In this context, one can understand why letterforms and typefaces would polarize opinion in the 1920s. Sanserif had been a rallying cry for modernist graphic designers for almost a generation, although it had not been tenable, at least as a reading face, until the recent development of new typefaces.

There were still reservations about the new faces, especially Erbar and Kabel, but Paul Renner's Futura was widely felt to be the way forward. This sanserif had all the characteristics that Tschichold was looking for. It was Roman, it was simple, it was based on a standardized unit, and it was "international," by which he meant that it was not nationalistic [Fig. 31]. There may have been problems with Futura (and all sanserifs) as a reading face because of the relationship between the familiarity of serifed letters and legibility, but Tschichold felt they could be overcome by increased availability and better-quality punches and molds.[62] There is no doubt that sanserif has a simplicity and uniformity that seemed to express many of the ideals of a standardized, egalitarian society, just as the image of the engineer represented a certain pragmatic efficiency over the superfluous additions of the artist, but there were many in the trade who objected to its use in reading texts. To Tschichold, this was no more than faint-heartedness when confronting a universal and democratic future, and he took every opportunity to dismiss the contributions of "artistic printers," whose preferred typefaces were alternately "disturbing," "individualistic," and "ornamental." "The simple geometric forms of sanserif express something too: clarity and concentration on essentials, and so the essence of our time."[63] Needless to say, *Die neue Typographie* was printed using a sanserif. Tschichold had spent some time thinking about it before accepting Akzidenz Grotesk, a utilitarian typeface from the later nineteenth century, as the best of the faces available to the printer.

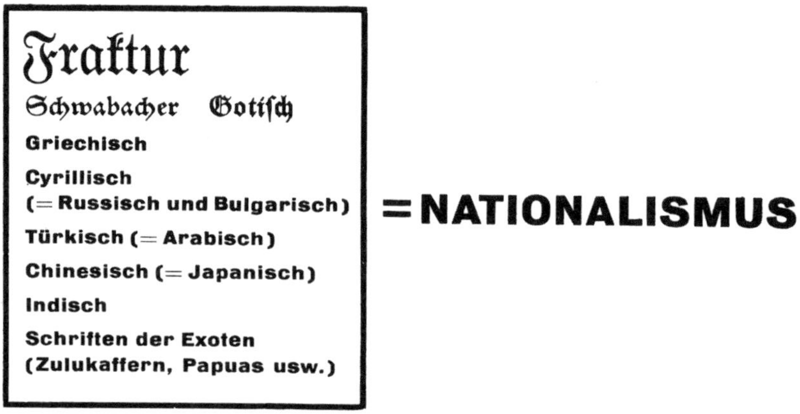

31

When Futura was launched, the Bauer foundry's publicity emphasized that the new face worked very well in conjunction with photography [Fig. 32].[64] Moholy-Nagy gave photography a key role in his 1923 and 1925 essays (Primary Text, nos. 3 and 5), as did Dexel in "Was ist neue Typographie?" (Primary Text, no. 9) and Burchartz in *Gestaltung der Reklame* (Primary Text, no. 12). Tschichold took up the subject in both "elementare typographie" (Primary Text, no. 7) and "Was ist und was will die neue Typografie?" (Primary Text, no. 15) as well as in *The New Typography*. Noting the "picture-hunger" of modern man, he writes: "The photograph has become such a remarkable characteristic of our age that it is now impossible to imagine its non-existence."[65] The adoption of photography was not merely a matter of convenience or the insatiable demand for illustrations. For Moholy-Nagy and Lissitzky, the photograph was a unique medium with its own modes of depiction and representation, but it also symbolized how the Romantic, individualist view of the world was being replaced by the rigor and objectivity of the machine. Photography also gave rise to new techniques and possibilities, such as photomontage, photograms, and the juxtaposition of positive and negative imagery, each of which suggested modes of vision and interpretation that had not been fully explored until the 1920s. As Moholy-Nagy wrote in *The New Vision*, "the limits of photography cannot be determined. . . . It is not the person ignorant of writing but the one ignorant of photography who will be the illiterate of the future."[66] Tschichold acknowledges the importance of these developments, especially in the field of advertising, as well as its impact on modes of seeing and identifying imagery. But he is most concerned with the new possibilities photography opened up for typography and layout, and the "synthesis between typography and photography" that Moholy-Nagy had dubbed "typophoto."[67] Tschichold shared Moholy-Nagy's optimistic view of the transformative role of photography on design and society:

The enormous possibilities of photography itself have so far hardly been recognized, outside a small group of a few specialists, and certainly not exhausted. There is no doubt that the graphic culture of the future will make a far greater use of photography than today. Photography will be as expressive of our age as the woodcut was of the Middle Ages. For this reason it is absolutely necessary for every graphic professional, even today, to develop creatively all the techniques of photography and reproduction as far as possible and prepare them for the higher demands that will surely be made of them in the near future.[68]

Part 1 closes with a chapter on standardization, which Tschichold views as the system of the future, without any exceptions. This matter of standardization and the establishment of recognized modular units in all areas of production was also a recurring theme in contemporary writings on architecture and design. Tschichold was aware of Le Corbusier's writings, and he echoes many of the Swiss architect's views.[69] When Le Corbusier writes, "Mass production demands a search for standards. Standards lead to perfection," one can begin to recognize the shared outlook of modernists across various art forms.[70] But Le Corbusier was hardly alone in promoting these views. Ernst May, Mart Stam, and Bruno Taut, all prominent in the public discourse on modern design and architecture, held similar views, not so much as a preference, but because standardization seemed the only solution to the challenges facing modern Germany. Tschichold shared their belief that standardization was no hindrance to creativity, especially when he turns to issues of paper size. Indeed, this was one of the most basic and yet most practical proposals in preparing the printing industry for yet more effective industrialization. In one of his more insistent passages, Tschichold lists all the advantages of standardized paper sizes, for the user, the printer, the tradesman, and the manufacturer.

32

On this point, Tschichold was joining in a controversy that began in the nineteenth century.[71] Recognizing the interrelated nature of modern industries, various state and professional bodies embarked on a campaign to establish standard types and sizes that would operate across the country to improve efficiency and coordination between firms. The need for industry-wide standards was given greater urgency during the First World War and led to the establishment of the Normenausschuß der deutschen Industrie (Standardization Committee of German Industry), renamed the Deutscher Normenausschuß (German Standardization Committee) in 1926. One of the first and most effective DI-NORM (or DIN) standards to be set was that for paper in 1922, as a result of which the sizing and terms A4, A3, A5, etc. were introduced.[72] Not everyone in the book trade was entirely happy with this, nor were some other users of paper, including artists, designers, newspaper editors, retailers, and printers of packaging, many of whom felt that their creativity and the distinctiveness of various products were being compromised under a uniform national format. To the modernists, there was no doubting the logic of standardization to the extent that it pointed the way toward the future organization of society. The radical journal *ABC*, edited by Mart Stam and El Lissitzky, even published an article on this in its second issue (Primary Text, no. 11). This was precisely the sort of matter that Tschichold felt his book could take up, and not just on the principles of utopian design and social engineering. Ten pages of *The New Typography* are devoted to a systematic explanation of DIN 476 and how the proportions might be exploited for effective design of letterheads, index cards, booklets, and other paper products.

In the second part of the book, Tschichold turns to more practical matters, discussing the implications for each category of printed material that requires the attentions of the designer. Starting with the typographic symbol, or logo, he moves successively through topics such as the business letterhead, the envelope, the postcard, the business card, advertising matter, the typo-poster, the pictorial poster, labels, advertisements, the periodical, the newspaper, tables and graphs, and the new book, each copiously illustrated with examples by some of the leading practitioners. Two years earlier, Herbert Bayer had been in touch with Tschichold about the "commercial letter," which he felt was developing in response to standardization into a new form "encapsulated by the designed concept of the 'letterhead.'"[73] The two were equally preoccupied with standardized envelopes and how envelope windows could become active features in the design. Bayer had sent him examples of the stationery he had designed for the wallpaper and flooring company Tapetenhaus Ruhl, which Tschichold duly illustrated. In many respects, these simple pieces of utilitarian paper were at the cutting edge of the New Typography, at the point where modern design entered the mainstream of everyday business life.

At the end of his journey through the various tasks of the modern designer-printer, Tschichold turns to book design, the discipline that he had been trained in and which still enjoyed a certain cachet as the most prestigious and serious pursuit of the trade. The "New Book," in his view, should reflect modern patterns of reading. Instead of traditional typesetting, which is suited to reading aloud or lengthy study of a text, modern books should be more like newspapers or even films, in which speed of movement and comprehension are more important than "feeling" each separate letter and word. He also felt that books were becoming increasingly visual and that photography could play as great a role in book design as it was already playing in advertising. Tschichold was even prepared to advocate a distinctly avant-garde approach to book design, citing the experimental typography of the Futurists and Dadaists. Poetry was in many respects the front line of this radicalism. Tschichold cites the "concrete" forms of Guillaume Apollinaire's *Calligrammes*, while reserving his highest praise for the Russians: Lissitzky's design for Vladimir Mayakovsky's collection *Dlia golosa* (For the Voice, 1923) [Fig. 33], with its "thumb index" similar to those used for parts catalogues and address books, and Rodchenko's *Pro eto* (About This), another

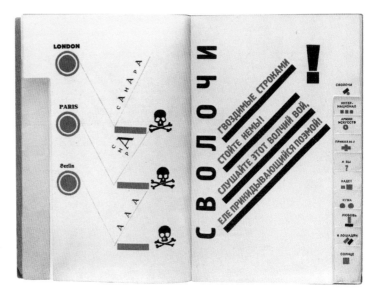

33

Mayakovsky collection, which was the first poetry book to be illustrated entirely by photography [Fig. 34].[74] At heart, however, Tschichold was most interested in reforming book design to make books cheaper and easier to use, which meant introducing standardized formats, greater integration of text and illustration, and attending to reasonable standards of material quality. He attacked the cult of fine printing and unnecessarily expensive materials that had made German books the most costly in the world. These values would remain a constant throughout his career. Despite Tschichold's rejection of the more extreme claims of modernism in the later 1930s, his concern for well-designed, attractive, and affordable books would come to the fore again in 1947, when he took over responsibility for the design of Penguin Books in London.

Tschichold closes the book with a bibliography that is basically a selection of modern books and periodicals illustrating the principles of the movement, and a list of names and addresses of the various designers that he regarded as its leading exponents.[75] These were the people

33 El Lissitzky. Vladimir Mayakovsky, *Dlia golosa* (For the Voice), 1923. Letterpress. Printed by State Printing House, Moscow-Berlin. The Museum of Modern Art. Gift of the Judith Rothschild Foundation. 280.2001.1–25.

34 Aleksandr Rodchenko. Vladimir Mayakovsky, *Pro eto* (About This), 1923. Published by Gosudarstvennoe izdatel'stvo, Moscow. Letterpress. The Museum of Modern Art. Jan Tschichold Collection, Gift of Philip Johnson. 813.1999. Cat. 17.

34

with whom he had been corresponding over the previous five years, or else they were designers whose work he had seen or heard about from his various friends and correspondents. And they were the designers whose work he had been collecting. A brief glance at the list of addresses is enough to indicate a map of the New Typography: of the sixteen designers listed, ten are in Germany, two are in France (although one of those is the Dutchman van Doesburg), and one each in Prague, Moscow, Vienna, and Wassenaar in the Netherlands. The same pattern can be observed in the recommended periodicals, which are exclusively avant-garde journals based in Czechoslovakia, France, Germany, Hungary, the Netherlands, and Switzerland. More significant, however, is the absence of the major printing and graphic design trade journals, such as *Gebrauchsgraphik*, which had been founded just four years earlier in 1924 and was perceived by many to be abreast of current trends.[76] For Tschichold, "modern design" was to be found in the little magazines —such as *ABC*, *De Stijl*, *L'esprit nouveau*, and *MA*—that promoted avant-garde art and architecture as part of a vision of the future [Fig. 35].

THE RESPONSE TO *THE NEW TYPOGRAPHY*

The New Typography did not attract the type of criticism that attended "elementare typographie" three years earlier. After all, *Typographische Mitteilungen* was a trade journal, and the traditionalists in the printing community may have felt that, because its role was at least partly educational, it should maintain certain recognized standards and advocate good practice within the profession. By contrast, *The New Typography* was a modest-looking book with a somewhat down-to-earth, practical, and serviceable purpose. It did, nevertheless, receive some hostile criticism from Tschichold's former teachers. Heinrich Wieynck felt moved to write four articles in response, expressing a view quite widely held among the print conservatives that the new movement was too rigid and programmatic and was thus a restriction on "the capacity for personal creativity." Nevertheless, Wieynck acknowledged that the book

35

was "an interesting document of its time" and a "milestone" in the development of its author.[77] Walter Tiemann had a different complaint. Affirming the high ideals of traditional printing, he suggested that the book would appeal to "the uncritical masses."[78] Less predictably, Tschichold came in for even stronger criticism from the left: the reviewer in *Die rote Fahne* (The red flag), the official organ of the Communist Party of Germany (KPD), took him to task for being insufficiently political in his analysis.[79] This was mild, however, in comparison to a review in the *Bauhaus* magazine, in which the anonymous reviewer attacked Tschichold for failing to "deny absolutely all capitalist advertising, root and branch, while private commerce remains in existence." The reviewer continues, in a somewhat patronizing tone that suggests it was written by a student: "You, Mr Tschichold, seem to be content with formal superficialities and speak already of a new philosophy just because you are able to fill a whole book with illustrations of tectonic-constructivistically designed printed examples. Forgive us, but this endless series of schematically applied constructivisms is deadly boring."[80] Ironically, Herbert Bayer, who had left the Bauhaus earlier the same year, wrote to Tschichold supporting all the design principles and the need for rules, but criticizing the inclusion of a political stance, stating that he considered it "false to introduce this subject with a worldview."[81]

Despite the mixed responses to the book, *The New Typography* confirmed Tschichold as a major spokesman for the movement that was now evident in every city in Central and Eastern Europe. It also meant that Tschichold was in demand for lectures, exhibitions, and participation in new projects. As already mentioned, he was an active member of the Ring and participated in both of their traveling exhibitions. He was also included in *Gefesselter Blick* (Captured glance), a book surveying recent developments in advertising design and echoing many of the ideas put forward by Moholy-Nagy, Lissitzky, and Tschichold.[82] Each of the twenty-six contributors to the book was invited to answer a simple question, to be reprinted next to illustrations of their work: "What principles do you follow in the design of your typography, or, do you actually have principles in this respect?" Tschichold's brief, condensed reply might be taken as a motto for his approach to design in general: "I attempt in my advertising work to attain maximum fitness for purpose and a unity of the individual, constructional elements."[83]

NEW INITIATIVES

Although not a member of the Deutscher Werkbund (DWB), Tschichold was appointed to the selection committee for the Werkbund's *Film und Foto* exhibition (FiFo), to be held in Stuttgart between May and June 1929. FiFo was one of the most ambitious attempts to showcase recent developments in photography [Fig. 36]. The theme was timely: photography was undergoing something of a technical revolution with the

36

introduction of high-speed 35mm film in rolls and the small Leica 1 cameras, and the critical discourse surrounding the aesthetics of film and photography was buzzing.[84] The New Typography and typophoto formed only one area of overlap: the very medium of photography was being reassessed as the quintessence of modernity. With around a thousand works on display from Europe, the Soviet Union, and the United States, the exhibition brought together many of the greatest and most innovative artists and designers with an interest in the medium. John Heartfield was allocated one room, as was Lissitzky, while Moholy-Nagy was given the responsibility of hanging much of the exhibition so as to clarify certain lines of development. It was so popular with professionals and the public alike that a version of the exhibition was shown over the next two years in Zurich, Berlin, Danzig, Vienna, Zagreb, Munich, Tokyo, and Osaka. Despite the success of the exhibition and the widespread circulation of Willi Ruge's striking poster, there was a distinct lack of illustrated publications to engage with the new work on display. Seeing an opportunity, Tschichold and Franz Roh, a critic and art historian from Munich, decided to publish a book on the new photography, *Foto-Auge* (Photo-eye) [Fig. 37]. This remains one of the most famous books on photography, not least because the cover, designed by Tschichold, contains Lissitzky's self-portrait photomontage "The Constructor." Included within were seventy-six photographs and composite works by many of the artist-designers associated with the New Typography, including Herbert Bayer, Burchartz, Heartfield, Hans Leistikow, Moholy-Nagy, Piet Zwart, and Tschichold himself. Tschichold was particularly proud of this cover and of the whole book, which was selected among the "50 Most Beautiful Books" of 1929.

Foto-Auge did not sell well, possibly as a result of the fallout from the international financial crisis, but Roh and Tschichold were committed to developing this area of publishing, setting up a book series titled "Fototek" along lines similar to *Foto-Auge*. Published by Klinkhardt and Biermann, Berlin, each volume had sixty illustrations and a cover

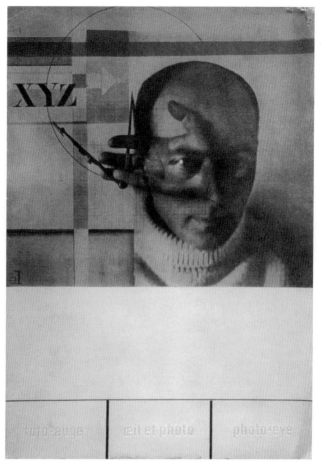

37

designed by Tschichold. Only two volumes were published, one on Moholy-Nagy and the second on Aenne Biermann, each with a restrained cover composed of a photograph and a single block of color within which the title and details were organized in an asymmetrical layout [Fig. 38]. The lack of sales was a major disappointment to the two editors, especially because the proposed future titles, including "Photomontage," "Police Photographs," "Typophoto in the USSR," and "El Lissitzky," suggested an ambitious survey of current themes in the

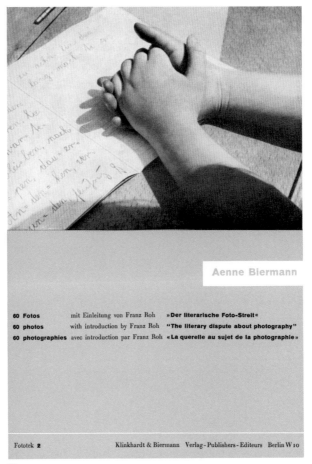

38

New Photography. It was through his plans for these photography books that Tschichold first became acquainted with Aleksandr Rodchenko, an artist-designer whose work he admired and whom he had praised in *The New Typography*. Tschichold lost no time in requesting examples of Rodchenko's photographs and graphic design work to illustrate one or another of his projected publications [Fig. 39]. He was also in touch with designers across Central Europe, building up his collection and gaining a more comprehensive overview of modern graphic design than

38 Jan Tschichold.
*Aenne Biermann:
60 photos*, 1930.
Published by
Klinkhardt &
Bierman, Berlin.
Photolithograph.
Private collection.

39 Aleksandr
Rodchenko. *Novyi
LEF: Zhurnal levogo
front iskusstv 6*,
1927. Published by
Gosudarstvennoe
Izdatel'stvo, Moscow.
Letterpress and half-
tone. The Museum
of Modern Art. Jan
Tschichold Collection,
Gift of Philip Johnson.
820.1999. Cat. 43.

39

perhaps anyone else. Indeed, this was probably Tschichold's most active period of collecting; he would soon be engaged in preparing new
books on typography and graphic design.

The New Typography itself had sold quite well. From an initial print
run of five thousand, it seems to have been "almost sold out" by 1930—
quite an impressive feat for a largely technical book aimed at printers,
designers, and typographers.[85] There were plans to produce a Russian
edition and a second German edition, possibly in A4 format with more

and better illustrations than in the first edition, but these proposals fell away as the chill of the international financial crisis began to be felt. There were other projects, however, not least two books that elaborated aspects of the New Typography for new and different readerships. *Eine Stunde Druckgestaltung* (Print design in an hour, 1930) was one of a series of introductory texts produced by Wedekind, the Stuttgart publishing company. Although mostly a book of illustrations using examples from his own collection, Tschichold's introductory essay (Primary Text, no. 15) is perhaps the clearest and most concise exposition of the New Typography. The full subtitle, "Basic Concepts of the New Typography with Illustrated Examples for Typesetters, Advertising Specialists, Users of Printed Matter, and Bibliophiles," gives an indication of the aims of the book.[86] It was also very well presented in an A4 format, with a silvered paper cover featuring the title in uppercase sanserif in black and red.

The second of Tschichold's books on typography and graphic design in the wake of *The New Typography* was *Typografische Entwurfstechnik* (Techniques of typographic design, 1932), which, despite its industrial appearance, with the DIN paper sizes marked out on a yellow A4 cover, was concerned primarily with typesetting by hand[87] [Fig. 40]. Unlike *Eine Stunde Druckgestaltung*, *Typografische Entwurfstechnik* is more of a technical manual, with guidelines on type selection, font size, layout, spacing, etc., and the text is aimed at people intending to work in a print workshop. As such, it could be regarded as a companion to *Schriftschreiben für Setzer* (Hand-lettering for compositors), a book on handwriting that Tschichold had published the previous year.[88]

These interests in the role of handcraftsmanship, however, should not be taken to imply that Tschichold was retreating from the issues brought to the forefront by *The New Typography*. He continued to give lectures and publish articles elaborating his views and giving clearer explanations of certain aspects of modern typographic design.[89] Despite these contributions, the old guard remained entrenched in their opposition to the movement, while the younger generation, although not in

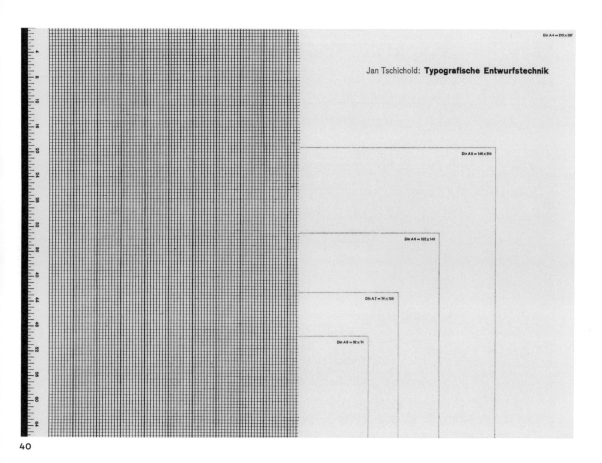

Din A 4 = 210 × 297

Jan Tschichold: **Typografische Entwurfstechnik**

Din A5 = 148 × 210

Din A6 = 105 × 148

Din A7 = 74 × 105

Din A8 = 52 × 74

40

40 Jan Tschichold.
*Typografische
Entwurfstechnik*
(Techniques of
Typographic Design),
1929. Letterpress
on vellum. Private
collection.

any way united in their aims, were still committed to a radical change
in style and practice. The division was brought to a head in 1933, when
Typographische Mitteilungen published the responses to a survey of
typographers, designers, and printers asking four broad questions: Has
"objective typographic design" (i.e., the New Typography) come to a
halt? How will typography develop in the future? Have sanserif typefaces lost their status as "the type for modern typographic expression"?
Is an imminent return of Fraktur likely? The forty-five respondents included some of the leading figures in the modern movement—Josef Albers,

Bayer, Burchartz, Renner, and Trump—and there was general support for the moderns overall. Nevertheless, the traditionalists used this forum to repeat many of their earlier complaints: the New Typography was too dogmatic; it was excessively rigid, made optical spacing redundant, and therefore imposed limits on individual creativity; and it was tainted with political ideology when it should be promoting "pure" typographic principles. Tschichold addressed some of the criticisms in his response, which was published in the March issue, providing a clear and level-headed but unrepentant exposition of his views:

> The change in typographic style which is called the "new typography" and is referred to in the survey by the expression "objective typographic design" cannot have reached a standstill if only for the simple reason that it has hardly got under way. We should not deceive ourselves that a penetration of the new ideas or indeed their practical realization can only be spoken about in terms of a minority of colleagues. The change in style should not be confused with a fashion, which disappears after a short while. We are not at all concerned with the new for its own sake, rather with the right, the good. The struggle is not directed against everything old, but against all that is unusable and bad, and not least against the falsely new! A turning away from unpleasantly monumental to nothing other than meaningful visual form would be desirable. The task of those dedicated to the new style is to make it more profound, and incidentally we want to ensure its dissemination. Something new is not to be expected and is entirely superfluous, since the new has so far been absorbed by so few, though for this reason its fruits have been all the richer. The need for a pleasant change in a merely modish sense attests to superficiality and a lack of understanding of the meaning of the change in style. Only the "bad economic conditions" are hampering the effects of the new.[90]

A CHAIN OF RIDICULOUS CIRCUMSTANCES

Typografische Entwurfstechnik (Techniques of typographic design) and *Schriftschreiben für Setzer* (Hand-lettering for compositors), both of which address the role of handcraftsmanship in the training of typesetters and graphic designers, must have emerged from Tschichold's teaching at the Berufsschule and Meisterschule in Munich. Although he lived in a comfortable apartment in the new, middle-class neighborhood of Borstei, a garden suburb in the north of the city, one senses from his letters and others' descriptions that Tschichold never felt truly settled in the Bavarian capital. He had made several firm friends, not least Franz Roh, his collaborator on the Fototek book series, who was a near neighbor. His family life was clearly happy and supportive, especially after the birth of his son Peter in 1929, but Tschichold's links were increasingly international by this time, and he may have felt constrained by the lack of opportunities in the city. Various aspects of his employment were frustrating. Renner, concerned above all to maintain stability and keep the two colleges out of controversy, was not supportive of Tschichold's very public participation in the debates of the day. The tension between his day-to-day job and the more stimulating activities of publishing, traveling, lecturing, and collecting examples of modern graphic design came to a head at the start of the new year in 1933 when Tschichold resigned from his post. Whatever he had in mind for employment and income, this did not materialize, and within a few weeks he had thought better of it and was forced to ask Renner to give him back his job. Despite the rift this caused between the two colleagues, Tschichold was reappointed, although with reduced benefits. But events overtook them before a new working relationship could be established.[91]

On January 30, 1933, President Hindenburg appointed Adolf Hitler as chancellor, and four weeks later, following a fire at the Reichstag building in Berlin, emergency powers were granted that allowed the suspension of civil liberties. In the general election on March 5, Hitler's coalition gained a narrow majority, and by the end of the month the chancellor and the Nazi Party were in absolute control of the country. Almost immediately, a warrant was issued for Tschichold's arrest. He was well known locally as a leftist with unconventional views, and in the press he had the reputation of being a "Bolshevik." Fortunately, he was away when the police called. Edith had to endure a series of heavy-handed searches of their house. Hearing of the danger, Tschichold hid out at a friend's house on his return, but he quickly realized that he would have to turn himself in to protect his family. He spent more than four weeks in prison with no clear indication of what would happen to him before his release as part of a general amnesty. In the interim, he was informed that his earlier resignation from the Meisterschule had been accepted, and he could not return to his position. He was now faced with prosecution on the grounds of his communist associations, although he had never been a member of the KPD. He had no income or prospects for employment in the fields of design or education. Through friends he was told that there might be a possibility for employment in Switzerland, and with some assistance the family obtained a travel permit and crossed the border in late July.

SWITZERLAND

The Tschicholds were safe, for the moment, but there was little work available and, in any case, refugees had certain restrictions on their opportunities for employment. Tschichold was given some work as a typographic designer for the publisher Benno Schwabe, and he gained a part-time teaching position at the Basel Gewerbeschule (Applied Arts School). These were reduced circumstances in every sense compared to what he was used to in Munich, but over the next few years he was able gradually to consolidate his position, gain additional work, and achieve a comfortable living for himself and his family. There were even some interesting commissions along the way, notably posters and catalogues for the Basel Gewerbemuseum, which allowed him to refine and elaborate some of his earlier principles [Fig. 41]. He also met and corresponded with a number of Swiss designers and photographers who shared his views. He got to know Herbert Matter, for example, before the photographer and designer emigrated to the United States in 1935, and also Max Bill, who had studied at the Bauhaus and was a fully committed modernist in his work and outlook. Tschichold also resumed his correspondence with designers from all over Europe and continued to exchange and collect examples of current work. Although circumstances in Germany were becoming increasingly difficult for artists, architects,

41 Jan Tschichold. *Die Konstruktivisten* (The Constructivists) poster, 1937. Lithograph. The Museum of Modern Art. Abby Aldrich Rockefeller Fund, Jan Tschichold Collection. 356.1937.

41

and designers, exciting work was still going on, above all in Czechoslo-vakia, where Sutnar, Zdeněk Rossmann, and František Kalivoda were at their peak. Kalivoda alone launched two magazines in the mid-1930s, *Ekran* (Screen, 1934) and *Telehor* (Television, 1936), each of which dem-onstrated a sophisticated grasp of the New Typography in asymmet-rical layout, sanserif type, and bold use of photography.

Tschichold was still in demand as a writer and speaker on typogra-phy and printing, and he was able to travel from his base in Switzerland to cities such as Copenhagen, Stockholm, and Prague. In 1935 he visited London, initially to assist with an exhibition of his own work at the pub-lisher Lund Humphries that was being organized by Edward McKnight Kauffer. Two years later, he was a guest of the Double Crown Club, an exclusive dining club for printers, designers, and bibliophiles, that was at the center of the typographical renaissance in the British printing and publishing industry. Type design and fine printing had been something of a special category in Britain, embodying the continuing values of design reform and the Arts and Crafts movement in the twentieth cen-tury. As in most other cultural areas, however, the British had remained somewhat aloof from developments in modern design from the Con-tinent. Nevertheless, Tschichold met and began to correspond with some of the leading figures in the British printing industry and, by exten-sion, with many others from the modern art and design worlds, such as Barbara Hepworth, Stanley Morison, Ben Nicholson, and Herbert Read. Whether this, in itself, was an invigorating experience, or whether he was already doubting the values that had informed his pioneering work in the 1920s, Tschichold seems to have become quite enamored of the British scene. He had apparently always admired *The Fleuron*, a magazine that ran from 1923 to 1930, edited by Oliver Simon and Stanley Morison, mainstays of the Double Crown circle [Fig. 42]. By 1937 Tschichold was having second thoughts on the relevance of the New Typography. If he did not repudiate his earlier views, he was at least willing to accom-modate traditional values in book design alongside the more radical

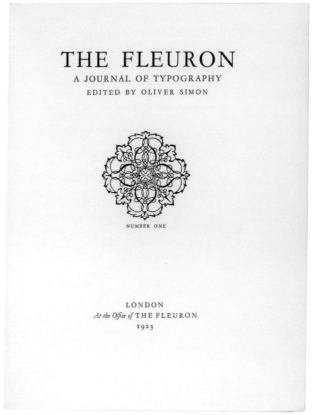

42

approach of the New Typography.[92] The modern movement in design was already in retreat, so Tschichold's change of heart must have been dispiriting to the few remaining supporters holding on to their principles, if not their jobs and livelihood. At this stage, at least, Tschichold did not broadcast his apostasy. Nevertheless, in Germany, the country where the great debates on design had been thrashed out in public, where tempers were raised over issues such as asymmetry and sanserif, and where idealistic claims were made repeatedly for design to work in concert with radical politics to change society, the movement had become almost invisible and possibly even irrelevant to the times.

1   The family originated in Poland, and Johannes's surname on his birth certificate was spelled "Tzschichhold." By 1920 he had simplified it to Tschichold. Information on Tschichold's life is drawn from his numerous autobiographical writings and from Christopher Burke, *Active Literature: Jan Tschichold and the New Typography* (London: Hyphen, 2007). For a bibliography of Tschichold's writings, see Jan Tschichold, *Schriften 1925–1974*, 2 vols. (Berlin: Brinkmann und Bose, 1991–92).

2   Rudolf von Larisch's most influential work was *Beispiele künstlerischer Schrift aus vergangenen Jahrhunderten*, 5 vols. (Vienna: Osterreichische Staatsdruckerei, 1900–26). Delitsch subscribed to the view that historic scripts or handwriting styles could be taken as an expression of national character (*volkerpsychologische momente*). See H. Delitsch, *Geschichte der abendlandischen Schreibschriftformen* (Leipzig: Hiersemann, 1928), 142 .

3   On Koch and the background to German calligraphy in the modern period, see Gerald Cinamon, *Rudolf Koch: Letterer, Type Designer, Teacher* (London: British Library, 2000).

4   "Jan Tschichold, 1924–1944," 2, manuscript; quoted in Burke, *Active Literature*, 19.

5   Jan Tschichold, "Flöhe ins Ohr" [Fleas in the ear], *Schriften* (Berlin: Brinkmann und Bose, 1992), 2:361–62.

6   Schnabel's "Palatino" series of poetry books were lithographic reproductions of calligraphic texts; some of the luxury editions included initials in gold added by hand. As such, they could be described as gift books for bibliophiles.

7   The Buchkunstbewegung was a movement in Germany in the early twentieth century to reform and improve the quality of book design, elevating the book arts to a position equal to that of the fine arts. Janus-Presse, founded in 1907, was one of the earliest private presses in Germany, soon followed by Bremer Press and Cranach Press, each offering a model of good typography, illustration, and binding. On this movement, see Jürgen Eyssen, *Buchkunst in Deutschland: Vom Jugendstil zum Malerbuch* (Hanover: Schlütersche, 1980), 23–26, 40–68.

8   *Internationale Ausstellung für Buchgewerbe und Grafik* (Bugra) was intended to mark the 100th anniversary of the Battle of Leipzig in October 1813. In fact, this huge book trade and graphic arts exhibition was held in Leipzig between May and October 1914.

9   "Jan Tschichold, 1924–1944," 3; quoted in Burke, *Active Literature*, 19. Berthold Wolpe

(1905–89) had a similar experience, but with the opposite outcome. After becoming Koch's pupil at Offenbach in 1924, Wolpe developed his career as a calligrapher and a book and type designer from within the Koch tradition, later becoming chief designer for the British publisher Faber and Faber.

10   A key text in this tendency to celebrate the Gothic aspects of German culture was Wilhelm Worringer, *Formprobleme der Gothik* [Form in Gothic] (Munich: Piper, 1912). Four years earlier, Worringer had published his doctoral thesis as *Abstraktion und Einfühlung: Ein Beitrag zur Stilpsychologie* [Abstraction and empathy: An essay in the psychology of style] (Munich: Piper, 1908), in which the final chapter was devoted to the Gothic.

11   On this debate, see Theodor Adorno, Walter Benjamin, Ernst Bloch, Bertolt Brecht, and Georg Lukács, *Aesthetics and Politics* (London: Verso, 2007), 16–58, and Siegfried Kracauer, *From Caligari to Hitler: A Psychological History of the German Film* (Princeton, NJ: Princeton University Press, 1947).

12   Tschichold acknowledged these art movements as key sources in the introduction to "elementare typographie," *Typographische Mitteilungen* (October 1925): 194.

13   Van Doesburg had several aliases, which he would use when the situation seemed appropriate. I. K. Bonset was his Dadaist name, invented in 1922, when there was much interaction between Dadaists and Constructivists. See Doris Wintgens-Hötte, "Van Doesburg Tackles the Continent," in *Constructing a New World: Van Doesburg and the International Avant-Garde*, ed. Gladys Fabre and Doris Wintgens-Hötte (London: Tate, 2009), 15.

14   According to Adolf Behne, more than 15,000 people attended the exhibition. See Klaus Kändler, Helga Karolewski, and Ilse Siebert, eds., *Berliner Begegnungen: Ausländische Künstler in Berlin 1918–1933* (Berlin: Dietz, 1987), 73.

15   The issue of *Egység* reproduced work by the INKhUK and OBMOKhU groups and published the "Realistic Manifesto" of August 1920 by Gabo and Antoine Pevsner and the 1921 "Program of the First Working Group of Constructivists" by Alexsei Gan. See Oliver Botar, *Technical Detours: The Early Moholy-Nagy Reconsidered* (New York: CUNY / Salgo Trust, 2006), 150–51.

16   *Veshch/Gegenstand/Objet* was published in 1922 by Skythen Verlag (Berlin) in an attempt to showcase recent Russian art and literature in the West. Only three issues were published:

the opening double issue (nos. 1–2) in March/ April and issue 3 in May 1922. Issue 3 was issued in Germany but refused distribution in the Soviet Union.

17 In February 1922, Moholy had a joint exhibition of recent abstract sculpture and prints with his fellow Hungarian émigré Laszlo (Peter) Péri at Galerie der Sturm in Berlin. The same year, he published *Buch neuer Künstler* [Book of new artists] with Lajos Kassák, and his work was featured in the journals *Der Sturm*, *MA*, and *Zenit*, among others.

18 The Groszherzoglich Sächsischen Kunstgewerbeschule was founded in 1908 under the directorship of Henry van de Velde with the support of the Grand Duke Wilhelm-Ernst of Saxe-Weimar. As a follower of the English Arts and Crafts movement and its celebration of handcraftsmanship as a spiritual as well as a manual activity, van de Velde placed craft workshop practice at the core of the curriculum. In 1919, the former Kunstgewerbeschule and the Groszherzoglich Sächsischen Hochschule (Academy of Fine Arts) were amalgamated to create the Staatliches Bauhaus. For the first six years, the Bauhaus occupied the buildings in Weimar designed by van de Velde.

19 The "Programm des Staatlichen Bauhauses in Weimar" of 1919, containing the famous woodcut of a Gothic cathedral by Lyonel Feininger, was written by Gropius more in the spirit of an art manifesto than an education program. After the opening line, "The ultimate aim of all visual arts is the complete building!," Gropius emphasizes a return to the crafts and "priority of creativity; freedom of individuality."

20 On the ceramics studio at the Weimar Bauhaus, see Juliet Kinchin, "Theodor Bogler Teapots, 1923," in *Bauhaus 1919–1933: Workshops for Modernity*, ed. Barry Bergdoll and Leah Dickerman (New York: MoMA, 2009), 110–13.

21 Theo van Doesburg, "Teaching at the Bauhaus and Elsewhere: From Copy to Experiment," *Het Bouwbedrijf* 2, no. 10 (October 1925): 363–66. Reprinted in Theo van Doesburg, *On European Architecture: Complete Essays from Het Bouwbedrijf 1924–1931* (Basel: Birkhauser, 1990), 71.

22 The motto "Kunst und Technik: Eine neue Einheit" was the title of a slide lecture that Gropius gave on August 15, 1923, to open the exhibition and the sequence of events known as Bauhauswoche (Bauhaus week).

23 László Moholy-Nagy, "Die neue Typographie," *Staatliches Bauhaus in Weimar, 1919–1923* (Weimar: Bauhaus, 1923), 141.

24 Walter Gropius to Jan Tschichold, August 17, 1925, Tschichold Papers. Tschichold was not alone among the left-leaning intelligentsia with a taste for Bauhaus furniture. Nikolaus Pevsner purchased nursery furniture by Alma Siedhof-Buscher at the 1923 exhibition, which probably marked the beginning of his fascination with both the Bauhaus and the modern movement in general.

25 Joost Schmidt reported that the presses belonged to van de Velde and were confiscated as the property of an alien. Helene Nonne-Schmidt and Heinz Loew, *Joost Schmidt: Lehre und Arbeit am Bauhaus 1919–32* (Dusseldorf: Marzona, 1984), 19.

26 *Typographische Mitteilungen: Zeitschrift des Bildungsverbandes der Deutschen Buchdrucker* [Typographic studies: The journal of the education association of German printers] was founded in Leipzig in 1903. As an educational tool for printers and typographers, it covered type, printing, illustration, and trademark design. Its circulation in the 1920s was in excess of 20,000.

27 *Kulturschau: Allgemeiner Anzeiger für die linksgerichtete Literatur* [Culture review: General advertiser for left-oriented literature], no. 4 (1925): 9–11.

28 El Lissitzky's text appeared in *Merz* no. 4 (July 1923): 47, and is translated in Lissitzky-Küppers, *El Lissitzky*, 359. Schwitters's text, which was published in *Merz* no. 11 (November 1924): 91, was a response to El Lissitzky's, although it was Schwitters himself who, as editor of *Merz*, had published it.

29 Tschichold to Imre Kner, June 12, 1925; quoted in Burke, *Active Literature*, 30.

30 Although Tschichold was in touch with El Lissitzky by this stage and could have checked the authorship of the article in *ABC*, it is not signed and seems out of character with either of the two authors. It is followed by a separate article on modern building by Stam. There is no mention of this article in Lissitzky-Küppers, *El Lissitzky*.

31 The manifesto was published in *Ermitazh*, no. 13 (August 1922): 3–4, although it had been written in the previous year. It appeared in translation in *Egység*, June 30, 1922.

32 Jan Tschichold, "Die neue Gestaltung," *Typographische Mitteilungen* (October 1925): 193.

33 Tschichold emphasized that it was El Lissitzky, not the Bauhaus, who was the true source and master of the New Typography. Ibid., 212.

34 El Lissitzky to Tschichold, October 22, 1925, Tschichold Papers. Quotation from "Five

Letters," translated by David Britt, in *Situating El Lissitzky: Vitebsk, Moscow, Berlin*, ed. Nancy Perloff and Brian Reed (Los Angeles: Getty Research Institute, 2003), 247.

35 *Zeitschrift für Deutschlands Buchdrucker* [The journal of German printers] and *Schweizer graphische Mitteilungen* [Swiss graphics studies] published attacks in 1926 describing Tschichold as a "Bolshevik." Cited in Friedrich Friedl, "Lernen von Jan Tschichold: Echo und Reaktion auf das Sonderheft 'elementare typographie,'" introduction to the reprint of Tschichold's "elementare typographie" (Mainz: Hermann Schmidt, 1986), 9.

36 Albert Giesecke, "Ein Verfechter des Konstruktivismus," *Offset: Buch und Werbekunst* 3, no. 11 (1926): 735–36, 738–39. Giesecke continued to attack Tschichold and the New Typography in general in articles throughout the 1920s and 1930s. See Jeremy Aynsley, *Graphic Design in Germany, 1890–1945* (London: Thames and Hudson, 2000), 184–85.

37 Postcard, Walter Dexel to Tschichold, December 4, 1925, Tschichold Papers.

38 Phoebus-Film was a film production and distribution company based in Berlin. In 1925 they began building cinemas in the major cities of Germany, but this activity ceased in 1927, when a scandal led to the company's decline. See Klaus Kreimeier, *The UFA Story: A History of Germany's Greatest Film Company 1918–1945* (Berkeley: University of California Press, 1999).

39 Tschichold, *The New Typography*, 181. See also Jan Tschichold, "New Paths in Poster Work," *Commercial Art* (June 1931): 29.

40 Tschichold wrote to Piet Zwart that he found Fritz Lang's *Metropolis* (1927) to be "one of the worst films of all time." Tschichold to Zwart, October 20, 1927, Tschichold Papers.

41 Jan Tschichold to Piet Zwart, November 30, 1929, Tschichold Papers.

42 *Die neue Typographie* was published in June 1928. The print run was five thousand, and according to the publisher's yellow publicity leaflet, it cost 6.50 marks, or 5 marks if purchased directly from the publisher. For information on the book and the circumstances of its publication, see Robin Kinross's introduction to Tschichold, *The New Typography*.

43 Karl Michael Scheriau, *Kunstgenossen und Kollegen: Entstehung, Aufbau, Wirkungsweise und Zielsetzung der Gewerkschaftsorganisation der deutschen Buchdrucker von 1848 bis 1933* [Comrades and colleagues in art: The origins, structure, impact, and aims of the union of German book printers, 1848 to 1933] (Berlin: Scheriau, 2000).

44 Adolf Behne, *Max Taut: Bauten und Pläne* (Berlin/Leipzig: Hübsch, 1927).

45 Tschichold, *The New Typography*, 11.

46 Ibid., 13.

47 Ibid., 28.

48 This reading would become a mainstay of the social history of art. See Frederick Antal, "Reflections on Classicism and Romanticism," *Burlington Magazine* 66, no. 385 (April 1935): 159–68.

49 Tschichold, *The New Typography*, 47.

50 Ibid., 53.

51 Ibid., 66–67.

52 Ibid., 67.

53 Ibid., 68.

54 Tschichold's date for Loos's essay, 1898, is an error. "Ornament and Crime" was first delivered as a lecture in 1910 and published in French three years later in *Les cahiers d'aujourd'hui*. It was not published in German until 1929, although the author's views were widely known and reported throughout the 1920s.

55 Tschichold, *The New Typography*, 69.

56 Quoted by László Moholy-Nagy, "Bauhaus and Typography," *Anhaltische Rundschau*, September 14, 1925; Hans Wingler, *The Bauhaus: Weimar, Dessau, Berlin, Chicago* (Cambridge, MA: MIT Press, 1969), 114.

57 Porstmann proposed the adoption of all lowercase initials in *Sprache und Schrift* [Speech and lettering], published by the Vereins Deutscher Ingenieure [Association of German Engineers] in 1920.

58 Tschichold, *The New Typography*, 80.

59 Gropius to Tschichold, November 9, 1925, Tschichold Papers.

60 Tschichold, *The New Typography*, 73.

61 Adolf Reinecke, *Die deutsche Buchstabenschrift: Ihre Entstehung und Entwicklung, ihre Zweckmäßigkeit und völkische Bedeutung* (Leipzig: Hasert, 1910), 79. On this debate, see Peter Bain and Paul Shaw, *Blackletter: Type and National Identity* (New York: Princeton Architectural Press, 1998).

62 On the long history of research into typefaces and legibility, see Herbert Spencer, *The Visible Word: Problems of Legibility* (London: Lund Humphries, 1968), 13–24.

63 Tschichold, *The New Typography*, 76–78.

64 Publicity material claimed that Futura was suited for use in combination with photography and photomontage. "Die Schrift unserer Zeit begleite das Bild unserer Zeit" [The type of our time joins the illustration of our time], *Futura Mappe* (Frankfurt: Bauerische Giesserei, 1927), unpaginated.

65 Tschichold, *The New Typography*, 87.

66 Moholy-Nagy seems to have reworked this quotation several times in the 1920s. One version appeared in "Die Photographie in der Reklame," *Photographische Korrespondenz* 63, no. 9 (September 1, 1927): 259. Walter Benjamin repeats it in "Kleine Geschichte der Photographie" [A short history of photography], *Die literarische Welt* (September–October 1931).

67 Tschichold, *The New Typography*, 92.

68 Ibid., 95.

69 The journal *L'esprit nouveau* and the books *Vers une architecture* and *L'art decoratif d'aujourd'hui* are cited in the list of recommended publications in *The New Typography*, 229 and 231.

70 Le Corbusier, "Mass Produced Buildings," *L'almanach d'architecture moderne* (Paris, 1925), translated in Tim Benton, Charlotte Benton, and Donald Sharp, eds., *Architecture and Design 1890–1939: An International Anthology of Original Articles* (New York: Whitney Library of Design, 1975), 134.

71 While the issues had been raised much earlier, the debate at the Deutscher Werkbund conference in Cologne in 1914 polarized opinion between those advocating craft principles, represented by Henry van de Velde, and those in favor of *Typisierung*, or standardization, advocated by Hermann Muthesius. See Frederic J. Schwartz, *The Werkbund: Design Theory and Mass Culture before the First World War* (New Haven, CT: Yale University Press, 1996), 121–50; Stanford Anderson, "Deutscher Werkbund—The 1914 Debate," in *Companion to Contemporary Architectural Thought*, ed. B. Farmer and H. Louw (New York: Routledge, 1993), 462–67.

72 The acronym DI-NORM was coined in 1918 to describe standards set by the Normenausschuß der deutschen Industrie, or standardization committee. This was later changed to DIN, reflecting the new title of the committee.

73 Herbert Bayer to Tschichold, April 7, 1926, Tschichold Papers.

74 Ibid., 224.

75 Tschichold, *The New Typography*, 229–35.

76 Under the editor Walter Curt Behrendt, *Die Form*, the journal of the Deutscher Werkbund, was more sympathetic to the New Typography. On its relaunch in October 1925, the new cover by Joost Schmidt declared its allegiance to the movement, and in the first year the journal published articles by Willi Baumeister, Max Burchartz, Walter Dexel, and Johannes Molzahn.

77 Heinrich Wieynck, "Die Wandlungen des Johannes," *Gebrauchsgraphik* 5, no. 12 (1928): 79.

78 "Bescheidenheit und Demut: Die Raben und die unkritische Masse," *Typographische Mitteilungen* 26, no. 4 (April 1929): 85.

79 *Die rote Fahne*, December 16, 1928.

80 *Bauhaus* 2, no. 3 (1928); quoted in Burke, *Active Literature*, 81.

81 Bayer to Tschichold, November 26, 1928, Tschichold Papers.

82 Organized by the architect-designers Heinz Rasch and Bodo Rasch, *Gefesselter Blick* was launched in February 1930 with an exhibition at the Graphische Klub, Stuttgart, after which it was shown in other cities. The accompanying book was dominated by members of the Ring and contained examples of advertising work by Baumeister, Dexel, Heartfield, Michel, Vordemberge-Gildewert, and Piet Zwart, among others.

83 Heinz Rasch and Bodo Rasch, *Gefesselter Blick: 25 kürze Monografien und Beiträge über neuer Werbegestaltung* (Stuttgart: Dr. Zaugg, 1930), 102.

84 Although developed before the First World War, the Leica 1 "Rollfilmkamera" only went into production later; it was launched at the Leipzig Spring Fair in 1925.

85 On the title page of Tschichold's book *Eine Stunde Druckgestaltung*, *Die neue Typographie* is listed as "almost out of print."

86 The subtitle, in German: *Grundbegriffe der Neuen Typografie in Bildbeispielen für Setzer, Werbefachleute, Drucksachen-verbraucher und Bibliofilen*.

87 Jan Tschichold, *Typografische Entwurfstechnik* (Stuttgart: Akademischer Verlag Fritz Wedekind, 1932).

88 Jan Tschichold, *Schriftschreiben für Setzer* (Frankfurt: Klimsch, 1931).

89 Apart from many articles in the British magazine *Commercial Art* and other German and Swiss journals, such as *Offset* and *Die Form*, Tschichold published an important article titled "Wo stehen wir heute?" [Where do we stand today?] in *Typographische Mitteilungen* 29, no. 2 (February 1932): 24–25.

90 *Typographisches Mitteilungen* 30, no. 3 (March 1933): 65.

91 In a letter to Imre Reiner from Basel, May 23, 1934, Tschichold referred to this as "a chain of ridiculous circumstances." Tschichold Papers.

92 Jan Tschichold, "Vom richtigen Satz auf Mittelachse" [From the right sentence to the central axis], *Schriften* 1 (1935): 178–85. Translated in Ruari McLean, *Jan Tschichold: Typographer* (London: Lund Humphries, 1975), 126–31.

Chapter 2
The New Typography, 1923–33: Theory and Practice

The position that an epoch occupies in the historical process can be determined more strikingly from an analysis of its inconspicuous surface-level expressions than from that epoch's judgments about itself.

—SIEGFRIED KRACAUER, *THE MASS ORNAMENT*, 1927

Significant literary activity can only be achieved from a rigorous alternation between doing and writing; it must cultivate the inconspicuous forms, rather than the universal gesture of the book, forms that better reflect literature's influence in active communities: in leaflets, brochures, magazine articles, and posters. Only this immediate form of language reveals itself as having emerged from the moment.

—WALTER BENJAMIN, *ONE WAY STREET*, 1928

Like the New Photography, the New Objectivity, and the New Frankfurt, the New Typography emerged in Germany in the 1920s at a moment when there was a hunger for some kind of rebirth of existing cultural forms. As with the other "new" tendencies, the New Typography sounded quite specific, but it actually addressed a broad spectrum of interests. Far from being concerned only with type design and layout, it sought to transform how we comprehend text and imagery through print. In that sense, it was not so much a practical reform of graphic design as an attempt to change fundamentally the ways in which we receive and interpret information. Furthermore, it was a movement that was driven by grand pronouncements, all-embracing theories, and manifestos that invoked a future world in which the way that text and illustration were presented to the public would play a central role in shaping a new consciousness.

MANIFESTOS AND VISIONARIES

While the underlying aims can be traced to the long tradition of "design reform," the term "Die neue Typographie" was given modern currency by the Hungarian artist-designer László Moholy-Nagy in a short essay (Primary Text, no. 3), little more than a paragraph, in the catalogue to the Bauhaus exhibition of 1923.[1] The essay lays out some of the principles of the movement, even before it had real form or aspirations beyond the need to bring design for print into a more dynamic relation with modern life. Opening with a series of statements on the need for "absolute clarity," Moholy-Nagy quickly moves on to much larger questions: the relation between words and meaning, the worldview of modern mankind, the opportunities new technologies offer for reproducing text and imagery, and the unlimited potential of film.[2] These grand claims were entirely within the spirit of the times. The Futurist manifestos before the war had set the tone for artists, architects, and designers to speak broadly of the future possibilities of the modern world when seen through the prism of their specific ideology. For the Italian Futurists, the future would be realized through the recognition that movement, violence, and dynamism were the defining characteristics of the age, and only when these forces were set free from the fetters of the old world would we arrive at the new awareness that was, in any case, our destiny.

As Marinetti wrote in *Les mots en liberté futuriste*, in effect the Futurist manifesto for graphic design: "I have initiated a typographical revolution directed against the bestial, nauseating sort of book that contains passéist poetry or verse à la D'Annunzio—handmade paper that imitates models of the seventeenth century, festooned with helmets, Minervas, Apollos, decorative capitals in red ink with loops and squiggles, vegetables, mythological ribbons from missals, epigraphs, and Roman numerals. The book must be the Futurist expression of Futurist thought"[3] [Fig. 43]. Marinetti was fighting a war against tradition, a war conducted on all fronts. That is why there were Futurist manifestos for each available art form and medium: painting, sculpture, architecture, cinema, music, smell, noise, and lust, as well as typography.[4] Although each manifesto was specific to the medium, the central aims were similar: the destruction

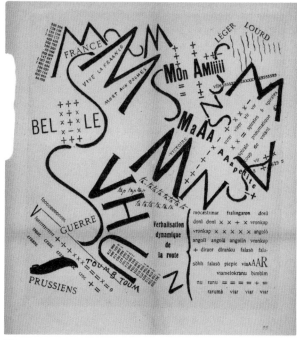

43 Filippo Tommaso Marinetti. "Après la Marne, Joffre visita le front en auto" (After the Marne, Joffre visited the Front in an automobile) from *Les mots en liberté futuristes*, 1919. Published by Edizioni Futuriste di Poesia, Milan. Letterpress. The Museum of Modern Art. Jan Tschichold Collection. Gift of Philip Johnson. 598.1977.3. Cat. 18.

43

of the old order and its replacement with the new by whatever means were most effective. In literature and typography, Marinetti sought disruption of the cognitive process but also the coordination of available resources related to sound, meaning, and print. This merging of form and content—of words as speech *and* words as print—was intended to antagonize the traditionalists, but it touched a nerve among progressives as well. Some could see this entire line of creative experiment as confirmation of a process begun by Stéphane Mallarmé in the previous century, while others were reluctant to surrender the privileged position that poetry enjoyed as a purely literary medium.[5] The Portuguese author Fernando Pessoa commented: "In order to be simultaneous, Marinetti comes out of literature; he wants to be simultaneous by a trick of typographic layout. An inferior form."[6]

For the Dadaists, what the future held mattered less than the need to undermine everything that belonged to the old world—the world that had created the conditions for a total war of unparalleled destruction. To Hans Arp, Hugo Ball, and Tristan Tzara, the central figures of Zurich Dada, the manifesto was a critique and insult, a denunciation of everything based on the flawed logic of bourgeois capitalism. Print and type served a purpose in the Dada interface with the world of officialdom, but it was deployed in a playful manner to subvert the logic and conventions of traditional reading practices. In this spirit, Ilia Zdanevitch's "transparent newspaper," advertising Tzara's *Soirée du coeur à barbe* (Evening of the bearded heart) [Fig. 44], a Dadaist event in Paris in July 1923, employs various typefaces and sizes in illogical lines, interspersed with random "cuts" or wood engravings to create a richly diverse pattern of words and images. This combination of visual elements forces the reader to decipher the information provided in a manner that is very different from the cognitive processes required in either traditional book design or display advertising. What began as an attempt to disrupt the interaction between text and reader also offered possibilities for new modes of engagement and meaning.

44

For the Constructivists, the various manifestos that appeared in Soviet Russia and Central Europe were attempts to establish new aesthetic principles based on modern industrial technologies around which a truly modern art, architecture, and design could flourish. In 1921–22, Aleksandr Rodchenko, Varvara Stepanova, and the other members of the "working group" came up with a "Program" to lay the foundations for a new technological art:

In order to master the creation of practical structures in a really scientific and disciplined way the Constructivists have established three disciplines: *Tectonics*, *Faktura*, and *Construction*.

A. Tectonics or the tectonic style is tempered and formed on the one hand from the properties of communism and on the other from the expedient use of industrial material.

B. *Faktura* is the organic state of the worked material or the resulting new state of its organism. Therefore, the group considers that *faktura* is material consciously worked and expediently used, without hampering the construction or restricting the tectonics.

C. Construction should be understood as the organizational function of Constructivism.[7]

A slightly more pithy and accessible statement was made by El Lissitzky and Ilya Ehrenburg to promote the journal *Veshch/Gegenstand/Objet* at the congress of "progressive artists" in Dusseldorf in 1922: "Our thinking is characterized by the attempt to turn away from the old subjective, mystical conception of the world, and to create an attitude of universality—clarity—reality. . . . The new art is founded not on a subjective, but on an objective basis. This, like science, can be described with precision and is by nature constructive. It unites not only pure art, but all those who stand at the frontier of the new culture. The artist is companion to the scholar, the engineer, and the worker."[8]

These manifestos furnished the critical environment within which Moholy-Nagy turned his attention to typography. In 1923, when he wrote his essay on the new typography, he had no experience in the craft of designing or setting letterforms—or in any aspect of printing for that matter other than his own linocuts. Just five years earlier, after service in the Austro-Hungarian army, he was recuperating from war wounds and preparing to return to his legal studies.[9] His ability to move so quickly to the center of the European avant-garde, making such confident assertions on the future role of typography in shaping a modern consciousness, says more about Moholy-Nagy as an original thinker and theorist than as a practitioner.[10] In this he is a true avant-gardist: someone whose role is to explore the very limits of aesthetic possibility rather than patiently develop the procedures to achieve it. Already by this stage, Moholy-Nagy believed that the traditional media of art and design, the materials with which we create and transmit our ideas, would be replaced by or subsumed under "light," the medium of the future.[11] This belief also explains Moholy-Nagy's particular interest in photography, in all its aspects, and why he saw the merging of type and photography as the immediate challenge facing graphic designers.

In 1925, after two years as a master at the Bauhaus, Moholy-Nagy published his first substantial contribution to the theory of new media: *Malerei, Photographie, Film* (Painting, photography, film)[12] [Fig. 45]. It was

45 László Moholy-Nagy. *Malerei, Fotografie, Film* (Painting, Photography, Film), Bauhausbücher 8, 1925. Published by Albert Langen Verlag, Munich. Printed by Hesse und Becker, Leipzig. Letterpress and photolithograph. Private Collection.

45

the eighth volume in the Bauhausbücher series, which he and Walter Gropius had launched in June 1925. The book itself was an important landmark in graphic design, employing Moholy-Nagy's signature style of bold vertical and horizontal rules, creating an asymmetrical grid that breaks up the various sections of type and photographic illustration into discrete areas while also operating under a dynamic overall design. The book is essentially a collection of seventy-four illustrations showing different applications of new media, with short texts outlining his views on such techniques as photomontage and photograms. The entire project, embracing typography, photography, and film, would become subsumed under a general term, "the New Vision," in which the visible world could be understood and interpreted anew by the fundamental shift that the camera lens had effected on our optical awareness.[13] To Moholy-Nagy, the New Vision had implications for print culture that were as significant as the invention of moveable type. To regard it as merely the application of new technologies to existing forms was to underestimate or misunderstand its potential to change our relationship with the exterior world.

With regard to typography and graphic design, one section of the book was of central importance: "Typophoto" (Primary Text, no. 5). "What is typophoto?" he asks. "Typography is communication composed in type. Photography is the visual presentation of what can be optically apprehended. **Typophoto is the visually most exact rendering of communication.**"[14] Recognizing the essentially linear nature of traditional typography, Moholy-Nagy seeks the full integration of text and image so as to "loosen up" the processes of communication. "The flexibility and elasticity of these techniques bring with them a new reciprocity between economy and beauty. . . . Photography is highly effective when used as typographical material. It may appear as illustration beside the words, or in the form of '**phototext**' in place of words, as a precise form of representation so objective as to permit of no individual interpretation. . . . The typophoto governs the new tempo of the new visual literature."[15] "Tempo" might be taken as the key term, for Moholy-Nagy's ultimate concern was to relate the modes of communication with the dynamism and movement inherent in modern life. Graphic design and typography may be static, fixed forms, but they should at least exploit the sense of time and movement that film was best equipped to represent. In *Malerei, Photographie, Film* Moholy-Nagy writes of "a state of increased activity in the observer, who—instead of meditating upon a static image and instead of immersing himself in it . . . is forced simultaneously to comprehend and to participate in the optical events. Kinetic composition . . . enables the observer . . . to participate, to seize instantly upon new moments of vital insight."[16] Kineticism, or the ability to communicate a sense of movement, would remain one of the underlying aspirations of the New Typography in its attempts to break through to a new conceptual understanding of modernity.

El Lissitzky, the emissary of Russian avant-garde ideas in the West, had already taken the lead in applying Constructivist aesthetic principles to print and, specifically, to typography. "The Topography of Typography," published in Kurt Schwitters's Dadaist journal *Merz* in 1923, one month before Moholy-Nagy's essay in the Bauhaus catalogue, is even more succinct, consisting of just eight statements, rather like biblical commandments to govern the new ways of printing and reading texts (Primary Text, no. 2).[17] Lissitzky's main focus was on the visual character of type, and the need to prioritize "seeing," not "hearing." Again, we are dealing with a visionary approach to graphic design and its potential to bring about a new enlightenment, a new sensibility, on the back of the reproductive technologies that were already available.[18] While Moholy-Nagy could foresee a time when film would replace books as our principal medium of communication, Lissitzky envisaged an "ELECTRO-LIBRARY" in which the printed surface "transcends space and time."[19]

To some extent, this type of futuristic thinking verges on science fiction, but it was inspired by the dramatic changes that photomechanical processes were bringing to the printing industry. This again was not new. Photography had been applied to mass printing since the 1870s, when the photosensitive process block was first introduced to transfer drawn and photographic imagery onto a printing surface.[20] This was closely followed by the introduction of the halftone process in the 1880s, which made it possible to print photographs quickly and cheaply, thus opening the door to mass-circulation illustrated magazines, such as the *Berliner Illustrirte Zeitung*.[21] Since then, the printing industry had been in a state of almost permanent revolution as new processes, equipment, and materials were developed.[22] A certain dichotomy remained, however, partly due to the structure of the industry but also because of the economic environment. Printing for a mass audience requires a considerable financial investment in machinery that often takes many years to recoup. In this context, the introduction of automatic typesetting systems (linotype, monotype, etc.) completely transformed the industry in the early years of the twentieth century, affecting not only the preparation of text for books and magazines but also the role of type foundries and the working relationships among editors, printers, proprietors, and the various suppliers of materials. The adoption of new technologies had to be balanced against the constant need for economy, increased speed of production, and innovation in the final product sold in shops and on city streets. While many people could see the potential of photography to change the printing industry, the existing infrastructure tended to define how it would change, if at all. Artist-designers could appreciate the freedoms offered by the paste-up process, which allowed text and images to be photographed and transferred to a rotary printing plate for offset lithography. These advantages were unlikely to change an industry wedded to different technologies, particularly hot metal typesetting. Nevertheless, many of the new typographers, including Lissitzky, were entranced by the idea of their designs existing on a fine plane of photosensitive fluid that might then be endlessly reproduced on paper—or on a nonphysical plane transcending space and time.[23]

In 1925, two years after "The Topography of Typography," Lissitzky provided a more comprehensive and practical statement of his views on modern typography, "Typographische Tatsachen" (Typographical facts), which was published in the *Gutenberg Festschrift*, a somewhat traditional, antiquarian-looking book marking the twenty-fifth anniversary of the founding of the Gutenberg Museum in Mainz.[24] Lissitzky's text (Primary Text, no. 4) was anything but traditional in either form or content. Opening with an almost unreadable stream of characters to emphasize the mental dexterity involved in word recognition, he goes on to discuss the relationship between thought and symbol, sound and letterform, and the remarkable skills involved in reading even something as mundane as a daily newspaper:

> YOU are accompanied from your first day onwards by printed paper, and your eye is superbly trained to find its way about in this specific field quickly, precisely, and without losing its way. You cast your glances into these forests of paper with the same confidence as the Australian throws his boomerang.

This reflection on the very act of reading is only a preamble to a larger appeal for greater freedom in the disposition of text on the page, and encouragement to treat typography with the same flexibility as speech:

> YOU can see how it is that where new areas are opened up to thought- and speech-patterns, there you find new typographical designs originating organically. These are: modern advertising and modern poetry. . . . YOU should demand of the writer that he really present what he writes; his ideas reach you through the eye and not through the ear. Therefore typographical form should do by means of optics what the voice and gesture of the writer does to convey his ideas.[25]

After Moholy-Nagy and Lissitzky, the third of these futuristic or visionary theorists of the New Typography was Kurt Schwitters, a Dada artist who had always maintained an interest in printed lettering, although not in any conventional sense. Since 1918 he had been assembling pictures from found material, mostly scraps of paper and cast-off objects he found on the studio floor or in the street. On one piece of paper he noticed the cryptic word "MERZ," thought to have been part of a line of text reading "COMMERZ UND PRIVATBANK."[26] Because his work in pictorial art, performance, and assemblage seemed to defy categorization, Schwitters fixed on this random term and used it to define its own category of creative work. "Merz" became the descriptive term for his poetry, music, pictures, constructions, publications, and eventually the graphic design business he would set up in Hanover in 1924. Although he was a singular figure in the world of art and design, Schwitters generally sought out associates to develop and show his work. He had not been very successful in aligning himself with any of the established Dada groups in Paris, Berlin, or Zurich, but in 1922 he participated in a series of events in the Netherlands organized by two members of De Stijl: Theo van Doesburg and Vilmos Huszar.

De Stijl, or neoplasticism, the Dutch movement to reform art and life, was based on a strict adherence to abstraction and the use of only the most basic formal elements—vertical and horizontal lines, the three primary colors, and the noncolors (black, white, and gray). Even in 1922, De Stijl was becoming recognized as the most substantial departure from existing conventions of visual art, and indeed the beginning of an entirely new formal vocabulary that had ramifications for architecture, furniture, interior design, and typography. Although he shared little or nothing with the austere aesthetics of De Stijl, Schwitters's association with van Doesburg marked the beginning of his entry into the burgeoning international avant-garde, to be followed with exhibitions, performances, and lectures across Europe in collaboration with figures such as Hans Arp, Raoul Hausmann, and Tristan Tzara. The most important link from this period, at least in terms of its impact on his graphic design, was with Lissitzky, whom he met in 1922, soon after the Russian had come to Western Europe.

Schwitters began publishing booklets and poetry in 1919, but in 1923 he decided to launch a journal, named (of course) *Merz*. Each issue had a different theme. Number 4, from July 1923, was devoted to *banalitäten* (banalities) and included poetry and artworks by Gerrit Rietveld, Philippe Soupault, Tristan Tzara, and Theo van Doesburg (and his alter ego, I. K. Bonset), as well as a photogram by Moholy-Nagy and some interesting typographic poetry by Schwitters himself [Fig. 46].

46 Kurt Schwitters. *Merz*, no. 4, 1923. Letterpress. International Dada Archive, Special Collections, University of Iowa Libraries.

46

Schwitters undertook the design and layout of the journal, which carried on many of the absurd features of Dada typography. Like other Dadaists, Schwitters's early experiments in printing employed deliberately illogical layouts, inconsistent typefaces, and the free use of wood display types alongside the standard illustrative cuts that were a staple of the nineteenth-century print workshop. However it began—and the Dadaists frequently broke into internecine disputes about who was first to use each of these innovations—it was soon apparent that the materials of the jobbing printer's case offered a rich repertoire of imagery for striking visual, textual, and aural effects. Like Zdanevitch, Schwitters had a particular liking for the pointing hand, which appears on several pages of *Merz*. He also liked the use of text in blocks, often set at right angles to one another, making it difficult to read the text continuously without either craning one's neck or rotating the page. Amid this largely Dadaist content, on page 47 of *Merz* no. 4 was El Lissitzky's "The Topography of Typography."

Merz retained a fairly consistent, drab appearance due to its dark-green paper cover until nos. 8–9 (April/July 1924), which was designed and coedited by Lissitzky. With its bold sanserif type, red and blue ink on white paper, and a strong rectilinear format, this issue of *Merz* had greater visual appeal than its predecessors [Fig. 47]. The contents were also closer in spirit to the international Constructivist movement, with illustrations of work by Lissitzky, Malevich, Mondrian, and Tatlin. But it was the layout and organization of the text and illustrations that distinguished this issue from previous issues of *Merz*. Lissitzky had provided a strong sense of an underlying grid on each page, even when the linear elements and blocks of text were sparse, leaving large areas of unprinted white paper as "negative space." This was particularly effective on pages with an exaggerated asymmetry that, like the paintings of Mondrian, makes one aware of the underlying order and balance despite the isolation of the positive features: in this case, relatively small blocks of text and illustration amid a sea of white [Fig. 48].

47

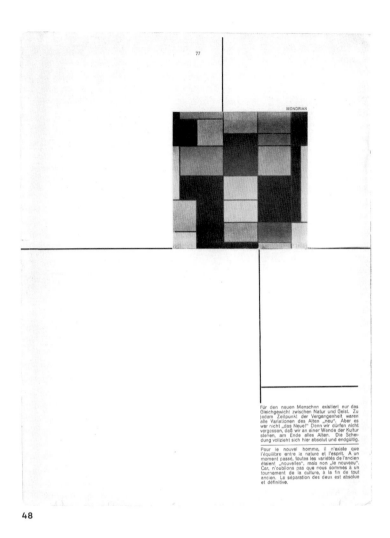

77

MONDRIAN

Für den neuen Menschen existiert nur das
Gleichgewicht zwischen Natur und Geist. Zu
jedem Zeitpunkt der Vergangenheit waren
alle Variationen des Alten „neu". Aber es
war nicht „das Neue!" Denn wir dürfen nicht
vergessen, daß wir an einer Wende der Kultur
stehen, am Ende alles Alten. Die Schei-
dung vollzieht sich hier absolut und endgültig.

Pour le nouvel homme, il n'existe que
l'équilibre entre la nature et l'esprit. A un
moment passé, toutes les variétés de l'ancien
étaient „nouvelles", mais non „le nouveau".
Car, n'oublions pas que nous sommes à un
tournement de la culture, à la fin de tout
ancien. Le séparation des deux est absolue
et définitive.

48

Schwitters remained on good terms with Lissitzky, but his own
foray into typographical theory was prompted by disagreements over
the Russian's "Topography of Typography." In response, Schwitters published his "Thesen über Typographie" (Theses on typography) in *Merz*
no. 11 in November 1924 as another series of statements—in this case,
ten maxims informing his approach to design (Primary Text, no. 6)[27]
[Fig. 49]. Opening with a general invocation to originality, Schwitters

49

writes: "Countless laws can be written about typography. The important
thing is: never to do it the way that someone else did it. Or you could say:
always do it differently than the others." Hereafter, he restates some of
the standard views on the need for "clarity," "simplicity," and "quality" in
design and type, but two points stand out. In the third thesis, Schwitters
is at pains to separate form and content in typographic design: "Design
is the essence of all art, the typographic design is not a reflection of the

textual content." This is quite a radical statement and perhaps could only have come from someone who was trained in the fine arts, having little or no experience in conventional typography, lettering, or book design. Then in thesis 5, he makes an equally important point about the active role played by unprinted areas in the overall composition: "Even the textually negative parts, the unprinted areas of the printed paper, are typographically positive values." Again, this probably reflects his background in the composition of abstract paintings and collages, but it was already becoming a feature of the New Typography, and one that gave the new work such a strong visual impact overall. After presenting his ten theses, Schwitters turns his attention to the lack of awareness of typographic matters among the general public and castigates older art and design magazines for their poor sense of design, typography, and layout, while praising several contemporary journals, such as *G* and *ABC*, for the quality of their design as well as their awareness of the impact of advertisements.[28] For Schwitters, all aspects of a publication, whether a book, magazine, or handbill, had to have overall coherence, and advertisements should not be allowed to disturb the unified character of the piece. This would be a recurring topic, with some journals devoted to the New Typography monitoring the advertisements printed within their covers and even taking over control of their design to ensure that they did not clash with the other contents.

THE EMERGENCE OF THE NEW TYPOGRAPHY

One of the problems in trying to establish an overview of graphic design in this period is that the field has been distorted by a canon set by art historians. There is no doubt that many of the key figures, above all Moholy-Nagy, Lissitzky, and Schwitters, loom large in the history of modern art. Furthermore, Tschichold himself emphasized the extent to which the New Typography developed from an exchange of formal and aesthetic values between Constructivist art and the emerging practice of graphic design. But the same canon that privileges a small group of artists on grounds that are often irrelevant to design chooses to ignore others who played a significant, if not an equally important, role within the commercial graphic design world. This perspective is not based solely on a perceived hierarchy between "artists" and "craftsmen." If that were the case, Tschichold would be the outsider, having studied in a trade school and practiced as a typographer and book designer all his life. In fact, many of the marginalized figures of the New Typography were also artist-designers, but in several important cases the "art" side of that equation has not been inducted into the canon of art history—at least, not in the Anglophone world. I am thinking of figures such as Willi Baumeister, Max Burchartz, Walter Dexel, and Johannes Molzahn, artist-designers whose work evolved along similar lines in the years following the First World War. Each of these figures recognized the possibilities that Constructivist aesthetics offered design for print, and thought deeply about the impact these ideas could have on everyday means of communication. Their paintings, however, have remained peripheral to the elite canon of modernist art. Without the artistic hierarchy that has developed subsequently, we might look back at the mid-1920s as a period when a broad spectrum of artist-designers felt they were on the verge of a breakthrough in visual communication that had ramifications far beyond the simple design of books, magazines, and advertising. Painting was even perceived by some as a self-indulgence at a time when visual culture was being revolutionized along a broad front.[29]

Baumeister trained in the Stuttgart Art Academy (Königlich Württembergische Akademie), where he formed a close friendship with Oskar Schlemmer, who was then studying landscape painting but would later become head of the Bauhaus theater workshop. Baumeister's training, however, was focused more on decorative mural painting than conventional easel painting, which may have given him a more flexible outlook later in his career with regard to commercial art for industry. After the First World War, he was closely involved in several avant-garde artists' associations, notably the Novembergruppe and Üecht, but the trajectory of his art was more specifically toward collage and assemblage and the design of simple geometric forms and figures in the precise manner associated with "the machine aesthetic." His breakthrough came in the early 1920s with a series of wall pictures (*Mauerbild*), employing precise linear forms in relief built up from the plaster on the wall. They were, in other words, a type of modernist mural or painted relief that had an affinity with the contemporary work of Fernand Léger and Le Corbusier in France.[30] This may explain the architectural metaphor that Baumeister employed when outlining his interpretation of new typography in an article for the Deutscher Werkbund's magazine *Die Form* in July 1926 (Primary Text, no. 8).[31] Opening with a discussion of the ways in which the modern city dweller perceives buildings and how architecture orients and choreographs the movement of a pedestrian, Baumeister connects these observations to the patterns in which our eyes enter and follow a text. While recognizing the freedom to organize the page or sheet of paper according to any principle of composition, he emphasizes the underlying imperative of reading from left to right:

> Many "modern" advertisements, letterheads, etc. are constructed according to the compositional principles of painting, even in a constructivist sense. However, artwork, even abstract art, has a compositional movement that results in a final balance of harmonized tension. The painting will be viewed. In contrast, the advertisement, the printed line, etc. will be read. And we know that reading is a movement. Everything that has movement—that is to say, direction—is unbalanced. The arrangement of the printed page has a very determined direction—in stark contrast to the rest of a painted composition. Thus, for printed text, the beautiful balance of free equilibrium cannot be the primary goal; rather, everything must be sacrificed for the directional line of the eye.[32]

As in his paintings, Baumeister was committed to the new aesthetic of technology, the machine, and standardization in graphic design. On the use of sanserif letterforms, for example, he had a very practical, if dogmatic, view that handwriting can never equal the purity and precision of metal type: "The preference for 'sans-serif' lies in the fact that the exact cut results in a clarity of text that painted lettering, artistic, and Fraktur could never attain."[33] Baumeister began designing advertisements and posters in the years immediately following the First World War. Like many modernists of his generation, he claimed that there was no distinction between fine and applied art and that the tasks facing the progressive artist-designer were often more sharply defined in the world of popular and commercial graphics.[34] His earliest posters were probably those designed for exhibitions in 1919 that he himself participated in, such as *1 Herbstschau neuer Kunst: Üecht Gruppe* (First Fall Exhibition of New Art from the Üecht Group) at the Sturm Gallery in Berlin and at the Kunstgebäude in Stuttgart. He soon found that his facility for typography, layout, and photography was in demand, providing a good income at a time when the economy made life as an artist precarious at best. By the mid-1920s, Baumeister had commissions for advertising designs from the Deutsche Linoleum-Werke (DLW, German Linoleum Works) and Robert Bosch, the electronics and engineering company based in Stuttgart [Fig. 50]. In fact, for much of the 1920s, Baumeister had a higher profile in Germany as a graphic designer than as an artist of easel or wall paintings.

As was typical across the country, art and design organizations were often most keen to promote themselves using the New Typography. One of Baumeister's most important commissions was to design the publicity surrounding the Werkbund exhibition *Die Wohnung* (The Dwelling), a complement to the landmark *Weissenhofsiedlung*, an international showcase of modern architecture held in Stuttgart in 1927.[35] Baumeister designed the logo, the catalogue (*Bau und Wohnung*), letterheads, envelopes, labels, and publicity brochures for the exhibition,

50

employing an elegant asymmetrical design with blocks of uppercase
sanserif lettering [Fig. 51]. His design for the poster, however, remains
one of the most striking images of the period. Taking a photograph
of a stuffy nineteenth-century bourgeois drawing room, Baumeister's
lithographic poster appears to deface the image with a huge red cross
to express the rejection of traditional values in interior design[36] [Fig. 52].
To confirm these sentiments, hand-painted script in red asks the question, *wie wohnen?* (how should we live?). As a simple expression of
the aims and values of the exhibition, it is clear, but as an eye-catching
image, it was almost unparalleled, especially for an official organization
such as the Deutscher Werkbund.

TEACHING THE NEW TYPOGRAPHY

In 1927, the year of his success at the Stuttgart exhibition, Baumeister
accepted a position teaching graphic design, typography, and printed
textiles in the Frankfurt Kunstgewerbeschule (School of Applied Arts).[37]

The school had recently amalgamated with the Städelschule fine arts academy, and the progressive director Fritz Wichert saw the merger as an opportunity to develop new facilities and teaching methods for graphic design. This initiative could be seen as an attempt to overshadow the Hochschule für Gestaltung Offenbach, which had established a reputation for traditional calligraphy and book design under the direction of Rudolf Koch. Wichert had already invested in a proper print and design studio, and in appointing first Paul Renner and then Willi Baumeister, he was making a commitment to modern graphic design, in contrast to the traditional values of their neighboring and rival college in Offenbach.[38] Wichert was closely involved in Ernst May's grand project, Das neue Frankfurt, to make the city a major center for new ideas in architecture, design, and social planning. The reform of the

51

52

Städel academy, embracing fine art and design, worked in tandem with these initiatives and served to make Frankfurt a more effective testing ground for applications of modernist architecture and design than in any phase of the Bauhaus.[39]

In 1926, the journal *Das neue Frankfurt* was launched as a mouthpiece for the radical program. Under the editorship of Ernst May and Fritz Wichert, there were contributions by Sigfried Giedion, Walter Gropius, El Lissitzky, and Frank Lloyd Wright, among many others, on a diverse range of topics related to contemporary art, design, technology, education, and urbanism.[40] The original design of the journal was set by Hans and Grete Leistikow, employing asymmetrical typography, sanserif type, and photomontage to project its modern and internationalist contents[41] [Fig. 53]. Indicating what a sympathetic regional council might

53

53 Hans and Grete Leistikow. *Das neue Frankfurt* (The New Frankfurt), vol. 3, nos. 7–8, cover, July–August 1929. Published and printed by Englert und Schlosser, Frankfort am Main. Lithograph. Private collection. Cat. 52.

achieve, the mayor wrote a rousing foreword to the first issue: "A new style as an expression of spiritual transformation needs a period of patient growth to be perfected. All that remains for the individual is to cooperate in the breakthrough to a new culture in all fields!"[42] In his opening article, Ernst May explained how he saw the city as a laboratory of modern ideas about design, technology, and civics. "Design in the city of Frankfurt will be the main object of our study. That does not mean that we will limit our circle of contributors to this city. On the contrary, our aim is to make our pages available to important figures from all parts of our country and from abroad who have similar aims in both theory and practice. . . . From the living conditions of our time, we find something new."[43] To make his point visually, May employed a sequence of illustrations recounting an evolutionary history of three design media: transport, interiors, and letterforms. He concluded his history of letterforms with an example of the official city documents, newly designed by Hans Leistikow demonstrating the New Typography in action [Fig. 54].

Graphic design was a recurring topic in *Das neue Frankfurt*. The third issue was devoted to advertising in the modern city and included articles by the architectural critic Adolf Behne and Walter Dexel, each taking opposing views, as well as a general article on the phenomenon by Ernst May.[44] An article on letterforms by Paul Renner also appeared in the following issue.[45] In fact, *Das neue Frankfurt* continued to publish articles on all aspects of design and social reconstruction, embracing some of the most radical views of architects and designers across Europe and the United States, while constantly emphasizing the interconnectedness of design and culture. Given these opportunities in Frankfurt, it is perhaps not surprising that when Baumeister was offered a position in the Bauhaus in 1929, he turned it down, even though his close friend Oskar Schlemmer was on the faculty in Dessau. The following year, he took over the design of *Das neue Frankfurt*.

SOMMER
DER MUSIK

FRANKFURT AM MAIN
11. JUNI BIS 28. AUGUST 1927

6. WOCHE

IM BACHSAAL
TÄGLICH 16 UHR
ORGELKONZERTE

Sonntag 17. Juli	Morgenfeier des Hessischen Sängerbundes Teatro dei Piccoli, Marionettenspiele Gamelan-Orchester und Javanische Tänze Tanz- und Gesangsgruppen aus Rußland	Bachsaal 9 Uhr Bachsaal 20 U. Saxophon 17 U. Opernh. 20 Uhr
Montag 18. Juli	Tanzabend »La Argentina«, Span. Tänze Quartett »Pro Arte«, Belg. Kammermusik Teatro dei Piccoli, Marionettenspiele Gamelan-Orchester und Javanische Tänze	Opernh. 20 Uhr Beethovensaal Bachsaal 20 U. Saxophon 17 U.
Dienstag 19. Juli	Tanzabend »La Argentina«, Span. Tänze Quartett »Pro Arte«, Belg. Kammermusik Teatro dei Piccoli, Marionettenspiele Gamelan-Orchester und Javanische Tänze	Opernh. 20 Uhr Beethovensaal Bachsaal 20 U. Saxophon 17 U.
Mittwoch 20. Juli	Tanz- und Gesangsgruppen aus Rußland Teatro dei Piccoli, Marionettenspiele Gamelan-Orchester und Javanische Tänze Hausfrauen-Nachmittag mit »Küchenmusik«	Opernh. 20 Uhr Bachsaal 20 U. Saxophon 17 U. Unterhalt.-Park
Donnerstag 21. Juli	Tage für mechan. Musik, Leitg. P. Hindemith Teatro dei Piccoli, Marionettenspiele Gamelan-Orchester und Javanische Tänze Streichorchester-Konzert, Leitg. Joh. Strauß	Beethovensaal Bachsaal 20 U. Saxophon 17 U. Unterhalt.-Park
Freitag 22. Juli	Tanz- und Gesangsgruppen aus Rußland Tage für mechan. Musik, Leitg. P. Hindemith Teatro dei Piccoli, Marionettenspiele Gamelan-Orchester und Javanische Tänze	Opernh. 20 Uhr Beethovensaal Bachsaal 20 U. Saxophon 17 U.
Samstag 23. Juli	Tanz- und Gesangsgruppen aus Rußland Teatro dei Piccoli, Marionettenspiele Tage für mechan. Musik, Leitg. P. Hindemith Streichorchester-Konzert, Leitg. Joh. Strauß	Opernh. 20 Uhr Bachsaal 20 U. Beethovensaal Unterhalt.-Park

IM
UNTERHALTUNGS
PARK: JEDEN TAG
KONZERT U. TANZ

TYP: LEISTIKOW

MUSIK IM LEBEN
DER VÖLKER
INTERNAT. AUSSTELLUNG

54

A similar pattern can be observed in other cities throughout Weimar Germany, as the various regional authorities sought to develop their historic academies of art and their trade schools to better equip students for a career in printing, publishing, and design. Baumeister's experience in Frankfurt, like Tschichold's in Munich, may have been particularly progressive, but similar developments in cities such as Berlin, Bielefeld, Essen, and Magdeburg suggest that the Bauhaus was more of a symbol of progressive theories of design than a model for design education. In fact, many colleges of craft and design throughout Germany were undertaking reforms of their curricula and teaching methods to address the challenges of modern industry. In Essen, for example, Max Burchartz developed plans to reorganize the curriculum of the Kunstgewerbeschule, turning it into a specialist college devoted exclusively to interior design and advertising graphics.[46] The schools and colleges were not consistent in their reforms, however, partly because the German regions retained a great deal of autonomy in educational as well as other matters.[47] Also, some colleges were better prepared to develop certain disciplines, often reflecting the regional patterns of industry and existing or previous collaborations with local manufacturers. This was particularly true in relation to design for print, for which the Bauhaus was singularly ill equipped to do more than teach the basic skills in hand presswork. The Bauhaus did not introduce a formal course in advertising design (*Reklame*) until 1927–28, by which stage the issues of the New Typography were already well developed in many applied arts schools and studios across Germany.[48] Explaining the background to the special insert in *Typographische Mitteilungen* in 1925, Tschichold states that at one point he had considered linking "elementare typographie" to the Bauhaus: "However, the Bauhaus is only one base in the battle for the New Culture. The ideas for which the Bauhaus in Dessau (formerly Weimar) stands are advocated by numerous artists, scientists, and technicians worldwide who are not members of the Bauhaus."[49] There may have been an element of sour grapes in this comment, but it is clear from many reports that the Bauhaus was held in rather low esteem by the modern graphic design community.[50]

In Magdeburg, the arts and crafts college (Kunstgewerbe- und Handwerkerschule) was introducing similar reforms under the guidance of the architect Bruno Taut. In 1923, he recommended the appointment of Johannes Molzahn, the son of a master bookbinder, who had studied photography and fine art at the Fürstliche freie Zeichenschule Weimar (Grand Ducal Drawing School in Weimar) before the war. Since 1919, Molzahn had been associated with various avant-garde groups, through which he met El Lissitzky, Oskar Schlemmer, and Theo van Doesburg. He was even consulted by Walter Gropius about establishing the Bauhaus in Weimar, probably because of his familiarity with the region. By the early 1920s, however, Molzahn was working as a commercial graphic designer with commissions from industrial manufacturers such as NEMA machine tools and lathes and Fagus shoe-lasts. His work for these clients was unmistakably in the manner of the New Typography, employing asymmetrical layouts, sanserif type, and photographic illustrations. It was in this capacity that, in 1923, he joined the college in Magdeburg.

Taut had been keen to introduce new teaching methods, and in Molzahn he found a willing contributor to his campaign. Unlike some artist-designers who dabbled in commercial graphics and teaching, Molzahn took his role very seriously. In 1925 he prepared a memorandum for the city council outlining the aims and requirements for establishing a full course in modern graphic design, along with a plan for the curriculum identifying "Werbegraphik, Satz, Druck und Lithographie" (advertising graphics, typesetting, printing, and lithography) as the fundamental skills.[51] Molzahn was also engaged in designing publicity for many of the cultural events in the city, such as the *Mitteldeutsche Handwerks Ausstellung*, a craft exhibition held in 1925, for which he created a striking image of an arm and hand composed of gears and drive belts, juxtaposing modern handcraft and machine production [Fig. 55]. This kind of design work helped build a bridge between the college and the

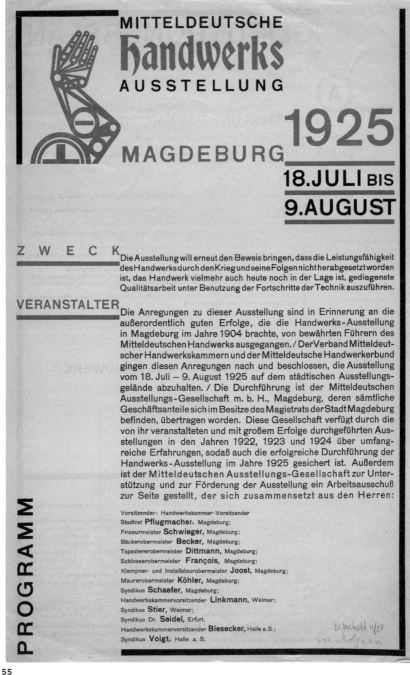

55

commercial and industrial activities of the region. Even the headed notepaper and invoices for his own office-studio had a didactic side, providing a statement of his aims and principles in design for modern life: "Increasingly, production and sales must also demand the creation of advertising according to the same principles that apply to the entire operating process: to achieve the maximum effect with the least expenditure of energy and material resources" (Primary Text, no. 13) [Fig. 56].

The policy of introducing the New Typography to studio teaching was given greater encouragement in 1927, when the director of the college, Jugendstil sculptor Rudolf Bosselt, was replaced by Wilhelm Deffke. As a well-established designer of posters, logos, and corporate graphics, Deffke was well aware of recent developments in print technology and the need to introduce new methods of teaching if graphic designers were to meet the demands of an expanding consumer society. He shifted the emphasis from broad-based craft training to four specialized departments, aiming to introduce the students to machine-related skills that were closer to professional practice in the areas of modern industrial design. In this he seems to have had the full support of the Prussian authorities and Bruno Taut. The following year, however, Molzahn moved to the industrial city of Breslau in Silesia, where he became head of graphic arts at the Staatlichen Akademie für Kunst und Kunstgewerbe (State Academy for Fine and Applied Arts), carrying on the same policies he had begun in Magdeburg.[52] As Molzahn's replacement, Deffke appointed Walter Dexel, another product of the postwar Constructivist avant-garde who had taken up commercial design.

Dexel had been based in Jena, where he designed a series of subtle typographic cards and posters for the Kunstverein (artists' association), using space bars and blocks of sanserif type to create simple but effective rectilinear compositions [Fig. 57]. He also produced posters, calendars, and brochures for the Thüringer Verlagsanstalt und Druckerei, printers in Jena, so he was well acquainted with the demands of designing for commercial print concerns [Fig. 58]. This worked well in Magdeburg,

56

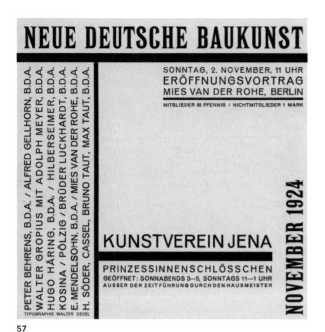

57

58

a city with a long tradition of publishing and book design. Dexel carried on many of Molzahn's initiatives, further developing the training of graphic designers for modern industry, although his classes seem to have been less progressive, at least in relation to the use of photography and new technologies. According to one of his students, Dexel placed greater emphasis on exercises in abstract design and typography than on new media and their application to graphic design.[53] Dexel was also able to build up his practice as an independent designer, working for local organizations, such as the Technische Vereinigung Magdeburg (Magdeburg Technical Association), as well as preparing the publicity for a number of major exhibitions [Fig. 59]. In 1929 alone, he designed posters and other graphic material for the sport exhibition, the *Bauten der Technik* (Building Technology) exhibition, and most effectively, *Fotografie der Gegenwart* (Photography of the Present), in all of which he demonstrated the most rigorous application of the New Typography in its purest form [Fig. 60].

57 Walter Dexel. *Neue deutsche Baukunst, Kunstverein Jena* (New German Architecture, Jena Art Society), 1924. Letterpress. The Museum of Modern Art. Jan Tschichold Collection, Gift of Philip Johnson. 550.1977. Cat. 73.

58 Walter Dexel. *Thüringer Verlagsanstalt und Druckerei G.m.b.H. Jena* calendar, 1927. Printed by Thüringer, Jena. Letterpress. The Museum of Modern Art. Jan Tschichold Collection, Gift of Philip Johnson. 652.1999. Cat. 74.

59 Walter Dexel. *Die Sport Ausstellung* (The Sport Exhibition), 1929. Printed by W. Pfannkuch & Co., Magdeburg. Lithograph. The Museum of Modern Art. Purchase Fund, Jan Tschichold Collection, 1937. 339.1937. Cat. 82.

59

AUSSTELLUNG AM ADOLF-MITTAG-SEE

FOTOGRAFIE

DER GEGENWART

28.NOVEMBER
—19.DEZEMBER

VERANSTALTET VOM AUSSTELLUNGSAMT DER STADT MAGDEBURG
UND VOM MAGDEBURGER VEREIN FÜR DEUTSCHE WERKKUNST E.V.

GEÖFFNET WOCHENTAGS 10 BIS 18 UHR SONNTAGS 10 BIS 19 UHR
EINTRITT 40 PF. SCHÜLER UND GESCHLOSSENE VERBÄNDE 20 PF.

ENTWURF: DEXEL / LINOLEUMDRUCK VON
W. PFANNKUCH & CO. IN MAGDEBURG

60

In the context of design education in Weimar Germany, the Schule Reimann in Berlin is an exception, but it followed a similar trajectory. As a private school offering training in the arts and crafts, it was not subject to the same local authority controls, but neither did it have the investment or funding to underwrite its running costs. As a result, the Reimann School admitted many more fee-paying students than its state school rivals, and it tended to emphasize manual studio skills, such as drawing and wood carving, rather than training students how to use modern machinery.[54] Graphic design and advertising were an important aspect of its curriculum from before the war. The poster class had been set up by the *Sachplakat* designer Julius Klinger, while Max Hertwig taught *Gebrauchsgraphik* (commercial graphics). Hertwig had a traditional approach to design education, placing emphasis on drawing for ornament and the preparation of artwork in black and white for process engraving. Throughout the 1920s, these prewar values were still in evidence, but they must have seemed outdated by 1928, when Tschichold's book appeared. Accordingly, Werner Graeff's appointment in 1930 to lead the graphic design studio marked the Reimann School's acceptance of the New Typography. Like Max Burchartz, Graeff had attended the Bauhaus and in 1922 defected to Theo van Doesburg's "alternative" classes in Weimar.[55] After this immersion in the theory and practice of De Stijl, he moved to Berlin, where he set up the journal *G: Zeitschrift für elementare Gestaltung* (Journal of Elemental Design), worked as a designer and photographer, and in 1928 joined the Ring.[56] At the Reimann School, at least until 1932, he introduced classes in photography and layout, as well as the aesthetics of film, thus confirming the early manifesto statements that linked the New Typography to broader theoretical and cultural movements.[57]

ADVERTISING AND THE NEW TYPOGRAPHY

Das neue Frankfurt was by no means the first journal to take up the theme of advertising and its impact on the modern city. In fact, this had been an issue beyond the specialist press for some time. The rise of a consumer culture attendant upon the massive expansion of the German economy in the last quarter of the nineteenth century and the years leading up to the First World War had attracted many commentators, alternately baffled and amazed by the plethora of branded goods and the insistent calls to buy one type of cookie, cigarette, or mouthwash over another.[58] This onslaught of advertising and branding had also created an atmosphere of distrust and anxiety, at least among social critics and policymakers, many of whom were concerned that the effects on the spiritual well-being of the population would outweigh the possible advantages of higher standards of living.[59] The immediate postwar period had been dominated by the crisis of defeat and occupation, closely followed by an economic collapse brought on by punitive reparations and the seizure of resources by the victorious powers. By 1924, however, the German economy was recovering from the hyperinflation of the previous two years and showing signs of expansion in most areas, with the result that industrial production was on the rise and goods and services were back in the competitive market. Mass production, the drive for exports, and the urge to increase domestic consumption were in such a dynamic relationship that it was widely recognized that advertising was not so much a by-product of capitalism as an essential element in regulating the system and representing a modern lifestyle. Writing on the effects of advertising on the reading public, Hans Siemsen remarked: "But those who read no books also have their literature. . . . They read the ad pillars and the billboards on buildings, roofs, and streetcars. Who knows Pascal? Everyone knows *Odol*."[60] Street advertising was a topic of particular fascination, especially when combined with electric illumination, which was transforming the cityscape by night as well as day.[61] The emerging group of graphic designers, however, were most interested in the massive expansion of advertising in print. Tschichold had relatively little to say about advertising, and what he did write was mainly concerned with practical questions of how to prepare designs for different types of printed matter. This was largely a reflection of his disdain for advertising as a tool of capitalism. In 1932, for example, he remarked, "On the evidence of the Soviet Union, the abolition of capitalist advertising would result in all communication becoming scientific, and without exception, such communications can be set very well in sanserif."[62] El Lissitzky could be similarly dismissive of the need for advertising and its effect on design. In 1924, while working on advertisements for Pelikan, he reports, "I am beginning to loathe the whole business. This is the face of capitalism . . . when they have sucked all they want out of me, they will spit me out on the street."[63] Of the generation coming to maturity in the 1920s, however, these views were unusual; most other commentators were greatly engaged by the very idea of advertising in all its forms.

Merz no. 11 (1924), the issue in which Schwitters published his "Theses on Typography," was devoted to "Typo Reklame," or typographic advertising. The issue opened with a series of quotations on advertising from the young artist-designer Max Burchartz, indicating the extent to which he was already becoming regarded as an authority on the subject. Trained in the Dusseldorf academy before the war, by 1919 he was a promising painter working in a loosely expressionistic manner and exhibiting at the Galerie der Sturm in Berlin. His focus changed markedly in 1921, when he enrolled at the Bauhaus, and even more so in the following year, when he transferred to Theo van Doesburg's alternative classes in Weimar. This was Burchartz's entrée into Constructivist circles. In September 1922 he participated in the International Congress of Constructivists and Dadaists in Weimar, alongside Lissitzky, Moholy-Nagy, and other luminaries of the European avant-garde. He also got to know Walter Dexel and others who were beginning to apply new ideas to graphic advertising. By this stage, Burchartz's paintings were strictly abstract and geometric, involving precisely organized interlocking squares of mostly primary colors; the debt to De Stijl, and particularly van Doesburg, was unmistakable. This was, of course, the same compositional discipline that prepared others for the New Typography, and Burchartz followed a similar route into commercial graphics. In 1924 he moved to Bochum, an industrial town in the Ruhr, where he set up one of the earliest graphic design / advertising studios, named Werbe-bau (advertising construction), with his colleague Johannes Canis. One of their first clients was the Dortmund printer C. L. Krüger, for whom Burchartz produced a series of brochures and advertisements that were largely variations on his abstract paintings but with the addition of the printer's name in bold uppercase sanserif and occasionally a photograph. These designs are a good example of the common ground between Constructivist art and the New Typography [Fig. 61].

61

Like many others in this emerging field, Burchartz felt motivated to evangelize for graphic design and to establish some of the theoretical principles that guided his work. Soon he was writing polemical pieces for journals such as *Die Form* and *Gebrauchsgraphik*, but the text for which he was best known—and which was quoted on the cover of *Merz*—was a pamphlet, or *Werbe-beratung* (advertising information sheet), he had published himself in June 1924 to promote his new business [Fig. 62].

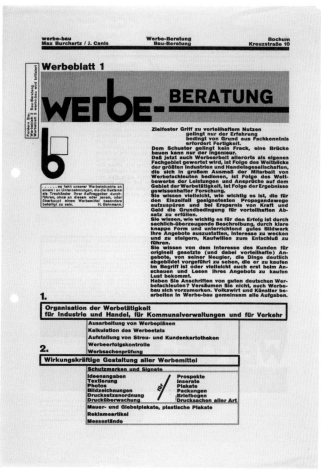

61 Max Burchartz. C. L. Krüger brochure, 1924. Lithograph. Private collection.

62 Max Burchartz, Johannes Canis. *Werbe-Beratung, Werbeblatt 1* (advertising information sheet), 1925. Letterpress. The Museum of Modern Art. Jan Tschichold Collection, Gift of Philip Johnson. 622.1999.

62

Titled *Gestaltung der Reklame* (Advertising design), it was one of the clearest statements on both the aims of advertising design and the role of the New Typography in realizing those aims (Primary Text, no. 12).[64] After emphasizing the importance of advertising in establishing a firm's identity and character, Burchartz provides a list of simple, memorable statements. Good advertising:

1. is factual;
2. is clear and concise;
3. makes use of modern methods;
4. packs a formal punch; and
5. is inexpensive.

Much of *Gestaltung der Reklame* offers practical advice, such as "its script is legible and clear; its wording is articulate and unambiguous despite its extreme terseness!" There are, nevertheless, clear recommendations that prioritize "modern methods." One key feature is the opportunities that photography offered, both as a tool to reconfigure text and imagery and as a medium for advertising in its own right: "Photography has thus far been rarely employed as means for artistic composition."

Burchartz was already an accomplished photographer before he took up graphic design, and photography continued to be an important part of his practice. As early as 1910, while still a student, he had begun experimenting with multiple-exposure photographs to suggest narrative and alternative views of the same scene.[65] By the time he had taken up graphic design in the 1920s, Burchartz recognized how the parallel movements of "Die neue Sachlichkeit" (the New Objectivity) and the New Photography would change the way that even the general public would begin to see everyday objects.[66] The most effective demonstration of this was Albert Renger-Patzsch's 1928 book *Die Welt ist schön*

(The world is beautiful), which brought the new aesthetics of photography and the previously unrecognized beauty of machine-made, industrial goods to a larger audience[67] [Fig. 63]. Renger-Patzsch was certainly one of the finest exponents of the New Photography, but his book was primarily the popularizer of an aesthetic that was already widespread among the new designers.

63 Albert Renger-Patzsch. "Shoe irons" from *Die Welt ist Schön: einhundert photographische Aufnahmen*. Published by Einhorn, Munich, 1928. Photolithograph. Private Collection.

63

The New Typography, 1923–33: Theory and Practice

In 1925, Burchartz and Canis were engaged by the Bochumer Verein (Bochum Association), a mining and cast steel company, to produce catalogues and publicity material. In one of the most ambitious campaigns, Werbe-bau designed a series of brochures and catalogues that were outstanding examples of photomontage in advertising [Fig. 64]. Tschichold recognized their quality immediately and illustrated several pages from the Bochumer Verein materials in *Die neue Typographie*. This was not Werbe-bau's only foray into the field. The company also

64

produced striking advertisements for Orion electrical goods and for Fortschritt, a manufacturer of office furniture, in which high-quality photography and minimal text, often set at right angles to the imagery, are used in a manner that would only become mainstream a generation later [Fig. 65]. These examples helped fulfill the claims of Burchartz (and Tschichold) that the New Typography was ideally suited to promoting the products of modern industrial manufacturing, especially when employed in concert with photography. Burchartz's advertising work

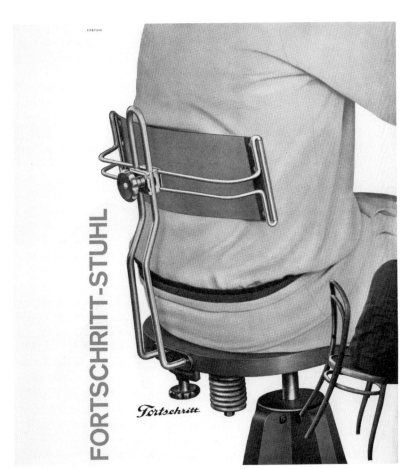

64 Max Burchartz, Johannes Canis. *Bochumer Verein* (Bochum Association) brochure, ca. 1925. Lithograph. Private collection.

65 Johannes Canis. *Fortschritt-Stuhl* advertisment, 1928–29. Lithograph. The Museum of Modern Art. Jan Tschichold Collection, Gift of Philip Johnson. 966.1999. Cat. 41.

65

probably reached its apogee in the designs he produced for the Wehag metal goods firm. Door handles, coat hooks, shelving, bellhousing, and nameplates are photographed with sophisticated lighting effects to accentuate their pristine, brushed metal finishes, while the products themselves seem to float within a range of abstract and evocative contexts. The catalogue cover setting the metal goods against a cracked egg is an early example of the way photomontage could prompt allusive or metaphorical associations with the product, just as the process had initially been used for artistic and political purposes [Fig. 66]. The Wehag advertisements also demonstrated that photography, with its gray tonality, need not conflict with the more precise definition of sanserif type if the full range of elements in the design were well handled. The use of photography with letterpress had been an ongoing issue, with many traditionalists adhering to William Morris's dictum that only wood engraving was appropriate for illustration within text because it maintained the same weight and textural richness as type and was produced using the same relief printing process. By 1930, that shibboleth had been laid to rest, at least among the new typographers.[68]

One of the surprising features in the critical and theoretical writing of the period is the enthusiasm with which the new typographers embraced the field of advertising, especially since so many leading figures were left-leaning to the point of anticapitalist radicalism. With the exception of Tschichold himself and Lissitzky, there is little evidence of any qualms about the role of advertising in either promoting inessential products at a time of widespread poverty or creating a market for surplus production.[69] In designers' polemical writings and private correspondence, one senses that the engagement with commerce offered by advertising design was more than merely financial opportunism. Indeed, to some of the designer-theorists, advertising was not merely a symptom of modern life but one of its most exciting visual features, as if the ways in which products were promoted was somehow a means of enlightenment or a conduit for a new state of being. The Hungarian

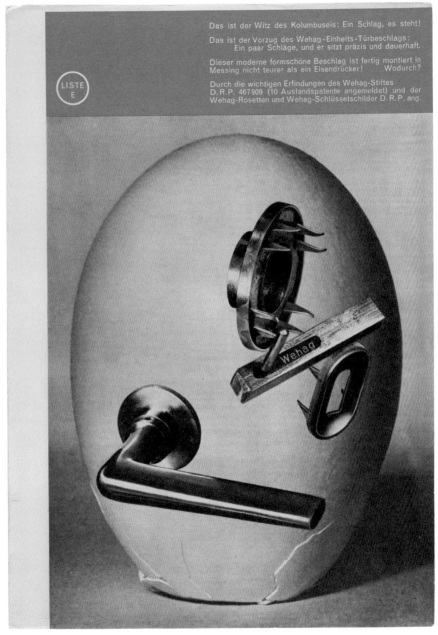

66

poet and Dada-Constructivist Lajos Kassák was one of the most enthu-siastic, despite his stated position as an anarchist—or at least an anti-establishment figure. It should be remembered that Kassák's first exper-imental journal, *A Tett* (The deed), was banned in 1916 for its antiwar stance. He then founded *MA* (Today) and gathered around him some of the most radical artists and poets of the Hungarian avant-garde. Never-theless, in a 1928 article published in *Reklámélet* (Advertising), he claims that advertising was the force that kept society functioning efficiently, regulating supply and demand, and generally acting as an independent force to raise the quality of manufactured goods for the consumer. "The Advertisement and Modern Typography" (Primary Text, no. 14) begins:

> In order to maintain the unobstructed production of modern industry, which is based on advanced technology and the rational organization of work, we must observe various laws of social justice and co-ordinate commerce properly. An industry which produces without consideration for social organization and commerce as a mediator will easily and periodically surely crash.... Producers have begun to rationalize their shops, and commerce has begun to make use of the greatest means of influencing the consumer: the modern advertisement [Fig. 67].[70]

Like Burchartz before him, Kassák has a few words of advice:

> The good, modern advertisement must:
> 1. be cheap and easy to produce
> 2. be factual, truthful and convincing; and
> 3. not praise the article, but qualify it, and make it familiar to the public.[71]

CORPORATE AND EVENT IDENTITY

One aspect of advertising for which the New Typography seemed particularly well suited was the developing field of corporate identity. Branding was already quite familiar in Germany, at least in the design community, from the debates at the Deutscher Werkbund before the war, and especially from the classic early example of an identity established by Peter Behrens in 1907 for the massive, heavy engineering and electrical goods firm AEG (Allgemeine Elektricitäts-Gesellschaft AG)[80] [Fig. 68]. Design for industry had moved on somewhat since then, but the central issues were still the same: How to establish a clear identity for a manufacturer, firm, or organization, especially when its products were either diversified or unfamiliar. How to create an appealing symbol, pattern, or color scheme that would remain distinctive yet be repeatable across various types of information graphics, packaging, and publicity. How to exemplify the ideals and products of a company in a competitive marketplace. As Burchartz demonstrated with Bochumer Verein and Wehag, the crisp rectilinear designs of the New Typography and

68 Peter Behrens. AEG logos, 1907–21.

68

the objective beauty of the New Photography helped communicate a sense of efficiency and modernity to industrial concerns. As a result, most of the leading practitioners in the new manner were given opportunities to demonstrate their skill in creating identities for commercial companies: Robert Michel for the seed supplier Samenhaus Kahl of Frankfurt; Joost Schmidt for YKO office furniture of Weimar; Walter Dexel for Thüringer Verlagsanstalt und Druckerei of Jena; Piet Zwart for Nederlandsche Kabelfabriek of Delft; and Paul Schuitema for Berkel weighing machines and meat products of Rotterdam [Figs. 69 and 70].

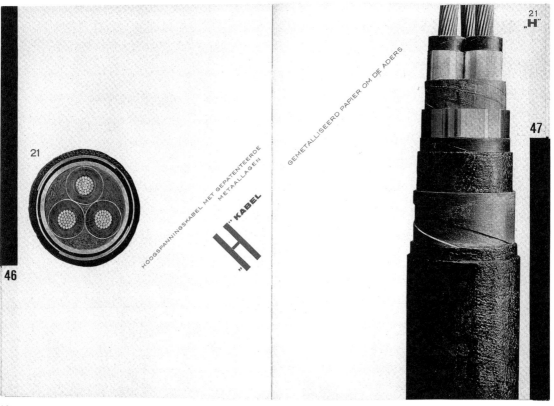

69

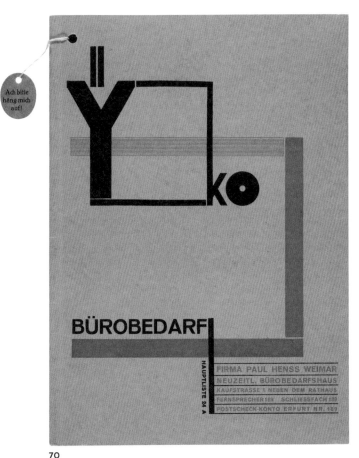

70

Creating a corporate identity was always more than designing (or updating) a logo and color scheme. There were already quite a few design manuals on the ways in which a diversified company could effectively project a strong, unified image. The New Typography came into its own in establishing that identity by using the most basic elements of sanserif type, bold blocks of color (especially red and orange, but not exclusively), asymmetrical layout, and uniform, standardized proportions for all printed material. These forms and media already had an affinity with the defining characteristics of industrial production, and they were relatively easy to apply to packaging, notepaper, business cards, brochures, invoices, reports, and envelopes—in short, the entire range of printed matter that a company generates. Tschichold had emphasized that each of these materials should conform to industry standards (DIN) in terms of paper size, and that the modern designer must be prepared to exploit format and dimensions for practical use in layout, typeface, and color scheme. Headed notepaper, envelopes, and invoices were the best examples. The new typographers not only observed the standardized dimensions but made effective use of them, creating reserved areas for addresses and reference numbers and tabulated sections for figures, demonstrating that the abstract features of the design operated under a larger organizational principle. The same was true of graphs, calendars, parts catalogues, and prospectuses, for which the layout seemed to follow a simple logic that held its own abstract beauty. George Orwell once wrote that "above the level of a railway guide, no book is quite free from aesthetic considerations," suggesting that such prosaic and ephemeral publications were produced without care or planning.[81] To the new typographers, the railway guide was precisely the sort of printed information sheet that could be rendered both efficient and aesthetically beautiful.

The belief that there was an abiding logic to this type of information graphics—and that, in the hands of a skilled designer, it would achieve a satisfying, abstract elegance—was further encouraged by the development of new methods of displaying statistics. In a prospectus for J. Ferbeck & Cie., "Europe's largest industrial corporation," Burchartz designed a photomontage of factory chimneys and the spire of Ulm Minster with measurement data [Fig. 71]. In other cases, the grid-like structure of the layout and the ease of tabulating text, numbers, and diagrams in the New Typography allowed for the straightforward presentation of factual and statistical information. These initiatives represented progress in tabulated information, but they pale in comparison with the more rigorous and scientific methods developed by Gerd Arntz,

71

Otto Neurath, and Marie Reidemeister at the Österreichisches Gesell-schafts- und Wirtschaftsmuseum (Social and Economic Museum) in Vienna. Between 1925 and 1934, the Vienna Method of Pictorial Statistics, subsequently known by the acronym Isotype (International System of Typographic Picture Education), established a new and accessible form of statistical display in which charts of simplified pictograms communicated comparative data clearly and memorably.[82] Although not exactly a branch of the New Typography, designers such as Jan Tschichold took an active interest in these developments in Vienna and incorporated aspects of the "Vienna method," as well as Soviet infographics, into their own work [Fig. 72]. Indeed, Tschichold corresponded with Neurath and Arntz, acquiring examples of their work, and he designed at least one book cover for the left-wing book club Der Bücherkreis that incorporated their system and pictograms.[83]

72

As it did elsewhere in Western Europe, the creation of corporate or brand identities generated considerable interest in Germany in the 1920s, when the country set about restoring its national infrastructure and attempted to establish international networks of trade. As mentioned earlier, there was an added appeal in that expanding industrial concerns were sometimes keen to adopt modern graphic design, especially when these design features came with related social connotations of modernity, progress, and a certain idealism. The Fagus shoe-last factory is a case in point. The product was very specialized and sold not to the public but to shoemakers, who one would expect were influenced by a concern with efficiency, quality, and reliability rather than modernity or style. Nevertheless, the owner, Karl Benscheidt, was keen to project a certain image, in contrast to his rival, the Behrens shoe-last company, especially since the two manufacturers were located in the same city. In 1911, Benscheidt contacted Walter Gropius and Adolf Meyer to redesign the exterior of the Fagus factory in a prominent site in Alfeld in Lower Saxony. Because of the war, the building was not completed until 1925, but Benscheidt had already commissioned publicity material to create a new image for the company. Following Gropius's recommendation, in 1922 he engaged Johannes Molzahn to establish a modern identity for the firm across the full range of their stationery and publicity. This was an opportunity for Molzahn to refine his work at the hands of a sympathetic client, and his designs became noticeably bolder and simpler as he gained greater familiarity with the demands of corporate identity. As noted earlier, Molzahn was already in thrall to American techniques of publicity, believing that there was a rational basis for advertising design for industry. By 1925, however, Benscheidt was looking for something different. At this point he turned to Herbert Bayer, again on Gropius's recommendation, who prepared some of the simplest and most memorable corporate graphics of the period [Fig. 73]. Based on a red rectangle on a white ground, with bold sanserif lettering in black, the Fagus identity can be traced across all the firm's printed materials.

73

A further indication of the New Typography in practice can be seen in various campaigns of "event identity," notably for cultural events such as the 1928 dance festival in Essen, for which Burchartz designed an outstanding photomontage poster [Fig. 74]. Progressive art projects tended to favor the new style in their promotional materials, partly due to the spirit of modernity implicit in the discourse around the New Typography, but there was also a sense that the different art and design media were engaged in a collective endeavor. Tschichold had been at pains to emphasize that the New Typography was a full participant in "the new art," to the extent that by 1928 this relationship between style, new media, and progressive cultural values had become firmly established in the mind of the public.[84]

A different but equally effective forum for the New Typography was the various trade fairs and international exhibitions held throughout Central Europe in the 1920s and early 1930s. These events were especially important in Weimar Germany because the punitive conditions of the peace settlement often prohibited German manufacturers from participating in international exhibitions, such as at the Paris World's

73 Herbert Bayer. *Fagus Schaftmodelle* (Fagus shoe-lasts) brochure, 1925. Printed by Bauhausdruck, Dessau. Letterpress. The Museum of Modern Art. Jan Tschichold Collection, Gift of Philip Johnson. 578.1999. Cat. 61.

74 Max Burchartz. *Tanzfestspiele zum 2. Deutschen Tänzerkongress Essen 1928* (Dance Festival at the Second German Dance Congress, Essen) poster, 1928. Printed by Graphische Anstalt F. W. Rohden, Essen. Photolithograph. The Museum of Modern Art. Purchase Fund, Jan Tschichold Collection. 326.1937. Cat. 44.

74

Fair of 1925. In response, the German government established a national exhibition organization (Deutsche Ausstellungs- und Messe-Amt) in 1927, "to reestablish international relations torn apart by the war."[85] In its first year alone, the committee organized 249 exhibitions throughout Germany, many of them on fair sites that were newly constructed as part of regional initiatives to promote local industries. As a result, Central European trade fairs had a certain synergy among the modernity of the wares, the buildings, the installation design, and the overall graphic identity. Dexel, Burchartz, and Molzahn were prominent among the many designers who produced their most innovative work for such events.

The most famous of these fairs in relation to the printing and publishing industry was undoubtedly *Pressa*, held in Cologne in the summer of 1928. This was a massive event, dominated by German printing and publishing houses, although nowadays it is probably best known for the photomontage installation and publicity that Lissitzky designed for the Soviet pavilion[86] [Fig. 75]. This was perhaps the most impressive demonstration of the ways in which text and photography could be organized so as to give greater expression to the narrative. It also indicated the shared skills and dynamic relationship that were emerging between graphic design and the practice of exhibition design. As Tschichold remarked, "With Lissitzky, all the possibilities of a new exhibition technique were explored: in place of a tedious succession of framework, containing dull statistics, he produced a new purely visual design of the exhibition space and its contents . . . by bringing a dynamic element into the exhibition by means of continuous films, illuminated and intermittent letters and a number of rotating models."[87] The reconstitution of the Deutscher Werkbund after the war also provided an impetus for exhibitions and fairs devoted to different aspects of contemporary design. The Stuttgart exhibition *Die Wohnung*, for which Baumeister undertook the publicity, was held in 1927 under this policy. The DWB was also behind the *Film und Foto* (FiFo) exhibition in Stuttgart two years later, in 1929, to which John Heartfield,

75

76 Johannes Molzahn. *Wohnung und Werkraum* (Dwelling and Workplace) advertisment, 1929. Letterpress on cellophane. The Museum of Modern Art. Jan Tschichold Collection, Gift of Philip Johnson. 797.1999. Cat. 55.

77 Johannes Molzahn. *Wohnung und Werkraum* (Dwelling and Workplace) poster for the Deutsche Werkbund Exhibition in Breslau, 1929. Printed by Druckerei Schenkalowsky, A. G., Breslau. Lithograph. The Museum of Modern Art. Purchase Fund, Jan Tschichold Collection. 346.1937. Cat. 53.

Lissitzky, Moholy-Nagy, and Tschichold were prominent contributors. This was the event that had prompted Tschichold and Franz Roh to publish *Foto-Auge*, devoted to graphics and photography, and to launch their book series, Fototek. An exhibition that is often overlooked in this series of memorable events is *Wohnung und Werkraum* (Dwelling and Workplace), held in Breslau (now Wrocław, Poland) in the spring of 1929, for which Johannes Molzahn designed the publicity. Using a distinctive logotype, an orange ground, and uppercase sanserif lettering as the unifying features, he elaborated this set of elements across all the printed matter: posters, notepaper, labels, large and small envelopes, brochures, exhibition diagrams, maps, and invoices [Fig. 76]. The most complex item in this extended family of graphics is the large poster, a photomontage depicting hands involved in various activities related to house building [Fig. 77]. In an article titled "Stop Reading! Look!" from the previous year, Molzahn prefigured this work as part of a larger discussion of the transformative role of photography in design: "A piece of paper, in the hand a pencil, and on the table the object—the looking eye; otherwise, a wrist and the tedious work of many, many hours. One hundredth of a second, through the highly sensitive eye of your camera and the picture of the object there on the table is captured on the thin coating of emulsion on the film."[88]

Molzahn, like Burchartz, Dexel, and Trump, set up his own graphic design firm in Magdeburg, and later in Breslau, as a complement to his teaching responsibilities. In fact, the urge to establish independent design studios was one of the defining characteristics of the New Typography in the 1920s. Many of the artist-designers who experimented in advertising quickly recognized that there was a market for those with a combination of formal design skills and the ability to prepare graphic material for printing. Kurt Schwitters set up his design studio, Merz-Werbe (Merz-Advertising), in Hanover in 1924, whereupon he was able to attract commercial clients such as Gunther Wagner (Pelikan writing and art materials), Bahlsen cookies, and Weise Söhne "acid pumps" of Halle, as well as the Hanover city council [Fig. 78]. On leaving the Bauhaus in 1928, Herbert Bayer designed new promotional material for himself under the heading Werbe Entwurf und Ausführung (Advertising Design and Realization), announcing that he was now an independent designer in Berlin [Fig. 79]. In 1930 Schwitters produced a brochure, *Die neue Gestaltung in der Typographie* (The New Design in Typography), advertising his services in a range of different printed materials and offering classes in the field. While not yet a profession, graphic design was emerging as a

78

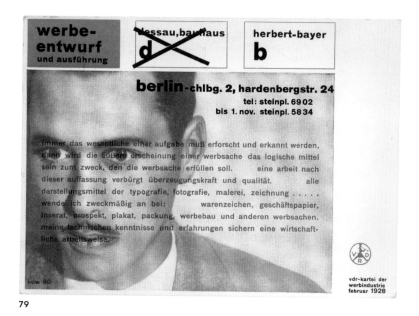

79

recognizable activity within the nexus of art, industry, and commerce [Fig. 80]. Furthermore, it was seen to be an important driver of the economy at a time when the effects of the financial crash of 1929 were beginning to be felt in Europe. Following *Reklame Schau*, the large "advertising exhibition" held in Berlin in 1929, the international exhibition *Kunst der Werbung* (Art of Advertising) in Essen in the summer of 1931 signaled the emergence of advertising theory into the public realm. Organized by Max Burchartz, Alfred Fischer, and Kurt Wilhelm-Kästner to coincide with a large contemporary art exhibition, the prospectus emphasized that this would not be like other advertising exhibitions and fairs. *Kunst der Werbung* had a didactic purpose: to explain the workings of the industry and offer examples of good practice. "The exhibition aims to improve advertising by systematically presenting exemplary advertising methods and artistic examples, and to promote sales. Such an exhibition will be of vital contemporary interest at this time of the most austere economic struggle, as the problem of advertising is one of its

80

most important factors in the struggle for economic livelihood and renewed prosperity."[89] Burchartz designed the publicity for the exhibition using the classic techniques associated with the New Typography: a photomontage of hands pulling strings, with textual information provided in lowercase, sanserif letters in blue and yellow [Fig. 81].

THE RING OF NEW ADVERTISING DESIGNERS

By the time Jan Tschichold's *Die neue Typographie* appeared in 1928, it was apparent that a movement was under way and that individual designers shared a range of specialist skills. Tschichold illustrated his manual with examples of work by many of the leading figures, including

81

Baumeister, Burchartz, Dexel, John Heartfield, Molzahn, Schwitters, and Piet Zwart.[90] Many of these designers had teaching positions in the various academies, *Hochschules*, and trade schools across Germany and Central Europe. In addition, German magazines and journals carried articles, manifestos, and discussion pieces on the new values in design, many written by the same designers Tschichold illustrated. New display typefaces were also appearing, not least Erbar-Grotesk, which had been released by the Ludwig & Mayer foundry in 1926, and Paul Renner's Futura, which the Bauer foundry released the following year. In addition, a series of fairs and exhibitions throughout Germany drew attention to the role of advertising in modern life.[91] Despite this activity, there was a feeling that the New Typography was still somewhat diffuse and fragmented. As with many cultural movements that emerge in different places and with various theoretical positions, there was some internal rivalry and a feeling that not everyone shared the same values. At this point, when the New Typography was rich in possibilities yet lacking coherence, Kurt Schwitters and Robert Michel proposed forming an association of like-minded designers.[92] Schwitters immediately set about contacting various figures he knew of, and by December 1927 he could claim: "We are now firmly established with 9 members, these are Vordemberge, myself, Trump, Burchartz, Michel, Baumeister, Tschichold, Dexel, Domela. We already have 2 magazines and 5 exhibitions. That's a lot for the beginning."[93] By January 1928, the group had a name: Ring neue Werbegestalter (Ring of new advertising designers). Many of these designers had known one another for some time, especially those who had been part of Constructivist art circles such as Gruppe K in the early 1920s. Schwitters took on the role of secretary and general factotum— or, to be more precise, these duties were often undertaken by Helma, his wife. Schwitters also wrote to printers, editors, and curators with a view to creating opportunities for the group. It was still unclear what the organization would do. After all, the members were spread across Germany in various cities and towns, and there were no clear aims, program, or calendar of events. What did emerge from the initial letter-writing campaign was the prospect of exhibitions of work by the Ring. After that, a simple set of rules was laid down, setting out subscriptions, the number of works each member could submit to exhibitions, and the possibility of creating an archive of photographs and design work.

The next stage was to invite foreign or corresponding members, thus enlarging the group and emphasizing its international stature. Again, the circle was expanded mostly by people with whom the members were already in touch. Tschichold proposed Lajos Kassák, El Lissitzky, Karel Teige, and Piet Zwart, designers whose work he planned to include in his forthcoming book. Zwart did in fact become the first foreign member, soon to be joined by Paul Schuitema, another Dutch designer. A number of others chose not to join the Ring but were willing participants in the group's activities. These included John Heartfield, Lajos Kassák, and Karel Teige, who were credited as "guests." As momentum gathered, other new members were proposed, including Werner Graeff, Johannes Molzahn, Hans Leistikow, and Theo van Doesburg.[94] Schwitters conducted the group's business in a light-hearted, enthusiastic manner, sending out postcards and seasonal greetings to various members with humorous comments about developments and possibilities. Schwitters was keen to launch a journal, but given the passive role that most members preferred to play, the idea was probably overambitious. Nevertheless, it was suggested that the Ring could use the journal *Das neue Frankfurt* as a mouthpiece for their activities, probably at the invitation of Leistikow and Ernst May. Schwitters also reached out to the Bauhaus with the possibility of collaboration with the Ring, but this proved to be a sore point between the two groups despite their shared ideals in design. Herbert Bayer and Joost Schmidt, the two people most closely involved with graphics at the Bauhaus, were rather frosty about any formal collaboration, as they had been in 1925 when Tschichold approached them about "elementare typographie."[95] The official response from the Bauhaus was quite high-handed:

> We do not disagree with your aims and stand firmly alongside your organization, but instead of participating we urge the current head of our advertising department and printing studio, Mr. J. Schmidt, to join your association as a representative of the Bauhaus. . . . We agree in principle to participate in your exhibitions on the condition that we are able to decide on our participation in each individual exhibition. . . . For organizational reasons, we cannot accept a commitment allowing you to participate automatically in our exhibitions. We will gladly consider your participation in each specific case and, wherever possible, bring it about.

Schwitters diligently reported this to the members and received a number of barbed comments in response, which he then circulated without attributing names:

Let's wait a bit, then we will be stronger and can bear the dirt that is thrown up after the Bauhaus. . . . There is a risk that our tendency could be viewed as being influenced by the Bauhaus. . . . In some areas of Germany, it is neither pleasant, nor beneficial, to be put in the same pot as the Bauhaus. . . . We should forego cooperation with the Bauhaus under these conditions. . . . The good thing about the Ring is its vitality without the Bauhaus. . . . In every commitment with the Bauhaus, only the Bauhaus has benefited.[96]

The first exhibition of the Ring opened on March 20, 1928, at the Kunstgewerbemuseum in Cologne—just two months before the massive *Pressa* exhibition at the nearby exhibition grounds—and included work by all nine members and several guest participants. The first showing was so successful that the exhibition moved on to the Nassau Kunstverein in Wiesbaden and subsequently toured through Barmen, Bochum, Hanover, Bremen, and Magdeburg. This immediate success led to other requests for the show, whereupon Schwitters approached his colleagues with a view to creating another exhibition. The second Ring exhibition was launched in Hamburg in the summer of 1928, after which, at the behest of Paul Schuitema, it traveled on to the Rotterdam Academy, then to Halle and Dresden. Thus, at the beginning of 1929 the Ring had two parallel exhibitions on tour throughout Germany and the Netherlands, stopping off in many of the cities that had already established studios of modern graphic design in colleges of fine and applied art. The climax of the exhibition program was in summer 1929, when an expanded version of the touring displays was shown at the Staatliche Kunstbibliothek (State Art Library) in Berlin under the title "Die neue Typographie." Along with the Ring members, the exhibition included work by Herbert Bayer, Moholy-Nagy, Karel Teige, and Theo van Doesburg.

Whether the Ring was the main catalyst or, more likely, the pub-lication of Jan Tschichold's *Die neue Typographie*, by the close of 1928 the movement had a fairly identifiable character and list of protagonists. The following year, in the summer of 1929, the Werkbund *Film und Foto* (FiFo) exhibition was held in Stuttgart, where many of the key figures were represented. *Film und Foto* also had a secondary life as a traveling exhibition that visited various cities in Central Europe before proceed-ing to Tokyo and Osaka in Japan.[97] In spring and summer 1931, two ex-hibitions devoted to aspects of photography had Ring members at the forefront, revealing the extent to which the medium was now central to the New Typography: *Das Lichtbild* (The Photograph), an exhibition of modern photography planned by Max Burchartz for the Folkwang Museum in Essen, featured a range of techniques and applications, although it is perhaps best known for the publicity image of a child's face.[98] This was a close-up portrait of Burchartz's daughter, Lotte, cropped to isolate only the left side of her face against the round brim of her hat. The second exhibition, *Fotomontage* (April 25–May 31, 1931), was organized by César Domela at the Staatliche Kunstbibliothek Berlin, where the Ring had held their last exhibition the previous year[99] [Fig. 82]. Again, several Ring members were prominent, as well as several of their guests and associates, especially the Russians, Gustav Klutsis, El Lissitzky, and Aleksandr Rodchenko. Domela took this opportunity to point out that photomontage had been a tool of the New Typography for some time and was certainly not a medium exclusive to avant-garde art. In the catalogue introduction, he writes: "Photomontage is not, as is often claimed, an invention, but something that emerged from the needs of its time, an age that requires new expressions and material combinations. . . . It finds its main use in the advertisement, both indi-vidual and political."[100]

In the middle of all this activity, a publication appeared that brought the field of modern graphic design in Germany into greater focus. This was *Gefesselter Blick* (Captured glance), prepared by Heinz and Bodo

82   83

Rasch in the wake of an exhibition at the Graphische Klub of Stuttgart in 1930. While Tschichold's *Die neue Typographie* gave guidelines on how to design in a new idiom, *Gefesselter Blick* provided a survey of the leading practitioners. In all, some twenty-six designers were invited to contribute examples of their work and to provide a brief account of their philosophy of design, often in the form of answers to simple questions. Because the publication was partly sponsored by the Ring, all their members were represented, along with the foreign members and guests: El Lissitzky, Paul Schuitema, Karel Teige, and Piet Zwart. There were a few figures from outside the mainstream, however. Three Swiss designers—Otto Baumberger, Max Bill, and Walter Cyliax—were included because the book was also supported by the Schweizerischer Werkbund. Moholy-Nagy was there, represented by some of his

Bauhausbücher publicity, but significantly, no other Bauhaus figures were included. As well as the compendium of designers and their work, *Gefesselter Blick* itself was something of a demonstration piece in new techniques and materials. Beneath a clear plastic cover, one could read the list of participants on a red flap on the left, with photomontages by Baumeister and Lissitzky to the right [Fig. 83].

Epigraphs from Siegfried Kracauer, "Die Ornament der Masse," *Frankfurter Zeitung*, 1927,
quoted in *The Mass Ornament: Weimar Essays*,
translated by Thomas Y. Levin (Cambridge,
MA: Harvard University Press, 1995), 75, and
Walter Benjamin, "Einbahnstraße," *Gesammelte
Schriften*, vol. 4 (Frankfurt: Suhrkamp, 1972), 85.
1   László Moholy-Nagy, "Die neue Typographie,"
Bauhaus Weimar 1919–1923 (Weimar/Munich:
Bauhaus, 1923).
2   Moholy-Nagy had already published an article
on the need for our sensory organs to catch
up with the potential of existing technologies.
László Moholy-Nagy, "Produktion—Reproduktion," *De Stijl* 5, no. 7 (July 1922): 98–99.
3   Tschichold, *The New Typography*, 53.
Tschichold reprinted Marinetti's manifesto in
Die neue Typographie under the heading "Typographic Revolution." He cited *Les mots en liberté
futuriste* (Milan: Edizioni futuriste di Poesia,
1919) as its source; however, the manifesto had
appeared as a pamphlet six years earlier, on
May 11, 1913.
4   See, for instance, Umberto Boccioni, "La
pittura futurista: Manifesto tecnico" [Futurist
painting: Technical manifesto], *Poesia*, April
11, 1910; Francesco Balilla Pratella, "La musica
futurista: Manifesto tecnico" [Futurist music:
Technical manifesto], *Poesia*, March 11, 1911;
Luigi Russolo, "L'art des bruits" [The art of nois-
es] (Milan: Direction du Mouvement Futuriste,
March 11, 1913); Valentine de Saint-Point, "Mani-

festo futurista della lussuria" [Futurist manifesto
of lust] (Milan: Direzione del Movimento Futurista, January 11, 1913).
5   Many poets had experimented with phonetic
or "pattern" typography, in which the words are
arranged across the page to represent a visual
motif or to suggest alternative or nonlinear
reading of the text. Stéphane Mallarmé's experiments in phonetic typography are best seen in
"Un coup de dés jamais n'abolira le hasard" (A
throw of the dice will never abolish chance), first
published in 1897, in which the words are positioned across the page in a manner that exploits
the negative space of unprinted areas as much
as the text itself.
6   Fernando Pessoa, "Intersectionism of the 1st
Degree" (1914), quoted without citation in Marta
Soares, Fernando Cabral Martins, and Antonio
Sáez Delgado, *Pessoa: All Art Is a Form of Literature* (Madrid: Museo Nacional Centro de Arte
Reina Sofia, 2018), 14. Pessoa reveals his hostility
to the entire Futurist campaign by adding, "Futurism isn't art; it's a theory of art accompanied by
illustrations that explain nothing" (14).
7   "Program of the First Working Group of
Constructivists," published in *Ermitazh*, no. 13
(August 1922): 3–4. Translated by Christina
Lodder in Charles Harrison and Paul Wood, eds.,
*Art in Theory 1900–2000: An Anthology of
Changing Ideas* (Oxford: Blackwell, 2003), 317.
Jan Tschichold published his version of this
program in "elementare typographie," 196–97.

8 El Lissitzky and Ilya Ehrenburg, "Statement of the Editors of *Veshch*," published in *De Stijl* 5, no. 4 (1922). Harrison and Wood, *Art in Theory 1900–2000*, 344–45.

9 Moholy-Nagy himself felt that his work only gained a degree of independence and maturity in 1920. Oliver Botar, *Technical Detours: The Early Moholy-Nagy* (New York: Graduate Center of the City University, 2006), 108.

10 Between 1918 and 1923, Moholy-Nagy had first become associated with the *MA* (Today) group around Lajos Kassák in Budapest and experimented with Dadaist and Constructivist painting, printmaking, and sculpture in Berlin before moving to the Bauhaus at Weimar in March 1923. On Moholy-Nagy's early work, see Botar, *Technical Detours*.

11 As early as 1919, Moholy-Nagy had written in a poem, "Light, total Light, creates the total man"; quoted in Sibyl Moholy-Nagy, *Moholy-Nagy: Experiment in Totality* (New York: Harper and Brothers, 1950), 12. His central preoccupation throughout the 1920s was the building of a machine known as the Light-Space Modulator to create an environment of shifting light and color patterns.

12 László Moholy-Nagy, *Malerei, Photographie, Film*, Bauhausbücher 8 (Munich: Albert Langen, 1925). The spelling of the title was inconsistent; "Fotografie" on the cover, but "Photographie" on the title page.

13 Moholy-Nagy's second book, *Von Material zu Architektur* (Munich: Albert Langen, 1929), coined the term "new vision," which, as he stated in the foreword, was a summation of the work he began in 1925.

14 Moholy-Nagy, *Painting, Photography, Film*, trans. Janet Seligman (Cambridge, MA: MIT Press, 1925), 39.

15 Ibid., 39–40.

16 Ibid., 23–24.

17 El Lissitzky, "Topographie der Typographie," *Merz* no. 4 (July 1923): 47.

18 It has always been something of a paradox that the Russian Constructivists, often the most ambitious and imaginative with regard to the potential of new technologies, had the least experience with advanced technical equipment and had to work with comparatively primitive processes, especially in the field of print.

19 Several commentators have pointed out that El Lissitzky appears to anticipate the internet in these statements. See Barrie Tullet, "Electro-Library Dreams," *Eye Magazine Blog*, June 16, 2010, http://www.eyemagazine.com/blog/post/electro-library-dreams.

20 The photographic line block was introduced by Charles Gillot in 1872.

21 In Europe, the halftone process was pioneered in Munich by Georg Meisenbach, who took out a patent in 1882. The *Berliner Illustrirte Zeitung* (*BIZ*) was launched in January 1892 and adopted photographic illustration throughout its issues in 1901. By 1914 it had a circulation of one million and had spawned many similar magazines. By 1928 its circulation was 1.8 million. Corey Ross, *Media and the Making of Modern Germany: Mass Communications, Society and Politics from the Empire to the Third Reich* (Oxford: Oxford University Press, 2008), 30.

22 For example, "3-color halftones" were introduced in 1885, the same year as the Linotype composing machine. Two developments that transformed the printing industry were the introduction of the Monotype composing machine in 1887 and offset lithographic printing, which was introduced in the United States in 1904–5. W. Turner Berry and H. Edmund Poole, *Annals of Printing* (London: Blandford, 1966), 249–70. For an outline of the German printing, publishing, and advertising industries in the years before the First World War, see Jeremy Aynsley, *Graphic Design in Germany*, 19–57.

23 Interestingly, "electrical inkless printing" was first demonstrated in 1899, and the first "photo-setting" machine was developed in 1925, employing "transparent alphabetical characters on glass," each of which seems to parallel some of the futuristic ideas proposed by El Lissitzky. Berry and Poole, *Annals of Printing*, 266–77.

24 El Lissitzky, "Typographische Tatsachen," in *Gutenberg Festschrift*, ed. Aloys Ruppel (Mainz: Gutenberg Gesellschaft, 1925), 152–54.

25 Lissitzky-Küppers, *El Lissitzky*, 359–60.

26 Kurt Schwitters, "Watch Your Step!," *Merz* no. 6 (October 1923): 57.

27 Kurt Schwitters, "Thesen über Typographie," *Merz* no. 11 (November 1924): 91.

28 *G: Material zur elementaren Gestaltung* [Material for elementary construction], edited by Hans Richter, was founded in 1923 in Berlin. It closed in 1926 after four issues. El Lissitzky and Mies van der Rohe were on the editorial board. *ABC: Beitrage zum Bauen* [Contributions to building], edited by Mart Stam, was founded in Zurich in 1924. It included contributions by El Lissitzky, Hannes Meyer, and Schwitters before it closed in 1928.

29 In January 1926, Lissitzky castigated Theo van Doesburg for having "turned traitor to architecture" and now "only want[ing] to be a painter." Lissitzky-Küppers, *El Lissitzky*, 73.

30 Baumeister was in touch with Léger, Le Corbusier, and the Purist group in the 1920s, and his work was featured in several issues of the journal *L'esprit nouveau*. See, for example, Waldemar George, "La peinture en Allemagne: Willy Baumeister," *L'esprit nouveau*, no. 15 (1922): 1790–94.

31 Willy Baumeister, "Neue Typographie," *Die Form* 1, no. 10 (July 1926): 215–17.

32 Ibid., 215.

33 Ibid., 216.

34 Brigitte Pedde, *Willi Baumeister 1889–1955: Schopfer aus dem Unbekannten* (Bonn: VG Bild-Kunst, 2013), 50.

35 Sponsored by the Deutscher Werkbund, Weissenhofsiedlung in Stuttgart was the setting for twenty-one model domestic buildings designed by seventeen architects, including many of the leading figures of modernist architecture and design: Peter Behrens, Le Corbusier, Walter Gropius, J. J. P. Oud, Hans Poelzig, Hans Scharoun, Mart Stam, and Bruno Taut. Ludwig Mies van der Rohe was in overall control of the project.

36 There were three variants on the design employing three different pictures of nineteenth-century interiors but retaining the same red cross and text.

37 Baumeister was replacing Paul Renner, who had moved to the Gewerbeschule in Munich eighteen months earlier.

38 Renner was appointed in 1925 but left for Munich the following year. See Christopher Burke, *Paul Renner: The Art of Typography* (New York: Princeton Architectural Press, 1998), 54–55, and Hubert Salden, ed., *Die Städelschule Frankfurt am Main von 1817 bis 1995* (Mainz: Hermann Schmidt, 1995), 112–14. See also *Der Städelschule Frankfurt am Main: Aus der Geschichte einer deutschen Kunsthochschule* (Frankfurt: Waldemar Kramer, 1982), chap. 4.

39 Under Ernst May, the Frankfurt city planning department completed around fifteen thousand family houses and apartments between 1925 and 1930, each in a simple utilitarian style and fitted with a version of the groundbreaking Frankfurt Kitchen, designed by Margarete Schütte-Lihotzky.

40 *Das neue Frankfurt* was published monthly by Englert and Schlosser in Frankfurt, inspiring similar journals in Berlin and Munich. In April 1932, the name was changed to *Die neue Stadt* under the new editor, Joseph Gantner. It was closed down by the Nazis in March 1933.

41 Hans Leistikow undertook the layout and typography, while his sister Grete prepared the photomontages.

42 Landmann, Foreword, *Das neue Frankfurt* 1, no. 1 (October 1926): 2–3.

43 Ernst May, *Das neue Frankfurt* 1, no. 1 (October/November 1926): 5–6.

44 *Das neue Frankfurt* 1, no. 3 (January 1927): 57–63.

45 Paul Renner, "Vom stammbaum der Schrift," *Das neue Frankfurt* 1, no. 4 (February/March 1927): 85–87.

46 Max Burchartz to Tschichold, December 9, 1926, Tschichold Papers.

47 The success of Bauhaus émigrés in creating an exceptional reputation for the college in the United States has distorted our understanding of design education in Weimar Germany, which was always more diverse and uneven than the narrow view of Bauhaus modernism. See Wingler, *Kunstschulreform 1900–1933* (Berlin: Mann, 1977), as well as numerous histories of individual colleges.

48 A class in "Reklame" was announced in 1927, but it appears that formal teaching in advertising design was not introduced until 1929. As an additional drawback, the structure of classes was changed each year between 1927 and 1932. Bergdoll and Dickerman, *The Bauhaus*, 331–34.

49 Jan Tschichold, "elementare typographie," 212.

50 See the comments by members of the Ring on p. 154. In *Bauhaus: Drucksachen, Typographie, Reklame* (Düsseldorf: Marzona, 1984), Gerd Fleischmann casts doubt on the significance of graphic design produced in the Bauhaus, and he has since stated: "The term 'Bauhaus typography' is inadequate in two ways: the Bauhaus never intended to create a style, and the Bauhaus was influenced from outside." "An Interview with Professor Gerd Fleischmann," *Typejournal*, February 7, 2017, typejournal.ru /en/articles/An -Interview-with-Professor-Gerd-Fleischmann.

51 *Johannes Molzahn, 1892–1965*, exhibition catalogue (Regensburg: Ostdeutsche Galerie, 1974), unpaginated. See also Siegfried Salzmann, ed., *Johannes Molzahn: Das druckgraphische Werk* (Duisberg: Wilhelm-Lehmbruck Museum, 1977).

52 On April 5, 1932, Molzahn submitted another memorandum to the Minister für Wissenschaft, Kunst und Volksbildung (Minister for Science, Art, and National Education) on the reorganization of the college in Breslau to better equip students to confront new demands and technologies. Salzmann, *Johannes Molzahn*, 27.

53 Eugen Gomringer, "Walter Dexel: Lehrer für visuelle Kommunikation," in *Walter Dexel*, exhibition catalogue (Hanover: Kestner Gesellschaft, 1974); quoted in Ruth Wöbkemeier, ed., *Walter Dexel: Bild, Zeichen, Raum* (Bremen: Kunstverein, 1990), 69–70.

54 On the Reimann School, see Aynsley, *Graphic Design in Germany*, 111–16.

55 Theo van Doesburg visited the Bauhaus in April 1921, hoping to be offered a teaching position. He was not successful and instead set up his own private classes in Weimar, promoting De Stijl principles and greater emphasis on design for industry. Wintgens-Hötte, "Van Doesburg Tackles the Continent," 13–15.

56 On Graeff, see Gerda Breuer, ed., *Werner Graeff 1901–1978: Der Künstleringenieur* (Berlin: Jovis, 2010).

57 Graeff was a prolific author on design, photography, and film. His books include *Innenräume* (Interiors) (1928), *Es kommt der neue Fotograf!* (Here comes the new photographer!) (1929), *Filmgegner von heute—Filmfreunde von morgen* (Film opponents of today—film friends of tomorrow) (1929), and *Das Buch vom Film* (1931).

58 On the expansion of advertising and the rise of branded goods in Germany, see Dirk Reinhardt, *Von der Reklame zum Marketing: Die Geschichte der Wirtschaftswerbung in Deutschland* (Berlin: Akademie, 1993), chap. 3, and Aynsley, *Graphic Design in Germany*, 49–57.

59 On this debate in relation to the Deutscher Werkbund, ca. 1907–14, see Frederic J. Schwartz, *The Werkbund: Design Theory and Mass Culture before the First World War* (New Haven, CT: Yale University Press, 1996), 121–50.

60 Hans Siemsen, "Die Literatur der Nachtleser," *Die literarische Welt* 2, no. 37 (September 10, 1926); quoted in Anton Kaes, Martin Jay, and Edward Dimendberg, eds., *The Weimar Republic Sourcebook* (Berkeley: University of California Press, 1994), 663–64. Odol mouthwash was created in 1892, thereafter maintaining highly visible advertising campaigns.

61 On the contemporary discourse on street advertising, especially illuminated billboards, see Janet Ward, *Weimar Surfaces: Urban Visual Culture in 1920s Germany* (Berkeley: University of California Press, 2001), 92–141.

62 Tschichold, "Wo stehen wir heute?"

63 Lissitzky-Küppers, *El Lissitzky*, 54.

64 Max Burchartz, *Gestaltung der Reklame* (Bochum, June 1924). This was the first in a series of publications produced by Werbe-bau on aspects of design and technology, titled *Flugblätter mit dem Buntquadrat* (Pamphlets of the colored square).

65 See Gerhard Glüher, "Untersuchungen zum fotografischen Werk des Gestalters Max Burchartz," in *Max Burchartz 1887–1961: Künstler,* *Typograf, Pädagoge*, ed. Gerda Breuer (Berlin: Jovis, 2010), 183–89.

66 See David Mellor, *Germany, the New Photography, 1927–33: Documents and Essays* (London: Arts Council of Great Britain, 1978), 9–17; John Willett, *The New Sobriety: Art and Politics in the Weimar Period, 1917–1933* (London: Thames and Hudson, 1987), 111–17, 139–49; Ralf Grüttemeier, Klaus Beekman, and Ben Rebel, eds., *Neue Sachlichkeit and Avant-Garde* (Amsterdam: Rodopi, 2013), 7–16.

67 Albert Renger-Patzsch, *Die Welt ist schön* (Munich: Kurt Wolff, 1928).

68 Morris's views on the need for wood engraved illustrations to accompany letterpress printing continued to be upheld by private presses in Britain and Germany throughout the interwar period. See William Morris, *The Ideal Book: Essays and Lectures on the Art of the Book*, ed. William S. Peterson (Berkeley: University of California Press, 1982), 40–58.

69 As noted in chap. 1, notes 73 and 74, reviewers of Tschichold's *Die neue Typographie* took up this line. The reviews appear in *Die rote Fahne*, December 16, 1928, and *Bauhaus* 2, no. 3 (1928).

70 Lajos Kassák, "The Advertisement and Modern Typography," *Reklámélet* (August 1928): 1. Reprinted in *The Advertisement and Modern Typography*, ed. Ferenc Csaplár (Budapest: Kassák Museum, 1999), 13–14.

71 Ibid.

72 Ibid., 3.

73 See C. Ross, "Visions of Prosperity: The Americanization of Advertising in Interwar Germany," in *Selling Modernity: Advertising in Twentieth-Century Germany*, ed. Pamela Swett, S. J. Wiesen, and Jonathan Zatlin (Durham, NC: Duke University Press, 2007), 52–77.

74 El Lissitzky, "Americanism in European Architecture," *Das Kunstblatt*, no. 2 (February 1925); quoted in Lissitzky-Küppers, *El Lissitzky*, 373.

75 Letter from Johannes Molzahn to Karl Benscheidt Jr., February 26, 1922; quoted in Annemarie Jaeggi, *Fagus: Industrial Culture from Werkbund to Bauhaus* (New York: Princeton Architectural Press, 2000), 95.

76 In 1929, Alfred Knapp, the official German representative at the international advertising congress, would claim that science had won out over art as the bedrock of the industry. See Swett, Wiesen, and Zatlin, *Selling Modernity*, 8.

77 In 1926, Ashley Havinden and William Crawford, head of the largest advertising agency in Britain, undertook a fact-finding tour of Germany, visiting type foundries, magazine publishers, and individual designers. See *Advertising and the Artist: Ashley Havinden* (Edinburgh: National Galleries of Scotland, 2003), 33.

78 Quoted in Aynsley, *Graphic Design in Germany*, 125.

79 *Die Form*, the journal of the Deutscher Werkbund, was first published in 1922, but it folded soon after. It was relaunched in 1925 with a cover design by Joost Schmidt. In 1928, a competition was held for a new cover design, which was won by Walter Dexel.

80 Frederic J. Schwartz, "Commodity Signs: Peter Behrens, the AEG, and the Trademark," *Journal of Design History* 9, no. 3 (January 1996): 153–84. Corporate identity and logo design were already appearing in teaching manuals for lettering artists. See, for example, Max Schramm and Hugo Jäkel, *Das Zeichnen schmuckender Berufe in der Fortbildungsschule auf methodischer Grundlage* [Drawing for the ornamental professions in continuing education schools] (Leipzig: Seemann, 1914).

81 George Orwell, "Why I Write," *Gangrel*, no. 4 (Summer 1946); collected in many editions.

82 On Isotype, see Otto Neurath, *International Picture Language* (London: Kegan Paul, 1936), and Christopher Burke, Eric Kindel, and Susan Walker, eds., *Isotype: Design and Contexts, 1925–1971* (London: Hyphen, 2013).

83 Cover for Otto Mänchen-Helfen, *Drittel der Menschheit* [A third of humanity] (Berlin: Bücherkreis, 1932).

84 "For the laws governing typographic design are the same as those discovered by modern painters as governing design in general." Tschichold, *The New Typography*, 30.

85 Janet Ward, *Weimar Surfaces*, 50–51.

86 Jeremy Aynsley, "Pressa Cologne, 1928: Exhibitions and Publication Design in the Weimar Period," *Design Issues* 10, no. 3 (1994): 52–76.

87 Jan Tschichold, "Display That Has Dynamic Force: Exhibition Stands Designed by El Lissitzky," *Commercial Art* 10 (January 1931): 21–22.

88 Johannes Molzahn, "Nicht mehr lesen! Sehen!," *Das Kunstblatt* 12, no. 3 (March 1928): 78. Article translated in *Visual Culture: Illustrated Press and Photography*, ed. Anton Kaes, Martin Jay, and Edward Dimendberg (Berkeley: University of California Press, 1994), 648–49.

89 Prospectus for *Kunst der Werbung*. Tschichold Collection, Museum of Modern Art, New York, 618.1999.

90 The full list of designers whose work is illustrated in *Die neue Typographie* is as follows: Otto Baumberger, Willi Baumeister, Herbert Bayer, Max Burchartz, Walter Dexel, John Heartfield, Lajos Kassák, El Lissitzky, László Moholy-Nagy, Johannes Molzahn, Joost Schmidt, Kurt Schwitters, Franz Seiwert, Karel Teige, Theo van Doesburg, and Piet Zwart.

91 Apart from the exhibitions organized by the Bund (BDG), the Kunstverein Jena held an exhibition on Neue Reklame (New Advertising) between May and June 1927, with a poster by Walter Dexel; the following year, *Pressa* in Cologne focused attention on design for print.

92 The idea was probably discussed in July 1927, when Schwitters was a guest of Michel and his wife, Ella Bergmann-Michel, in the Taunus Mountains. Broos, "Das kurze, aber heftige Leben des Rings 'neue Werbergestalter,'" 7.

93 Schwitters to Piet Zwart, December 1927, cited in ibid., 7.

94 Van Doesburg refused, probably because he was accustomed to being the leading figure in such organizations.

95 Tschichold approached Bayer with a view to publishing "elementare typographie" in the Bauhausbücher series, but Bayer was discouraging, saying that it could only appear after a publication of his own on Bauhaus typography. Bayer to Tschichold, October 30, 1925, Tschichold Papers.

96 Circular letter to Ring members, July 21, 1928, cited in Broos, "Das kurze, aber heftige Leben des Rings 'neue Werbergestalter,'" 9.

97 A version of FiFo was shown in Zurich, Berlin, Danzig, Vienna, and Zagreb, and then in Tokyo and Osaka in 1931.

98 *Das Lichtbild* was mounted by the Verein zur Veranstaltung kultureller Ausstellungen (Association for Cultural Exhibitions) at the Folkwang Museum, Essen, between July 11 and August 23, 1931. Apart from Burchartz himself, other exhibitors included César Domela-Nieuwenhuis, John Heartfield, Hannah Höch, Lucia Moholy, and László Moholy-Nagy.

99 César Domela-Nieuwenhuis's catalogue cover for *Fotomontage* depicted the practice of photomontage.

100 César Domela-Nieuwenhuis, *Fotomontage* (Berlin: Staatliche Kunstbibliothek, 1931), 6.

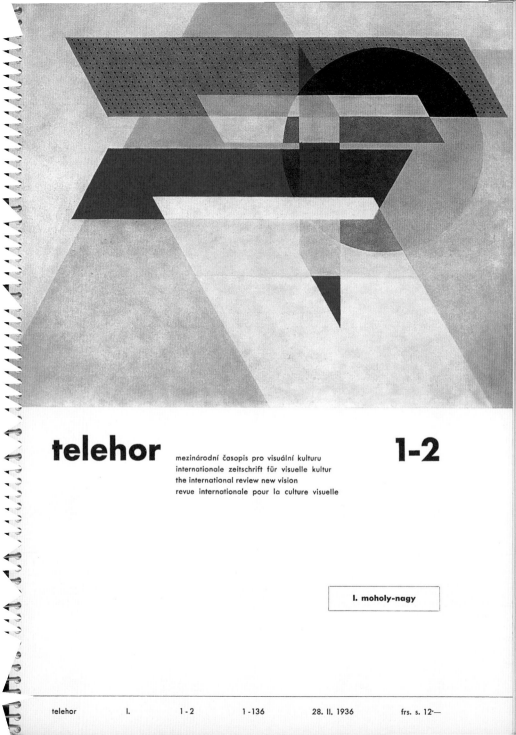

telehor

mezinárodní časopis pro visuální kulturu
internationale zeitschrift für visuelle kultur
the international review new vision
revue internationale pour la culture visuelle

1-2

l. moholy-nagy

Chapter 3

The Final Years: The Fall and Rise of the New Typography

If the early to mid-1920s were the pioneering phase of the New Typography, a time when many of the grand theories were being thrashed out among a relatively small group of artist-designers, the years between 1928 and 1931 were the high watermark of the movement as a radical and reforming force. The German economy had been growing consistently, albeit from a very low point in 1923–24, but growth slowed down markedly after 1931 as the effects of the international crisis began to be felt. Despite the economic downturn, conditions were still right for innovation in publishing, zadvertising, and graphic design. After all, the manifestos of modern advertising made it clear that the New Typography could make promotion of goods and services more efficient and cheaper to produce. Exhibitions showing new work were appearing in many towns and cities across Central Europe, and designers still had work in hand. But there were signs of a loss of momentum among the designers themselves. Hans and Grete Leistikow had moved to the USSR in 1930 along with the May Brigade, a team of Frankfurt architect-designers who had followed Ernst May to the Soviet Union with the aim of building new cities, while the Russians were finding it increasingly difficult to participate in events and publications in the West.

The Ring ceased to play an active role after 1931. Although individuals carried on their work in various fields, there was less excitement about the revolution in print. In 1932, the trade journal *Typographische Mitteilungen* held a survey questioning whether "objective typographic design" had ground to a halt. The overwhelming response to the question was that the New Typography was still a vital force in design, but the traditionalists who had objected to Tschichold's publications in the 1920s were regaining their voice. This debate within the printing trade, however, would prove to be a sideshow. By the time the results of the survey were published in March 1933, Hitler had been appointed chancellor of Germany; the National Socialist Party had gained control of the instruments of state and introduced the Enabling Act, or Law to Remedy the Distress of the People and the Reich, granting Hitler special powers to override the rule of law.[1] The effects of this change were felt in the print world almost immediately. That same month, on March 14, 1933, Joseph Goebbels established the Reichsministerium für Volksaufklärung und Propaganda (Ministry for Education and Propaganda), which created seven separate divisions to monitor content in the news and entertainment media.[2] Newspapers, books, and magazines were overseen by Division 4, which controlled the press; Division 6 had jurisdiction over the arts. Control was tightened in October when the Schriftleitergesetz (Editors' Law) was enacted, requiring journalists, editors, and photographers to submit their work to a committee of the Reichskulturkammer (Reich Chamber of Culture) for approval.[3] In the realm of design, the effects were felt even more quickly. On March 11, a warrant was issued for Jan Tschichold's arrest, and a few days later he was taken into "protective custody." After just over four weeks in prison, he was released under an amnesty and immediately began making plans to leave the country. In July, he and his family left Germany for Switzerland.

By this time, the Bauhaus in Berlin was closed, Moholy-Nagy had moved to the Netherlands, and the various figures associated with the Ring and the New Typography were becoming dispersed throughout

Europe, the Soviet Union, and North America. On April 4, 1933, Paul Renner was arrested and later sacked from his post as director of the Munich Meisterschule. Renner had a history of principled opposition to Nazi ideology and was critical of the Nazis' attitude toward national styles in design. His 1932 book *Kulturbolschwismus?* had been drawn to the attention of the authorities, and just a few days before his arrest he had been reprimanded for including too much Roman and not enough Gothic type in an exhibition of German printing and book design in Milan.[4] Johannes Molzahn left his position in the Staatliche Akademie für Kunst und Kunstgewerbe in Breslau and emigrated to the United States, where he was able to find work at the University of Washington in Seattle and at the School of Design in Chicago. In an attempt to anticipate the problems that would arise once the Nazis took power, Wilhelm Deffke advised the lecturers at the Magdeburg Kunstgewerbe- und Handwerkerschule to join the party, which they did on May 1, 1933, but this merely delayed the inevitable. Walter Dexel, whose work had been denounced as degenerate, was removed from his post eighteen months later.[5] In 1933 Max Burchartz was relieved of his professorship in the Folkwangschule in Essen, and although he also joined the party and was prepared to undertake propaganda work for the Kriegsmarine (German navy), he was not reappointed to the school.[6] Kurt Schwitters lost his main client, the Hanover city council, in 1934, and his work was held up for ridicule in publications and in the *Entartete Kunst* (Degenerate Art) exhibition of 1937. In January 1937, having been informed that he was required to attend an interview with the police, Schwitters left Germany for Norway, where his son was living. Even the Reimann School attracted the opprobrium of the Nazis, and in 1937 it moved to London.

Only Georg Trump seems to have survived in his post. Having established successful typography departments at the Handwerker und Kunstgewerbeschule in Bielefeld and the Höheren Grafischen Fachschule in Berlin, in 1934 he took over Renner's position as director of the Meisterschule in Munich, where he managed to steer the college through the next five years until he was called up for military service in 1939.[7] Herbert Bayer was probably the only one of the leading figures to actually thrive under the Nazis. He undertook a series of prestigious exhibition projects in the mid-1930s, culminating in the *Deutschland-Ausstellung*, a major propaganda display at the Berliner Funkturm timed to coincide with the Olympics in 1936. Regardless of his political sympathies or any moral qualms he may have had about this work, the *Deutschland-Ausstellung* catalogue remains one of the finest pieces of mass consumption photomontage in the period, giving a lie to the view that the Nazis could not accept modern art, architecture, or design. Clearly, when it served their purposes, the New Typography, photomontage, and Roman (as opposed to Gothic) lettering were perfectly acceptable.[8] Nevertheless, the purge of modern designers from the colleges of arts and crafts was virtually absolute within the first two years of the Nazi regime.

THE NEW TYPOGRAPHY BEYOND GERMANY

Despite the suppression of the New Typography within Germany, the movement carried on in neighboring countries. Tschichold's presence in Switzerland had little impact initially because, as a resident alien, restrictions were placed on the amount of work he could undertake. Nevertheless, despite the attack on "elementare typographie" in the *Schweizer graphische Mitteilungen*, there had been serious interest in the New Typography in Switzerland.[9] At the end of the First World War, Max Dalang, inspired by the American model, set up a professional advertising consultancy in Zurich that became one of the first full-service agencies in Europe. Dalang also established the Schweizer Reklameverband (Swiss Advertisers Association) to ensure high standards across this developing industry.[10] Several exhibitions and publications in the early 1930s also demonstrated that the central ideas of the New Typography were familiar in Switzerland. There had been an exhibition devoted to *Neue Typographie* in the Gewerbemuseum Basel in 1927, and in 1930 another exhibition showcased *Neue Werbegraphik* (New Advertising

Design).[11] It should also be remembered that *Gefesselter Blick* was partly sponsored by the Swiss Werkbund, thus placing the three Swiss designers, Otto Baumberger, Max Bill, and Walter Cyliax, alongside their German counterparts.

Max Bill, a Swiss national who attended the Bauhaus in Dessau, had returned to Zurich in 1929 to set up an architecture and design practice called *bill-reklame* (Bill advertising). Bill's strict adherence to the principles of Bauhaus modernism led to the creation of several sanserif typefaces and a successful career as an advertising designer and teacher. In 1944, he became a professor at the Kunstgewerbeschule in Zurich, where he was able to refine his teaching methods based on the central ideals of the New Typography: sanserif typefaces, objective photography, asymmetrical composition, and active use of negative space.[12] In fact, Bill's unwavering support for these principles would bring him into conflict with Tschichold when the latter became more vocal in his rejection of modernism in book design. This led to a bitter dispute in 1946, in the course of which Bill accused Tschichold of being a traitor to the cause, which in turn polarized opinion among graphic designers and printers throughout the succeeding decade. Although Tschichold became one of the most influential typographers of the postwar period, especially after his work with Penguin in 1947–49, Bill and his colleagues at the Zurich and Basel Kunstgewerbeschules laid the foundations of what became known as "Swiss Style" or "The International Typographic Style," one of the most influential approaches to display and advertising design across Western Europe and North America.[13]

In the hands of Bill, Armin Hofmann, Ernst Keller, and Josef Müller-Brockmann, emphasis was placed on the strict use of a grid as the controlling framework for layout, the division of the printed field according to classical ratios, high-quality objective photography, and crisp sanserif letterforms with little or no ornament. On face value, the style is not very different from the New Typography as Tschichold had defined it in the 1920s. It also benefited from several related developments: the expansion of design education in the 1950s, which enshrined many of these principles into a formal graphic design curriculum, and the rise of an international market in which the uniformity of Swiss Style advertising crossed borders and cultures with ease. A series of sanserif typefaces also provided the raw material for the new style, above all Univers, created in 1954 by Adrian Frutiger, and Neue Haas Grotesk (later renamed Helvetica), created by Eduard Hoffmann and Max Miedinger in 1957. Helvetica would become the most ubiquitous typeface for advertising and display throughout the Western world. Two of the leading European graphic design journals, *Graphis* and *Neue Grafik*, were based in Zurich, which also helped the widespread acceptance of Swiss Style graphics in advertising.[14] This movement would, in effect, revive the principles of the New Typography for a new age, but without the grand millenarian theories to reform society or the aspiration to employ new technologies to develop new ways to receive and comprehend text.

In Poland, the New Typography developed in a manner roughly parallel to its development in Germany. After the First World War, with the reestablishment of the Polish state, there was a resurgence of artistic activity, with avant-garde groups springing up in many of the major cities. The real start of Constructivism in Poland, however, was the Blok group, which held exhibitions and launched a journal of the same name from Warsaw in March 1924. *Blok* was one of the most ambitious art and design journals in this period, notable as much for its striking appearance as its contents [Fig. 84]. The two central figures were Henryk Berlewi and Władysław Strzemiński, both of whom recognized the potential of Constructivist art to transform typography and visual communication. They both practiced as independent graphic designers as well as engaging in the theoretical debates of the day. Of the two, Strzemiński was the more sophisticated intellectually. He had known many figures in the Soviet avant-garde, notably Kazimir Malevich in Vitebsk, which influenced his approach to art and design during the 1920s as he devel-

84

oped his own ideas. By 1930, he had begun a correspondence on "functional typography" with Jan Tschichold, which resulted in their exchanging examples of their work over the next few years. Strzemiński's designs for *Praesens* (Present time, 1926–30) were among the finest expressions of the New Typography in Poland, but by this time the journal was winding down, and Strzemiński was keen to link up with the international movement [Fig. 85]. He designed books and wrote on typography, reviewed work by Tschichold and others in Polish journals, and even organized an international *Typo-Show* in Łódź. This last project went ahead in 1932, but the early effects of the oncoming economic depression were being felt in Poland as elsewhere. "The general crisis in the arts seems to aim especially at discrediting everything new and creative," Strzemiński wrote, lamenting the barriers to aesthetic ambition as well as reduced practical opportunities.[15]

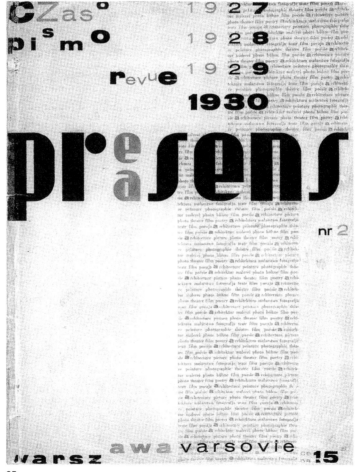

85

Despite these constraints, Strzemiński continued to work in an innovative manner throughout the 1930s, and to write repeatedly on aspects of the New Typography. His article "Druk funkcjonalny" (Functional printing) of 1934, reprinted here in translation (Primary Text, no. 16) is a good example of the ways in which he was able to trace a long trajectory through the history of printing that conferred a certain logic, if not inevitability, to the modern style. Strzemiński stayed in touch with Tschichold throughout the latter's Swiss exile, becoming one of his most active correspondents. Tschichold recognized that they had very different approaches to typography, but that did not diminish their mutual respect. Writing from Basel in May 1934, Tschichold told Strzemiński:

> You are pursuing a very different direction than I am, in that you distribute the typographic forms on the surface according to primarily painterly principles. Furthermore, you limit yourself to an expansive spatial composition. In any case, your work rarely shows group elements without at least one of them standing right up to the edge. Such design could perhaps be described as expansive, whereas another kind, in which the lines and groups move on relatively neutral ground, could be described as compressive. . . . In my eyes, both kinds are equally valid. In my work, I tend to take the technical requirements as a starting point, and deduce the design principles from there.[16]

After 1933, and until it was annexed by Nazi Germany in 1938–39, Czechoslovakia was the most sympathetic environment for modern architects and designers. The government was still committed to fostering innovation in all spheres of industry and culture, a policy that had been apparent when the republic was created under the leadership

of Tomáš Masaryk and Edvard Beneš in 1918. One of the first initiatives had been the establishment of the Government Printing Office
(Státné tiskorna) under the direction of the typographer Karel Dyrynk.
The office was responsible for introducing both fine typefaces and a
progressive character to official documents. But this broader policy
toward the modernization of state institutions and adoption of an
outward-looking, free-trade ethos was also conducted through encouragement of independent entrepreneurs such as Bata, the shoe manufacturer; textile producers such as Alfred Löw-Beer and the Stiassni
family; and glassworks such as Vereinigte Lausitzer and Kavalier.[17] Along
with these industrial concerns, a range of progressive art and design groups had arisen in the 1920s and 1930s, within which the New
Typography found several accomplished adherents. Tschichold had
been in touch with Karel Teige as early as 1925, when he referred to
the Czech in "elementare typographie," and he also used Teige's cover
for *Zivot* (Life) as an example in *Die neue Typographie*. Teige, however, was always an ambitious and wide-ranging innovator who did not
restrict himself to a single medium or movement.

Ladislav Sutnar, Zdeněk Rossmann, and František Kalivoda were
of a different sort: equally committed to modern design in all its
manifestations but particularly keen to develop their skills in the field
of graphics. The Czechoslovakian avant-garde had also placed a high
premium on experimental photography, which found its way into both
avant-garde work and mainstream publications. Sutnar's covers for
the George Bernard Shaw series, published in Prague by Břetislav Klika,
and Rossmann's equally innovative catalogue for the 1929 *Žena doma*
(Woman at Home) exhibition indicate the extent to which the most innovative photomontage found an outlet in the mass market [Fig. 86].
Kalivoda produced two short-lived experimental journals in the mid-
1930s, inspired by the dynamic relationship he detected between
graphics, photography, and film. *Ekran* (Screen, 1934) is the simpler of
the two, but it demonstrates a firm grasp of the New Typography in

86

its handling of text and photographic illustration. *Telehor* (Television, 1936), produced in only one double issue, employed the most recent techniques of industrial printing and binding, in this case "Spirex," a method of binding with spiral wire that had been developed in Germany in the 1920s, and a clear plastic cover, with text in four languages set in sanserif lowercase type throughout. The journal has since been recognized as a landmark of modern graphic design [Fig. 87].

telehor   mezinárodní časopis pro visuální kulturu
internationale zeitschrift für visuelle kultur
the international review new vision
revue internationale pour la culture visuelle

1-2

I. moholy-nagy

telehor   I.   1 -2   1 -136   28. II, 1936   frs. s. 12'—

87

The double issue of *Telehor*, fittingly devoted to Moholy-Nagy
given his fascination with new technologies and the potential of the
moving image, is one of the finest surveys of his work, incorporating
four original essays and a film script by the artist, a critical commen-
tary by Sigfried Giedion, and a range of illustrations, many of them
unique. It should be remembered that Kalivoda was only twenty-three
years old when he brought these disparate elements together and
still a student in the technical university in Brno. Moholy-Nagy was
apparently delighted with the result and "decorated an entire wall"

87 František
Kalivoda. *Telehor*
(Television), nos. 1–2,
1935. Lithograph.
Private collection.

of his London apartment with pages from the journal.[18] He also present-ed Kalivoda with one of his most important paintings, *Construction A1 6*, in oil on perforated aluminum. Despite the strong affirmation of classic modernist ideals that *Telehor* represented, Moholy-Nagy (like Tschichold) was disheartened by the current situation. In his letter to Kalivoda, he writes: "We have published many programmes, issued many manifestos to the world. Youth has every right to know why our claims have failed, why our promises have remained unfulfilled. At the same time youth has the duty of continuing the quest for new forms to advance the course of art."[19]

Lajos Kassák, an early supporter of the movement in Hungary and Austria, continued to promote modernist graphics in the avant-garde journal *MA*. During the 1930s, however, the New Typography moved into the mainstream of Hungarian commercial graphics and advertising. Kassák and several of the *MA* circle took on more commercial book de-sign, although much of that work was restricted to publications on modern art and literature. A better indication of the wider acceptance of the New Typography might be found in the work of Lajos Kozma (1884–1948), an architect-designer whose designs for the publisher Imre Kner (1890–1944) were among the most highly admired Hungarian fine press books of the period. Kner, a fastidious publisher with high stan-dards in design and production, was a close friend and correspondent of Tschichold's, but he advocated a more conservative, historicist style in his own books. Accordingly, Kozma's work for Kner was in a neo-Baroque manner, involving the use of eighteenth-century typefaces, historic orna-ments, and engraved illustrations. By 1930, however, Kozma was receiv-ing more commissions for architectural projects, particularly for pro-gressive industrialists like the Markus family. Not only did he design the Markus family house in a severe modernist style, he employed the New Typography in the firm's advertising and publicity [Fig 88]. Indeed, this shift in taste might equally be traced in the contents and cover designs of the leading Hungarian architecture and design journals. *Tér és Forma*

88

(Space and Form), launched in 1928 with covers designed by the Bauhausler Farkas Molnár (1897–1945), encapsulates the full acceptance of the New Typography in its asymmetry, its use of sanserif letterforms, abstract color blocks, and photographic illustration [Fig 89].

The New Typography continued to thrive in the Netherlands, where it was also aligned with radical, left-wing views. Schuitema received commissions from commercial clients throughout the 1930s, including the electronics firm Philips, for which he produced photomontage advertisements and brochures. Individual developments in his work were apparent in his use of a more colorful palette than previously, but his use of photomontage continued as a central feature. His finest designs

88 Lajos Kozma. *Korszerü Vas-és Fém Portálok* (State of the Art Metal and Iron...) *Markus Lajos RT* brochure, ca. 1930. Lithograph. Private collection. Cat. 30.

89 Farkas Molnár. *Tér és Forma* (Space and Form) Hungarian architecture and design journal, vol. 4, no. 7, July 1931. Lithograph. Private Collection.

89

were for *Links Richten* (Points left), the magazine of a worker-writers collective, posters for the transport workers union, and advertising design for the furniture cooperative d3 Meubelen (d3 furniture) for whom he designed tubular steel chairs as well as catalogues[20] [Fig. 90]. Zwart also carried on his commercial practice, but with more urgency after he was sacked in 1933 from his teaching position at the Rotterdam Academy and had given up his most supportive client, NKF. Fortunately, he had several new clients, including the Bruynzeel kitchen furnishing company. He was initially commissioned to produce calendars and brochures, but in 1937 branched out into designing modular kitchens that went into production as Dutch counterparts to the Frankfurt Kitchen. Along-

ph. dekker fabrikant
ir. j. w. effinger adviseurs
paul. schuitema

fabriek . burgemeester roosstraat 50
rotterdam . telefoon 40365

stalen meubelen

90

side this, Zwart had been commissioned by the post office to design
their information graphics and publicity. In 1938 he produced *Het boek
van PTT* (The PTT book), a light-hearted story for children about how
to make best use of the post office services, which became the model for
a long tradition of innovative graphics in governmental organizations
in the Netherlands.[21] In 1942, Zwart was arrested and interned by the
German occupying forces. He survived the war and was released at the
end of hostilities in 1945. H. N. Werkman, another Dutch experimental
typographer, was less fortunate. Just a few days before the liberation
in March 1945, he was executed by the Gestapo near Groningen for
producing resistance material on his press.[22]

THE ANGLOPHONE RESPONSE

In the UK, the situation was very different. Resistant to change, suspicious of developments on the Continent, and bolstered by a profound belief in the value of their own design traditions, the British were nevertheless undergoing their own printing renaissance. During the 1920s, the Monotype Corporation, under the guidance of Stanley Morison, had made great strides in improving the standards of British book type and typography. But this was largely a reform of book design based on recutting classic typefaces, notably Bembo, Garamond, and Poliphilus, while introducing several new faces, especially those by Eric Gill (Gill Sans, Joanna, and Perpetua).[23] A landmark in this reform movement was the introduction of Times New Roman, which appeared in *The Times* on October 3, 1932. Gill was, in many respects, the living embodiment of certain tendencies in British design. A committed believer in the continuing relevance of the Arts and Crafts movement, he emphasized the role of handcraftsmanship in all spheres of design, and the working patterns of the medieval guild system. These views were declared unequivocally by his adoption of a smock, sandals, and a paper hat, as worn by medieval stonemasons, even when meeting clients in government agencies or the captains of industry. In 1931, Gill published his overview of book and type design, "An Essay on Typography," identifying "two worlds": the typography of industrialism, as opposed to the "humane typography" of the private press movement, which he felt were locked in a life-or-death struggle.[24] "The conflict between industrialism & the ancient methods of handicraftsmen which resulted in the muddle of the 19th century is now coming to its term. But tho' industrialism has now won an almost complete victory, the handicrafts are not killed, & they cannot be quite killed because they meet an inherent, indestructible, permanent need in human nature." Gill's use of archaic language, ampersands, and paragraph marks instead of indented lines, are a clear indication of his revivalist attitude to typographic design. This designer of the most successful sanserif face in Britain (Gill Sans) ends his book with a somewhat depressing statement: "The business of printed lettering has now, under the spur of commercial competition, got altogether out of hand and gone mad. There are now about as many different varieties of letters as there are different kinds of fools. . . . Lettering has had its day. Spelling, and philology, and all such pedantries have no place in our world. The only way to reform modern lettering is to abolish it."[25]

Although several articles on contemporary German graphic design were published in Britain, some by Tschichold himself in *Commercial Art*, the yearbook of *The Studio* magazine, there was little serious interest in London or in other centers of British publishing.[26] In fact, many luminaries of the reform movement in Britain were suspicious, not to say downright hostile, of what they regarded as "Hunnishness" in design as much as in national character.[27] Even the Design and Industries Association, ostensibly a progressive organization partly inspired by the example of the Deutscher Werkbund, took a dim view of the insistent and direct approach of contemporary German advertising.[28] Paradoxically, this more traditional reform movement may have been instrumental in pushing Jan Tschichold toward his own conversion. After visiting London at the invitation of the Double Crown Club in 1937, where he was warmly received by Morison and Oliver Simon, Tschichold began expressing doubts over the larger claims of the New Typography.[29] Even the influx of European émigrés—including Walter Gropius, László Moholy-Nagy, and Piet Mondrian, in the years leading up to the war in 1939—did little to shift the British from their adherence to classic typefaces, traditional book design, and a design culture that was still defined by the activities of handcraftsmanship.

The United States is another story, but one with some similarities to the UK. The private press movement, begun in Britain, had been as successful in the United States as it had been in Germany both before and after the First World War. The finest of the writers on the history of type, Daniel Berkeley Updike, author of *Printing Types: Their History, Forms and Use*, was himself a typographer and book designer following in the tradition of William Morris's Kelmscott Press, as were Frederic

Goudy and Bruce Rogers.[30] There was even a concern for the higher aesthetic claims of typography. In 1926, speaking at the annual conference of the American Association of Museums held at the Metropolitan Museum in New York, John Dana, director of the Newark Museum, asked, "Will the work of the printer never find in art museums the high place it should have there? Printing produces in mere words more things that interest the eye and the brain than do all other crafts combined. In its more studied forms it is as beautiful as are the outgivings of art, and add to beauty an irresistible appeal to the mind. Yet the printer's products occupy no high place among 'museum pieces.' Is this because printing is an industry? Or of today? Or of this country?"[31]

Alongside the continuing appeal of the private press movement in the United States came the massive expansion of the advertising industry, which had dazzled the Europeans by its range, its confidence, and the quasi-scientific way that it pursued its goals. In the postwar period American advertising established many of its key institutions and expanded into new media, such as radio, and the burgeoning market for illustrated magazines that were increasingly accessible to the mass of the population.[32] The leading US historian and commentator of the period, Douglas C. McMurtrie, was certainly aware of developments in Europe. As director of advertising and typography at the Ludlow Typograph Company, which manufactured a Linotype machine setting system, McMurtrie spoke of "the contribution of the present generation in adapting typography in the trend and tune of the age, the marvels worked by the creators of the New Typography, the immense possibilities of this new art and its character of permanency."[33] McMurtrie had been a member of the Continental Type Founders Association, which imported new sanserif faces from European foundries such as Erbar, Rudolf Koch's Kabel, and Georg Trump's City. Yet his own typefaces, such as Ultra Modern, released by Ludlow in 1929, seem closer in spirit to Art Deco or Moderne rather than the severe modernism of the Germans[34] [Fig. 91]. This is understandable, given the warm reception of contemporary

French design in the United States following the 1925 Paris Exhibition.[35] Nevertheless, it marks a contrast between the French and the German models in the US perception of contemporary European design. This is revealed quite sharply in Frederic Ehrlich's large-format book, *The New Typography and Modern Layouts*, of 1934. In his preface, Ehrlich writes:

> In presenting this volume . . . the Author has completed a task which he hopes will accomplish two things: one, clarify the confusion, doubt, and uncertainty that exists regarding the precepts and history of the New Typography in European countries and its inception in America. The other is to acquaint the reader with the basic balances that have resulted from the first efforts and experimentations of a group of foreign typographers; the subsequent development of their humble beginnings into balances based on structure developed along an Americanized version of the likes and appreciation of the American advertiser.[36]

In many respects, Ehrlich's book could be seen as an attempt to emulate Tschichold's 1928 *Die neue Typographie*, because it sets out to provide a theoretical and historical context for recent developments in graphic design. A chapter on "The Modern Movement in the Arts" includes sections on "The Revolutionary Trend in Painting," "Industrial Arts Break Away from Traditional Practices," and "Influences of These Revolts in the Arts on Typography." Any hope that Ehrlich's publication would communicate the central aims of the New Typography, however, is cast into doubt when one considers the design of the title pages and the 1,200 designs that the author selected to illustrate his book [Fig. 92]. In line with the dominant contemporary taste in the United States, Ehrlich's book offers a compendium of labels, book covers, and advertisements in a "moderne" style. Things go further awry in the text, which is

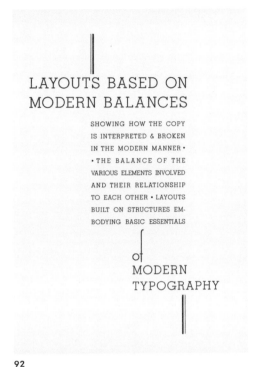

91

92

a lengthy dismissal of many principles that Tschichold and his contemporaries stood for. On oblique text in advertisements, Ehrlich writes: "When the symptoms of dynamic indigestion became quite evident, this phase of unreasoned and riotous composition was laid to rest in the graveyard of advertising monstrosities. It also marked and signaled the end of the various phases, inept failures, the revolts and rebellions through which modernism has passed or was part of."[37] Photography is barely mentioned, and the movement is patronizingly summed up in a musical metaphor: "Apparently the pioneers had the right notes, the proper instruments, but were unable to find the correct harmonies. The tendency was toward discords. Very few examples qualified as a symphony in type.... Their enthusiasm to create something new and startling made them overstep the bounds of common sense and good taste against their better judgment."[38]

The schism between "moderne" and modernism in the United States was brought into sharper relief by Alfred H. Barr and the circle around the Museum of Modern Art in New York. Barr and his associates Philip Johnson and Edgar Kaufmann Jr. would accept no examples of "moderne" into the museum and established rigorous criteria for the modern movement in design based on their travels in Central Europe in the late 1920s and early 1930s.[39] It was in this spirit that MoMA mounted its own exhibition of modern typography and graphic design on May 23, 1935, selected by Otto Fuhrman, Gustav Stresow, and MoMA curator Ernestine Fantl, under the title "European Commercial Printing of Today." Although the material for the exhibition had been assembled from various European countries (Czechoslovakia, England, France, Germany, Italy, Russia, Spain, Sweden, and Switzerland), German works dominated, perhaps because the exhibition was sponsored in part by the Bauer Type Foundry of Frankfurt am Main, who had opened their New York office in 1927. No object list or installation photographs appear to have survived, but there is a clear indication of the contents of the show from a contemporary review. The day after the opening, the *New York Times* critic quoted the labels indicating that the modern movement in printing and layout had its beginnings "in several countries simultaneously," although for the most part the movement had "found a well-established educational system as well as creative ingenuity" in Germany. As a result, "after years of experimentation the Germans have developed a refined, almost chaste style." The label went on: "The average French printer could never be enlisted in the movement for modern typography; it has remained in France the instrument of a very small group of highly talented artists"; and "Czechoslovakia has proved alert to new currents and the same appears true of Russia and Spain."[40]

The United States would become the most receptive culture for the New Typography, but, apart from a few notable individuals, such as Mehemed Fehmy Agha and Alexey Brodovitch, who had a considerable influence on US magazine design, this country would have to wait until European émigrés, such as Herbert Bayer, Herbert Matter, and Ladislav Sutnar entered into the mainstream of American graphic design and advertising.

Bayer was the co-organizer with Walter Gropius of the exhibition *Bauhaus 1919–1928* at MoMA in 1938, for which he also designed the graphics. From this, Bayer launched a successful career as a graphic designer in the US, as well as practicing as an architect and design consultant in Aspen until his death in 1985. Matter designed exhibits and photographed architecture and design from the MoMA collection, after which he became a much-sought-after photographer for magazines such as *Vogue* and *Harper's Bazaar*. He was also a design consultant for the furnishing firm of Knoll Associates and professor of photography at Yale University. Ladislav Sutnar would be stranded in New York while supervising the construction of the Czechoslovakian pavilion at the World's Fair of 1939; his country was annexed by the Nazis and their allies in March of that year. Despite being temporarily stateless, Sutnar became art director of Sweet's Catalog Service, and in 1944, with his colleague Knud Lonberg-Holm, published *New Patterns in Product Information*, which clarified the subdiscipline of information graphics through the use of grids, tables, and symbols.[41] The meeting point for many of these disparate tendencies and individuals was The Composing Room. Founded in New York in 1927 as a forum for designers and art editors to promote their work, it became a venue for some of the most innovative graphic design, hosting classes and lectures, mounting exhibitions, and publishing its own bimonthly journal.[42] By the late 1930s, several European émigrés, including Bayer, Matter, and Sutnar, had become members of The Composing Room, seeing here a space for conversation, new ideas, and professional opportunity. It is a pattern that has become enshrined in the broader history of twentieth-century American culture. As a result of the merger of European modernism and American values, the design styles that came to be known universally as Midcentury Modern and Swiss Style proved to be the true descendants of the New Typography.

1   The "Gesetz zur Behebung der Not von Volk und Reich" was signed by President Hindenburg on March 23, 1933.

2   On the Reichsministerium, see Richard J. Evans, *The Third Reich in Power* (London: Penguin, 2005), 138–40. See also David Welch, ed., *Nazi Propaganda: The Power and the Limitations* (London: Croom Helm, 1983), 4–6.

3   These were merely the first of a series of measures to control print media in Germany and to bring the printing industry into line with Nazi Party policy. Measures also included the removal of Jewish printers, photographers, and journalists from their posts; the acquisition of media outlets by groups and individuals nominated by the party; and the "Gesetz über Wirtschaftswerbung" (Commercial advertising law) enacted October 27, 1933, which required all advertisers (and advertisements) to be registered and approved by an "advertising council" (Werberat) based in Berlin. See Michael Imort, "'Planting a Forest Tall and Straight like the German *Volk*': Visualizing the *Volksgemeinschaft* through Advertising in German Forestry Journals, 1933–1945," and Pamela E. Swett, S. Jonathan Wiesen, and Jonathan R. Zatlin, eds., *Selling Modernity: Advertising in Twentieth-Century Germany* (Durham, NC: Duke University Press, 2007), 102–26.

4   Burke, *Paul Renner*, 126–33.

5   Dexel was able to find work teaching at the Staatlichen Hochschule für Kunsterziehung in Berlin-Schöneberg and later at the Hochschule für Bildende Künste, Braunschweig, where in 1945 he was, in turn, dismissed by the occupying powers and had to undergo denazification.

6   Breuer, *Max Burchartz*, 169–70.

7   Hans Lehnacker, ed., *Vita Activa: Georg Trump, Bilder, Schriften und Schriftbilder* (Munich: Typographische Gesellschaft, 1967), 183–84.

8   The popular view that the Nazi Party advocated the use only of Fraktur, or Gothic, scripts and typefaces is oversimplistic. It did support the use of Fraktur in the early years as a symbol of Nordic culture but recognized the limitations once subject peoples were required to read Nazi literature. In January 1941, Hitler decreed that "Gothic type" was a Jewish form and that Antiqua (Roman) would henceforth be the accepted script.

9   Hermann Hoffmann, in *Schweizer graphische Mitteilungen* (January 1926), had described Tschichold's work as "communist style." Cited in Friedl, "Lernen von Jan Tschichold," 9.

10   Tschichold collected examples of Swiss advertisements, although it is not clear whether this was after his own move to Switzerland.

11   *Ausstellung neue Typographie* at the Gewerbemuseum Basel included work by German and Swiss designers, much of it drawn from the schools in Basel, Zurich, and Munich, as well as the Bauhaus.

12   In 1953, Bill was one of the founders of the Hochschule für Gestaltung at Ulm, seeking to restore pre-Nazi design and cultural values through a revival of Bauhaus teaching methods for the postwar industrial and commercial environment. He resigned in 1957 over the school's deviation from the classic curriculum.

13   On "Swiss Style" and the continuities from the New Typography of the 1920s, see Richard Hollis, *Swiss Graphic Design: The Origins and Growth of an International Style, 1920–1965* (New Haven, CT: Yale University Press, 2006).

14   *Graphis*, founded in Zurich in 1944, became one of the most successful international graphic design journals of the 1950s and 1960s, a position helped by the publication of their annuals, which were devoted to photography, posters, etc. *Neue Grafik*, an "International Review of graphic design and related subjects," was founded by Josef Müller-Brockmann and ran from 1958 to 1965.

15   Strzemiński to Tschichold (?), dated 1932; quoted in Paulina Kurc-Maj, ed., *Zmiana pola widzenia: Druk nowoczesny i awangarda* [The changing field of view: Modern printing and the avant-garde] (Łódź: Muzeum Sztuki, 2014), 85.

16   Ibid., 89.

17   For an example of the high modernist ambitions of one Czech industrial concern and its attempts to create integrated communities around functionalist aesthetics and working practices, see Katrin Klingan, ed., *A Utopia of Modernity: Zlin* (Berlin: Jovis, 2010).

18   Klemens Gruber and Oliver Botar, eds., *Telehor: L Moholy-Nagy—Kommentarband* (Zurich: Lars Muller, 2013), 29.

19   László Moholy-Nagy, *Telehor* 1–2 (28 February 1936): 30–31.

20   Dick Maan, *Paul Schuitema: Visual Organizer* (Rotterdam: 010 Publishers, 2006), 105–12.

21   Piet Zwart, *Het Boek van PTT* (Leiden: Posterijen Telegrafie en Telefonie, 1938).

22   Tschichold was in contact with Werkman in August 1926, when he requested copies of Werkman's occasional journal, *The Next Call*. Burke, *Active Literature*, 86. Werkman belonged to a different tradition and was not included in any of Tschichold's publications.

23   S. H. Steinberg, *Five Hundred Years of Printing*, rev. ed. (London: British Library, 1996), 170–72.

24 "An Essay on Typography" appeared first in Eric Gill, *Printing and Piety: An Essay on Life and Works in the England of 1931, and Particularly Typography* (London: Sheed and Ward, 1931). A second, expanded edition appeared in 1936, retitled *An Essay on Typography*. "Two worlds" is discussed in "The Theme," prologue to the 1936 edition, unpaginated.

25 Gill, *An Essay on Typography* (1936), 132–33.

26 In 1930 and 1931, Tschichold wrote several articles for *Commercial Art*, published by *The Studio*, as well as individual pieces for more specialist journals, such as *Axis, Circle*, and *Penrose Annual*.

27 Joseph Thorp, ed., *Design in Modern Printing: The Year Book of the Design and Industries Association 1927–28* (London: Benn, 1928), 73. This book, which appeared the same year as Tschichold's *Die neue Typographie*, gives an indication of British reform attitudes toward contemporary graphics and book design. Emery Walker's work at the Doves Press is held up as a paradigm, although the press had all but ceased working by 1909 (ibid., 41).

28 Thorp ridicules German advertising as hammer blows "to batter through the defences of the immediately-to-be-sold-to public" (ibid., 137–39).

29 Tschichold had already suggested that "every compositor should still be able to set up an ordinary symmetrical page," thus accommodating the traditional approach. Tschichold, "Vom richtigen Satz auf Mittelachse," 127.

30 Daniel Berkeley Updike, *Printing Types: Their History, Forms, and Use*, 2 vols. (Cambridge, MA: Harvard University Press, 1922).

31 "Wants Progress in Art Museums; Many Institutions a Century behind the Times, Says John C. Dana of Newark. NEW CONDITIONS STRESSED Neglect of the Printing Art Deplored—A Tribute to the Beauty of Typography," *New York Times*, May 19, 1926, 24. I am grateful to Juliet Kinchin for drawing my attention to these contemporaneous quotations from US newspapers.

32 For example, the Art Director's Club of New York, founded in 1920, held juried exhibitions each year and published the *Annual of Advertising Art in the United States*.

33 "New Typography Address Subject. Modern Trend in Advertising Composition Stressed by D. C. McMurtrie," *The Gazette* (Montreal), April 17, 1930, 5.

34 On the stylistic character of McMurtrie's type designs and the displays at the 1933 Chicago Century of Progress Exposition, see Lloyd C. Engelbrecht, "Modernism and Design," in *The Old Guard and the Avant-Garde: Modernism in Chicago, 1910–1940*, ed. Sue Ann Prince (Chicago: University of Chicago Press, 1990), 129–32.

35 On the reception of French Art Deco in the United States, see Marilyn Friedman, "Defining Modernism at the American Designers' Gallery, New York," *Studies in the Decorative Arts* 14, no. 2 (Spring–Summer 2007): 79–116; Carma Gorman, "'An Educated Demand': The Implications of 'Art in Every Day Life' for American Industrial Design, 1925–1950," *Design Issues* 16, no. 3 (Autumn 2000): 45–66; Kristina Wilson, *Livable Modernism: Interior Decorating and Design during the Great Depression* (New Haven, CT: Yale University Press, 2004), and "Rethinking American Modernist Design, 1920–1940," *Studies in the Decorative Arts* 14, no. 2 (Spring–Summer 2007): 2–5.

36 Frederic Ehrlich, *The New Typography and Modern Layouts* (New York: Stokes, 1934), 7.

37 Ibid., 52–53.

38 Ibid., 30.

39 See comments by David Hanks, Barry Bergdoll, and Juliet Kinchin in David A. Hanks, ed., *Partners in Design: Alfred H. Barr Jr. and Philip Johnson* (New York: Monacelli, 2015), 28–55, 136–47, and 148–73.

40 "Typography Show Has Modern Mood. Specimens of Printing from European Countries Put on Exhibition Here," *New York Times*, May 24, 1935, 19.

41 K. Lonberg-Holm and Ladislav Sutnar, *Catalog Design: New Patterns in Product Information* (New York: Sweet's Catalog Service, a division of F. W. Dodge Corp., 1944).

42 From 1934 The Composing Room published its own bimonthly journal, *PM: An Intimate Journal for Production Managers, Art Directors, and Their Associates*. In 1939 the journal title was changed to *A-D* (Art Director). Steven Heller, "Dr Leslie's Type Clinic," *Eye* 4, no. 15 (Winter 1994): 68–80.

Primary Texts on
the New Typography

Where relevant, formatting of text has been
retained from original publications.

1
Filippo Tommaso Marinetti

Rivoluzione tipografica (Typographical revolution)

From *Distruzione della sintassi—Immaginazione senza fili—Parole in libertà* (Destruction of syntax—wireless imagination—words in freedom), May 11, 1913. Republished in *Les mots en liberté futuriste* (Milan: Edizioni futuriste di "Poesia," 1919). Translation by Lawrence Rainey from *Futurism: An Anthology*, 149–50.

I have initiated a typographical revolution directed against the bestial, nauseating sort of book that contains passéist poetry or verse à la D'Annunzio—handmade paper that imitates models of the seventeenth century, festooned with helmets, Minervas, Apollos, decorative capitals in red ink with loops and squiggles, vegetables, mythological ribbons from missals, epigraphs, and Roman numerals. The book must be the Futurist expression of Futurist thought. Not only that. My revolution is directed against the so-called typographical harmony of the page, which is contrary to the flux and reflux, the leaps and bursts of style that run through the page itself. For that reason we will use, in the very same page, *three or four different colors of ink*, and as many as twenty different typographical fonts if necessary. For example: *italics* for a series of swift or similar sensations, *boldface* for violent onomatopoeias, etc. The typographical revolution and the multicolored variety in the letters will mean that I can double the expressive force of words.

I oppose the decorative and precious aesthetic of Mallarmé and his search for the exotic word, the unique and irreplaceable, elegant, suggestive, exquisite adjective. I have no wish to suggest an idea of sensation by means of passéist graces and affectations: I want to seize them brutally and fling them in the reader's face.

I also oppose Mallarmé's static ideal. The typographic revolution that I've proposed will enable me to imprint words (words already free, dynamic, torpedoing forward) every velocity of the stars, clouds, airplanes, trains, waves, explosives, drops of seafoam, molecules, and atoms.

And so I shall realize the fourth principle contained in my "First Manifesto of Futurism" (February 20, 1909): "We affirm that the beauty of the world has been enriched by a new form of beauty: the beauty of speed."

2
El Lissitzky

Topographie der Typographie (Topography of typography)

From *Merz* no. 4 (July 1923): 47.

1. The words on the printed surface are taken in by seeing, not by hearing.
2. One communicates meanings through the convention of words; meaning attains form through letters.
3. Economy of expression—optics rather than phonetics.
4. The design of the book-space, set according to the constraints of printing mechanics, must correspond to the tensile and compressive stresses of the content.

5. The design of the book-space using process blocks is what establishes the new optics. The supernatural reality of the perfected eye.
6. The continuous sequence of pages: the bioscopic book.
7. The new book demands the new writer. Inkwell and goose-quill are dead.
8. The printed surface transcends space and time. The printed surface, the infinity of books, must be transcended. THE ELECTRO-LIBRARY.

3
László Moholy-Nagy

Die neue Typographie (The New Typography)

From *Staatliches Bauhaus in Weimar 1919–1923* (Weimar and Munich: Bauhausverlag, 1923), 141.

Typography is an instrument of communication, so it must be as clear and effective as possible. The emphasis must be on absolute clarity, because that is what distinguishes the character of our writing from that of ancient pictograms. Our mental relationship with regard to meaning in the outside world is both individual and exact (although this individual-exact attitude is in a state of transition toward one that is more collective-exact), in contrast to the old individual and amorphous mode of communication, and subsequently the collectively amorphous mode. So first and foremost, we require absolute clarity in all typographic work. The message must never suffer from a priori aesthetics. Letters or type must never be forced into a predetermined framework, such as a square.

The printed image corresponds to the content through the specific psychological and optical laws that determine its meaning. The essence and purpose of printing require the unrestricted use of all linear directions (i.e., not only horizontal articulation), all typefaces, font sizes, geometric shapes, colors, etc. Given the elasticity, variability, and vitality within the contents of a sentence, we must create a new typographic language that is subject, first of all, to the inner laws of the expression and also to its effect on the viewer.

The most important asset for contemporary typography is the use of zincographic techniques, which enables the creation of photographic reproductions in all formats by mechanical means. What the Egyptians began with their inexact hieroglyphs, which could be interpreted according to tradition and personal ability, leads directly to the precise expression resulting from the inclusion of photography into today's printing process. Books with photographic reproductions already exist (mostly scientific), but the photographs are only a secondary explanation of the text. Recent developments supersede this phase, and now photographs, small and large, take their place in the text where previously we employed individually interpretable concepts and set expressions. The objectivity of photography liberates the receptive reader from the crutches of the author's personal descriptions and forces him, more than ever, to form his own opinion.

One could even say that such a use of photography must lead shortly to the replacement of a substantial part of literature with film. Indications of this development are already apparent; for example, many fewer letters are written nowadays because of the use of the telephone. It is not a valid objection to claim that film needs a burdensome apparatus; this is only apparently so. Film will soon be as common a technique as book printing is now.

An equally substantial transformation can result from the use of photography in poster design. The poster must take into consideration all the psychological effects of its immediate impact. The greatest potential for this will be achieved by the correct application of the camera and various photographic techniques: retouching, masking, superimposing, distorting, enlarging, etc.

The two new opportunities for poster design are (1) photography, today's means of providing the greatest and most striking narrative device, and (2) the contrasting and vivid use of typography, with its countless variations of surprising letter order, uniform and mixed typefaces, different typesetting materials, colors, and so on, depending on the particulars or required effect of the message.

4
El Lissitzky

Typographische Tatsachen (Typographical facts)

From *Gutenberg Festschrift* (Mainz, 1925). Translation from Sophie Lissitzky-Küppers, *El Lissitzky: Life, Letters, Texts* (Greenwich, CT: New York Graphic Society, 1968), 359–60.

ABCDEFGHIJKLMNOPQRSTUVWXYZ Inordertocommunicateyourthoughtsin writingyouhaveonlytoformcertaincombinationsfromthesesymbolsandstringthem togetherinanunbrokenchain

but—NO.

YOU see here that the pattern of thought cannot be represented mechanically by making combinations of the twenty-six letters of the alphabet. Language is more than just an acoustic wave motion, and the mere means of thought transference. In the same way, typography is more than just an optical wave motion for the same purpose. From the passive, non-articulated lettering pattern one goes over to the active, articulated pattern. The gesture of the living language is taken into account.
E.g.: the Hammurabi tablets and modern election literature.

YOU have divided up the day into twenty-four hours. There is not another hour for extravagant effusion of feelings. The pattern of speech becomes increasingly concise, the gesture sharply imprinted. It is just the same with typography. *E.g.: Prospectuses, advertising brochures, and modern novels.*

YOU are accompanied from your first day onwards by printed paper, and your eye is superbly trained to find its way about in this specific field quickly, precisely, and without losing its way. You cast your glances into these forests of paper with the same confidence as the Australian throws his boomerang. *E.g.: the page of a large daily paper.*

YOU ask for clear patterns for your eyes. Those can only be pieced together from plain elements. The elements of letters are:

the horizontal —
the perpendicular |
the diagonal /
the curve C

These are the basic line directions on the plain surface. Combinations occur in the horizontal and perpendicular directions. These two lines produce the right (unambiguous) angle. It can be placed in alignment with the edges of the surface, then it has a static effect (rest). It can be placed diagonally, then it has a dynamic effect (agitation). These are the axioms of typography.
E.g. this page

YOU are already overcoming the prejudice which regards only letter-press-printing (from type) as pure typography. Letterpress belongs to the past. The future belongs to photogravure printing and to all photomechanical processes. In this way the former fresco-painting is cut off from the new typography.
E.g.: advertisement pillars and poster-walls.

YOU have observed that in the organic pattern all the facets exhibit the same structural unity. Modern typography is improving structural unity.
E.g.: The paper (art paper), the type (absence of flourishes), the ink (the new spectrum-clear products).

YOU can see how it is that where new areas are opened up to thought- and speech-patterns, there you find new typographical designs originating organically. These are: modern advertising and modern poetry.
E.g.: some pages of American and European magazines and technical periodicals. The international publications of the dada movement.

YOU should demand of the writer that he really presents what he writes; his ideas reach you through the eye and not through the ear. Therefore typographical form should do by means of optics what the voice and gesture of the writer does to convey his ideas.
E.g.: As you have more faith in your grandparents' generation, let us consider this small example by Master Francis Rabelais, abstractor of the quintessence:

O,i?... am the great tamer of the Cimbri
  ::;. ted through the air,
because the dew annoyed him.
    he appeared, went
putting clods in the troughs.
    ! of fresh butter, which
with great tubs;
Gargantua, Book 1, Chapter 2.

5
László
Moholy-Nagy

Typophoto

From *Malerei, Photographie, Film*, Bauhausbücher 8 (Munich: Albert Langen, 1925). Translation from Moholy-Nagy, *Painting, Photography, Film*, trans. Janet Seligman (Cambridge, MA: MIT Press, 1969), 38–40.

Neither curiosity nor economic considerations alone but a deep human interest in what happens in the world have brought about the enormous expansion of the news-service: typography, the film and the radio.

The creative work of the artist, the scientist's experiments, the calculations of the business-man or the present-day politician, all that moves, all that shapes, is bound up in the collectivity of interacting events. The individual's immediate action of the moment always has the effect of simultaneity in the long term. The technician has his machine at hand: satisfaction of the needs of the moment. But basically much more: he is the pioneer of the new social stratification, he paves the way for the future.

The printer's work, for example, to which we still pay too little attention has just such a long-term effect: international understanding and its consequences.

The printer's work is part of the foundation on which the new world will be built. Concentrated work of organization is the spiritual result which brings all elements of human creativity into a synthesis: the play instinct, sympathy, inventions, economic necessities. One man invents printing with movable type, another photography, a third screen-printing and stereotype, the next electrotype, phototype, the celluloid plate hardened by light. Men still kill one another, they have not yet understood how they live, why they live, politicians fail to observe that the earth is an entity, yet television [Telehor] has been invented: the 'Far Seer' tomorrow we shall be able to look into the heart of our fellow-man, be everywhere and yet be alone, illustrated books, newspapers, magazines are printed—in millions. The unambiguousness of the real, the truth in the everyday situation is there for all classes. **The hygiene of the optical, the health of the visible is slowly filtering through.**

What is typophoto?
Typography is communication composed in type.
Photography is the visual presentation of what can be optically apprehended. **Typophoto is the visually most exact rendering of communication.**

Every period has its own optical focus. Our age: that of the film; the electric sign, simultaneity of sensorily perceptible events. It has given us a new, progressively developing creative basis for typography too. Gutenberg's typography, which has endured almost to our own day, moves exclusively in the linear dimension. The intervention of the photographic process has extended it to a new dimensionality, recognised today as total. The preliminary work in this field was done by the illustrated papers, posters and by display printing.

Until recently type face and type setting rigidly preserved a technique which admittedly guaranteed the purity of the linear effect but ignored the new dimensions of life. Only quite recently has there been typographic work which uses the contrasts of typographic material (letters, signs, positive and negative values of the plane) in an attempt to establish a correspondence with modern life. These efforts have, however, done little to relax the inflexibility that has hitherto existed in typographic practice. An effective loosening-up can be achieved only by the most sweeping and all-embracing use of the techniques of photography, zincography, the electrotype, etc. The flexibility and elasticity of these techniques bring with them a new reciprocity between economy and beauty. With the development of **phototelegraphy**, which enables reproductions and accurate illustrations to be made instantaneously, even philosophical works will presumably use the same means—though on a higher plane—as the present day American magazines. The form of these new typographic works will, of course, be quite different typographically, optically, and synoptically from the linear typography of today.

Linear typography communicating ideas is merely a mediating makeshift link between the content of the communication and the person receiving it:

COMMUNICATION ← TYPOGRAPHY → PERSON

Instead of using typography—as hitherto—merely as an objective means, the attempt is now being made to incorporate it and the potential effects of its subjective existence creatively into the contents.

The typographical materials themselves contain strongly optical tangibilities by means of which they can render the content of the communication in a directly visible—not only in an indirectly intellectual—fashion. Photography is highly effective when used as typographical material. It may appear as illustration beside the words, or in the form of "**phototext**" in place of words, as a precise form of representation so objective as to permit of no individual interpretation. The form, the rendering is constructed out of the optical and associative relationships: into a visual, associative, conceptual, synthetic continuity: into the typophoto as an unambiguous rendering in an *optically* valid form.

The typophoto governs the new tempo of the new visual literature.

In the future every printing press will possess its own block-making plant and it can be confidently stated that the future of typographic methods lies with the photo-mechanical processes. The invention of the photographic typesetting machine, the possibility of printing whole editions with X-ray radiography, the new cheap techniques of block making, etc., indicate the trend to which every typographer or typophotographer must adapt himself as soon as possible.

This mode of modern synoptic communication may be broadly pursued on another plane by means of the kinetic process, the film.

6
Kurt Schwitters

Thesen über Typographie (Theses on typography)

From *Merz* no. 11 (November 1924): 91.

Countless rules can be written about typography. The important thing is: never to do it the way that someone else did it before you. Or you could say: always do it differently than the others.

First some general theses about typography:

I. Typography can be an art under certain conditions.

II. First and foremost, there is no parallel between the content of the text and its typographic form.

III. Design is the essence of all art; the typographic design is not a reflection of the textual content.

IV. The typographic design is an expression of the stresses and strains of the textual content. (El Lissitzky)

V. Even the textually negative parts, the unprinted areas of the paper, have typographically positive values. There is typographic value in every particle of material, i.e., each letter, word, piece of text, number, punctuation mark, line, symbol, illustration, space, and overall field.

VI. From the point of view of artistic typography, the ratio or overall balance of typographical values is important, but the quality of the type itself, the intrinsic typographical value, is of no importance.

VII. From the point of view of the type itself, quality is the main requirement.

VIII. Quality of the type means simplicity and beauty. Simplicity implies clear, unambiguous, purposeful form, and the abandonment of all unnecessary features. Beauty means a good balance of formal relationships. The photographic image is clearer and therefore better than the drawn image.

IX. A display or poster constructed from existing letters is, in principle, easier and therefore better than a drawn poster. Even the impersonal type of printing is better than the individualist script of an artist.

X. With regard to content, the main requirement of the typography is that it emphasize the purpose for which the content is to be printed. The typographic poster thus results from the demands of the textual content.

It is incomprehensible that, up till now, the requirements of typography have been so neglected, taking into account all the demands of expressing the textual content. Today, as a result, quality goods are advertised by barbaric advertising. And it is even more incredible that almost all the older art magazines do not understand typography as well as art. Conversely, the leading modern art journals use typography as one of their main advertising mediums. I mention here especially the magazine *G*, edited by Hans Richter (Berlin-Friedenau, Eschenstrasse 7); *Gestaltung der Reklame* [Advertising design], published by Max Burchartz, Bochum; the magazine *ABC*, Zurich; and I could name a few others. The journal *Die Reklame* [Advertising] long ago recognized the importance of advertising and poster design for the impression that is communicated of the goods being praised, and has since employed advertising artists. Unfortunately, however, these advertising artists of the past were individualists who had no idea of consistency of design in the overall display and typography. With greater or lesser skill, they designed details, sought extravagant compositions, drew ornate or otherwise unreadable letters, painted conspicuous and distorted illustrations, thereby compromising the advertised goods in the eyes of objective people. It is irrelevant here that, from their point of view, good work may have been produced when the approach was entirely wrong. Today, the advertiser has begun to recognize the error of choosing individualists and, instead of artists, they use art for advertising purposes, or, to put it more clearly: TYPOGRAPHY. Better no advertisement than an inferior one; because the reader draws his conclusions from the impression of the advertising and not from the textual content on the goods.

7
Iwan Tschichold

Elementare Typographie (Elemental typography)

From "Sonderheft 'elementare typographie,'" *Typographische Mitteilungen* 22, no. 10 (October 1925): 198, 200.

1. The new typography is purposeful.
2. The purpose of each piece of typography is communication (which means what it represents). The message must appear in its shortest, simplest, and most urgent form.
3. In order to make typography serviceable for social purposes, it is necessary to establish the *internal organization* of the materials (the ordering of content) and the *external organization* of the materials (which sets the means of typography in relation to each other).
4. Internal organization is restricted to the elemental means of typography: letters, numbers, signs, rules from the typecase, and the composing machine. In today's optical world, one of the elemental means of the new typography also includes the exact image: photography.
The elemental letterform is the sanserif in all its variations: light—medium—**bold** and from condensed to expanded. Letterforms that belong to certain styles

or bear specific national characteristics (Gothic, Fraktur, Church Slavonic) are not designed elementally and are somewhat limited in their ability for international communication. The Medieval-Antiqua (old style roman) is the most common form of typeface for the majority of people today. For continuous text it still has the advantage of better legibility over many sanserifs, although without being designed elementally.
Until a truly elemental form that is easily readable in continuous text has been created, an impersonal, factual, unobtrusive form of Medieval-Antiqua (i.e., one with minimal temporal or personal character) will be preferable to a sanserif.

Extraordinary savings could be achieved by the exclusive use of lowercase letters (and the elimination of all capital letters), a way of writing that is recommended for our future by all innovators in the field of script. See the book *Sprache und*

Schrift by Dr. Porstmann (Beuth-Verlag, Berlin SW 19, Beuthstraße 8. Price: 5.25 marks). Our writing loses nothing by using only lowercase letters but instead becomes easier to read, easier to learn, and much more economical. Why for the single sound of "a" are there two signs: A and a? One sound, one sign. Why two alphabets for one word; why double the number of signs when half could achieve the same thing?

By using very different sizes and shapes, without regard to previous aesthetic attitudes, the logical structure of the printed area is made visually perceptible. The unprinted parts of the paper are just as much means of the design as are the printed forms.

5. *External organization* is the creation of the strongest contrasts (simultaneity) through the use of opposing forms, sizes, and weights (which must correspond to the value of the content), and the creation of the relation between the positive (colored) formal values and the (white) negative values of the unprinted paper.

6. Elemental typographic design is the creation of logical and visual relations between the letters, words, and phrases as presented by the task at hand.

7. In order to increase the urgency and sensational effects of the new typography, vertical and diagonal line directions can be used simultaneously as a means of internal organization.

8. Elemental design excludes the use of any *ornament* (including "swollen" and other ornamental lines). The use of lines and elemental forms per se (squares, circles, triangles) must necessarily have a basis in the overall construction. The *decorative-artistic-fanciful* use of elemental forms is not synonymous with elemental design.

9. The ordering of elements in the new typography should in the future be based on the standardized (DIN) paper formats of the Standards Committee of German Industry (NDI), which alone make possible the organization of the printing industry encompassing all typographic designs. (See: Dr. Porstmann, *Die Dinformate und ihre Einführung in die Praxis,* Selbstverlag Dinorm, Berlin NW 7 , Sommerstraße 4a. 3 marks.)

In particular, the DIN format A4 (210 × 297 mm) should be the basis for all business and other letters. Business letters have also been standardized: DIN 676, "Geschäftsbrief," obtainable direct from Beuth-Verlag, Berlin SW 19, Beuthstraße 8; 0,40 mark. The DIN standard "Papierformate" is number 476. The DIN formats have only recently been introduced. In this special issue there is only one piece that is consciously based on a DIN format.

10. In typography, as in other fields, elemental design is never absolute or definitive. The design concepts change with the transformation of the elements. Inventions that create new elements, such as photography, ensure that typographic design will also constantly change.

8
Willi Baumeister

Neue Typographie (New typography)

From *Die Form* 1, no. 10 (July 1926): 215–17. Translated by Annika Fisher.

Its success is resounding. Symmetrical layout had to yield: it was an order of rest and repose. Reading, however, is a *movement from left to right*.

•

Typography is based, above all, on the division of a limited surface. At the start of his work, the typographer faces the same task as the painter. The principles of surface division are different. The printed page contains images and text. For posters, the image predominates. In typography, the message must be constructed pictorially. A primary and unifying order creates clarity, which we cannot do without. The traditional order is symmetrical. The symmetrical arrangement of a printed page, as an advertisement, a poster, etc., is no different from the decoration of a facade. The distribution of energy in the arrangement allocates forces and tensions to both sides. Forces and tensions cancel each other out in favor of balance. This system does not feature

a starting point and offers no entry for the eye. One is constantly drawn to the central axis. This arrangement in no way facilitates the process of reading. A street at right angles to the facade of a symmetrical building forces us closer, until we finally enter the door: its purpose is fulfilled. The movement was spatial. In this spirit, a symmetrically ordered printed surface likewise compels us to approach it spatially, at a right angle to the surface. But, in terms of reading left to right, it does not lead us into the printed surface of text.

The insertion of the eye into the absolutely planar system of the printed page can only be achieved by shifting its center of gravity, namely, toward the beginning: the starting point for the text. Thus, the upper left. The ornate initials of ancient manuscripts were functional and therefore correct. The initial was the eye-catcher, and the following text hung upon it like train cars hitched to a locomotive. The fundamental movement goes from the top left to the bottom right. Consequently, the resulting diagonal becomes the determining line of the entire order. The use of larger initial letters is the formation of eye-catchers made out of letters. The danger, however, is that the enlarged initial letters lose their connection with the following text. To support the contrast, it is necessary to surround these amplified letters with unprinted space, if possible. The so-called air between headlines and text blocks has an essential importance. If the enlarged initial letters keep the same lower edge as the following letters, this is more correct than the reverse relationship to the upper edge. But we can read the text most smoothly if we place the following smaller letters in the lower two-thirds axis of the eye-catcher letter. The golden ratio is 1:1618. In this way, the general movement from left to right is surrendered, and the connection of the big letters with the smaller ones is tighter, that is to say, more correct. This rule is not compromised by exceptions. The weight of the font must be meaningfully determined. For example:

Steam engines
Steam
Engines

The rectangular format dictates a block layout as a consequence. The use of forms similar to the given surface has

an extraordinarily beneficial effect—a well-known, unstated tenet in modern painting. Awareness of such effects also caused Cubism and Constructivism to use the straight line and the right angle.

Many "modern" advertisements, letterheads, etc. are constructed according to the compositional principles of painting, even in a Constructivist sense. However, artwork, even abstract art, has a compositional movement that results in a final balance of harmonized tension. The painting will be viewed. In contrast, the advertisement, the printed line, etc. will be read. And we know that reading is a movement. Everything that has movement—that is to say, direction—is unbalanced. The arrangement of the printed page has a very determined direction—in stark contrast to the rest of a painted composition. Thus, for printed text, the beautiful balance of free equilibrium cannot be the primary goal; rather, everything must be sacrificed for the directional line of the eye.

In the earlier style of letterhead arranged with symmetrical decoration, company logos were positioned as central medallions or most commonly to both sides. Balance created calm. If I want to activate a logo or a block of text as a complex, then a nonaxial shift through lines or bars is necessary. The complex comes about through rotation.

The preference for "sans-serif fonts" lies in the fact that an exact cut results in a clarity of text that painted lettering, artistic writing, and Fraktur could never attain. The block of text is clearly expressed, which allows for an exemplary design compared to the other types. It is wrong to set text in capital letters—even for longer titles and headlines. The exclusive use of capitals is questionable since it reduces readability.

Jacob Grimm, already very early, had advocated for the exclusive use of lowercase letters. The well-known Viennese architect Loos, champion of the new architecture in Europe, had all his writings printed in lowercase about 20 years ago. Subsequent advocates include Stefan George and the Bauhaus. This method of writing would bring about a very advantageous simplification. Moreover, today we perceive uppercase Latin letters as antiquated. Lowercase "Latin" letters are a type of bastardization that has a sense of movement in comparison to the starkly geometric letters of the Romans. Our preference for the static has changed over time. The Egyptians built their conically tapered pyramids and temples atop large surfaces. The Romanesque arch and the Gothic pointed arch are feats of engineering that no longer have any sense of risk from today's perspective. The potential of iron construction, and particularly methods with iron and concrete, provide us with new impressions.

Expansive terraces; cornices; canopies without supports. The reduced base of a cyclist; the rising hot-air balloon with its massive volume on top; airships and planes have altered our sense of the static.

This feeling also asserts itself in our sentence structure. We tend to move our emphasis to the start of the sentence, although initially for no logical reason. This demonstrates that the correctly attuned sensibility always finds its parallels in the spirit of the times.

If two rows of the same length are to be typeset, then, because of the order of the blocks, the eye is forced to trace back the entire long length of the line to the left after reading the upper line in order to arrive at the beginning of the next line. If, however, one were to stagger the lower line to the right, then the eye would have a correspondingly shorter way to travel to reach the start. Therefore, the graduation of lines of text is highly recommended:

I consider the underlining of words wrong in principle because the underscore (the bar), like any other decorative sign, only expresses itself. The underscoring bar only indirectly emphasizes the word that it is meant to reinforce. Additionally, the bar visually minimizes the appearance of the word. If one wants to emphasize something, increased size and weight should be sufficient. Undoubtedly, however, a bar can occasionally have rhythmic or compositional value.

In almost all cases, I consider the arrangement of vertically aligned characters and words as incorrect because legibility is greatly impacted.

The unprinted complexes in advertisement have a very special function.
The primary means of contrast through
white and black is especially applied
to new typography. The best ornaments
of all time show us how not only the
painted ornament but also the combination of the ornament together with
vacant spaces can form a unity. The
Greek meander ornament forms an
outstanding example. The new tendencies in typography are elementary.
Returning to the original requirements
of typesetting, no arrangement can
be found other than that based in the
sense of the movement of reading, the
movement from left to right.

9

Walter Dexel

Was ist neue Typographie? (What is new typography?)

From *Frankfurter Zeitung*, February 5, 1927. Reprinted in Walter Dexel, *Der Bauhausstil: Ein Mythos: Texte 1921–1965* (Starnberg: Josef Keller, 1976), 130–37. Translated by Annika Fisher.

The avoidance of any personal touch is in line with the new typography, which is a matter-of-fact, impersonal affair. The new typography should not imitate manuscripts, nor use rare, uncommon type, nor involve a personal alphabet (although many of our most modern members place decisive value on such individuality), nor should it be propaganda for any new, improved font; my opinion matters as little in the scope of our activities as does the use of lowercase. We have only one duty: to be objective—and to be typical.

Our primary objective is the quickest and finest readability, and our best type is one that everyone can immediately decipher. At the moment when "lowercase script" becomes familiar to everyone, we will apply it, for we recognize it as a step towards economic progress. But as long as lowercase writing demands any extra effort from the average reader, it is still not the best possible instrument of communication for us.

Our insights are of as little interest to our audience as our taste or our artistry. These days, science and art are invoked much too often. It is of no concern to art if we want it known that coffee is wholesome, that [Elisabeth] Bergner will perform in the theater tomorrow, or that a cigarette costs around 5 pfennigs.

If these messages were transmitted to us by radio instead of by posters or advertisements, then we would not demand that the announcer "broadcast" this information or that he give his voice a special tremolo when he speaks of Bergner or when he praises Manoli [cigarettes]. We would even vehemently refuse to tolerate such a presentation and demand only one thing of the announcer: "Sir, speak clearly and make it short!"

In my opinion, the exact same thing is true for any visual, optical communication—it should be very clear, very objective, and very short. Streams of words and an overabundance of art have become widespread in the field of typography and advertising. They have obfuscated basically simple and self-evident things in such a way that we have had to fight a difficult battle, step by step, to regain our ability to say something both clearly and briefly. The hard effort of limiting oneself just to what is necessary is only felt by those who are in the midst of this struggle.

Well-executed, logically formed typography conveys a pleasing impression of balance and harmony beyond its content. Although not a matter of art, such typography is a matter of skill and workmanship. Our means may seem limited—our lack of ability to visually differentiate is a result of distortion; we have been bombarded for too long by only the heaviest guns and the coarsest means. In truth, every task requires its own particular solution. Formulae are rarely viable and we should be wary of all dogmas, even if they are factually correct, such as:

> "one reads
> > from the top left
> > > to the bottom right
> > > > and everything must
> > > > > be structured
> > > > > > accordingly."

It is by no means always important that a printed message be read from the first to the last word in succession. For example, in a notice from an art association, the reader should immediately learn who the artist is that is being shown. If this artist in question does not interest him, he can save himself the effort of scanning all further information.

The examples shown here for the Jena Art Association serve a dual purpose: first, they are sent to the homes of each member as notifications; and second, they are complemented in the most pleasant way through a strip of some color and are glued to cardstock of a different color in order to form an effective announcement to display at universities, reading rooms, stores, shop windows, and so on. Thus a good visual effect from a distance is also a necessity, otherwise one could argue that such bold sanserif letters would not be required on a postcard. The following text block, for example,

has already become a logo, which the initiate can merely notice without reading, and which only really concerns the newcomer.

Thus, apart from the name of the artist, the only essential information remaining in the message are the dates and an indication of whether the works are watercolors, paintings, graphics, or in some other medium. The arrangement of the individual blocks can never be arbitrary, but neither does it need to be monotonous or stereotypical. There are always new ways to emphasize the most important parts, be it through the greatest possible emptiness of the surrounding space or through adding a solid line or underlining text.

KUNSTVEREIN JENA
PRINZESSINNENSCHLÖSSCHEN
GEÖFFNET: SONNABENDS 3—5, SONNTAGS 11—1 UHR
AUSSER DER ZEIT FÜHRUNG DURCH DEN HAUSMEISTER
14. DEZEMBER 1924
BIS 11. JANUAR 1925

OSKAR SCHLEMMER
GEMÄLDE ZEICHNUNGEN BÜHNENENTWÜRFE FIGURINEN

Today, modern means are generally understood to include, in addition to the letter type (usually SANS SERIF in all **WEIGHTS** and POINTS, Mediaeval Antiqua, **EGYPTIENNE**, and a number of other clear fonts), all kinds of strokes, points, squares, and arrows—in short, all symbols that can be found in the typesetter's case

and, above all, the surrounding empty or negative space, which we regard as an active factor in achieving the necessary contrasts.

By and large, over the years, I personally have increasingly moved away from using strokes and squares. They are only justified in some cases. Usually, the right arrangement of space and the strong differentiation in font sizes achieves the same result. Unquestionably, there is today a misuse of lines of all weights, arrows, squares, and dashes. All these means are crutches, "modern gestures," which, in the interest of

the best possible readability, should be rejected as complicating elements. Used purely decoratively, as they too often are, these forms can be valued no differently than the ornamental trim and closing vignettes on the program of a small town's singing club. To simply replace the concluding picture of a birdie with a central square achieves nothing—nothing at all.

Also the unrestrained use of all line directions.

the vertical orientation of whole lines <u>should be rejected on principle.</u>

As well as the

V	S	P	O	L
E	U	L	F	E
R	B	A		T
T	S	C		T
I	E	E		E
C	Q	M		R
A	U	E		S
L	E	N		
	N	T		
	T			

These are our childhood shoes, which we should have outgrown by now. If it is a necessity of space, then common words, such as "hotel" or "bar" or

Primary Texts on the New Typography

the like, can occasionally be written with vertical letters, but only those words that we immediately grasp after seeing just the initial two letters. In all cases where there is no shortage of space, other solutions must be found. They always exist; it is just inconvenient sometimes to look for them.

To accentuate the entire composition or to clarify and delineate the text, lines and space bars may occasionally be indispensable. In these cases, their necessity will be determined objectively. An instance may be a brochure for an exhibition of artists at Der Sturm, which contains an abundance of names that are difficult to organize and require a compositional scheme. Such conditions lead naturally to the enlarged "S" of the word Sturm that appears in the middle of the flier in the largest possible font. (But even this arrangement could be read as a gimmick and should not be employed very often.)

For all tasks that have to serve other functions in addition to simple communication, such as book covers, magazine titles, letterheads, billboards, etc., different rules obviously apply. Here I am only concerned with messages using the word and the letter, that is, a narrowly defined special field.

In many cases, pictorial means of representing the object will be equally called into question. All photographic techniques and the mechanical transfer of images are, because of their clear objectivity, ideally suited to inform us both quickly and in complete detail. In the future, they will often be preferable to mere words.

BAUER
DONAS
FILLA
MARC LEGER
KLEE UHDEN
TOPP WAUER
PUNI WALDEN
PERI FISCHER

KUNSTVEREIN JENA
PRINZESSINNENSCHLÖSSCHEN
GEÖFFNET: SONNABENDS 3–5, SONNTAGS 11–1 UHR

6. JULI – 3. AUGUST 1924
AUSSTELLUNG **STURM**
DER

ARCHIPENKO
BAUMEISTER
HEEMSKERCK
KOKOSCHKA
DELAUNAY
SCHWITTERS
MARCOUSSIS
MOHOLY-NAGY
GLEIZES
BRAQUE
MOLZAHN
SCHREYER
CHAGALL

SONNTAG, 6. JULI, 11 UHR
ERÖFFNUNG: VORTRAG
HERWARTH WALDEN
EINTRITT FÜR MITGLIEDER FREI
FÜR NICHTMITGLIEDER 1,50 MARK

Warum 4 Alphabete (Why 4 alphabets?)

Insert to *Foto-Auge*, 1929.

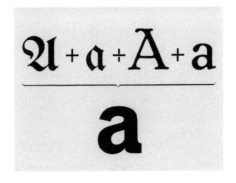

why 4 alphabets, if they are all pronounced the same (latin majuscule, latin miniscule, german majuscule, german miniscule)? why install 4 different keyboards, if each produces exactly the same notes? what a waste of energy, patience, time, and money! what a complication in typewriters, typefounding, printers' cases, composing machines, proof corrections, etc.! why write nouns with capital letters when in england, america, and france they do without that? why mark the beginning of a sentence with two signs (a period and a capital letter) instead of making the period bolder? why even write with capitals when you cannot speak with capitals? why are overburdened children tormented by 4 alphabets, while there is insufficient time in schools for the vital material?

lowercase script is "more difficult to read" only insofar as it is still unfamiliar. it is only "more aesthetic" as in the bygone days of architecture when movement up and down and along roofs and turrets was once desired.

would our suggestion be too purist? on the contrary: we are for the enrichment of all life's genuine emotions. but, in the end, all 4 keyboards produce the same excitement for life.

and as for the "german way of life"? did our own most characteristic asset, german **music**, require the generation of a german (and quadrupled) notation?

11

Normalisierung der Papierformate (Standardization of paper sizes)

From *ABC: Beiträge zum Bauen*, no. 2 (1924): 1–2 (unsigned). Translated by Annika Fisher.

The aim of the standardization of paper sizes is economic organization—to facilitate the stacking of the same units in binders and folders, within filing cabinets and bookshelves, and spread out on the walls of exhibitions and billboards. Moreover, we do not only have to standardize the surface area by setting up a series of fixed formats, we have to standardize the use of these areas as well. This means that we must adjust ourselves to the use of a few determined paper sizes to fulfill our communication, representation, and recording needs. Thus, the simplest form of the geometric system of ordering becomes the starting point—everything that needs to be ordered must fit into it. The simpler this system is, the more it will prevail over today's arbitrariness.

The conditions for such a system are:

1. The formation of a series from which each size format can be derived by halving or doubling the next format.
2. The geometric similarity of all formats with each other, namely the ratio of the sides as $1:\sqrt{2}$ or $1:1.41$.
3. The establishment of a standard measure.

This standard measure must be a unit of length, since area is determined most simply by multiplying the lengths of the sides. We choose the metric system because it is our current standard of measurement. From this precondition, we obtain the following series, for which we can round the ratio of $1:1.41$ to $1:1.40$.

1000 × 1400	mm	
700 × 1000	"	
500 × 700	"	
350 × 500	"	
250 × 350	"	
175 × 250	"	
125 × 175	"	

Take this magazine and create the formats of our series by folding and unfolding it. Try to apply our series

If we compare our series with the previously suggested formats known to us, including the measurement standards of the Association of Swiss Machinery Manufacturers (VSM), which are supported by international agreement, we see that while conditions 1 and 2 are met equally by all, the proposals diverge in their choices of a standard measure.

which works in relation to the meter, was intended as a secondary series to be used only in dire need.

We contend that employing a simple relationship to the metric measurement system in order to create the most comprehensive standardization possible is more important than the perpetuation of today's business

1.	Standard Measure	1 cm	(Ostwald/Bührer)	Main Format	226 × 320	mm	
2.	"	1 dm	(Wyssling)	"	200 × 280	"	
3.	"	1 m	(VSM, Series B)	"	250 × 353	"	
4.	"	1 m²	(VSM, Series A)	"	210 × 297	"	

In choosing the standard measure of rows 1, 2, and 4, the desire to replace the entrenched folio and quarto formats by a median main format (of about 210 × 300), the business letter, was decisive. A simple correspondence to the metric system was sacrificed for this intermediary main format that originated out of the preexisting measurement system. For this reason the primary sequence A of the VSM, which is to be introduced to the Swiss federal administration on the instructions of the federal assembly, arrives at dimensions with very complicated measurement ratios (compare *Technik und Betrieb*, no. 2). Series B,

letter. In any case, for technical operations the letter will increasingly assume the character of a note or memo (the basis of the inquiry, the offer, the contract, or the bill), in addition to the graphic documents outlining the description, the estimate, the parts list, the conditions for the job, etc.

Experience has shown that for these kinds of materials even the old folio, especially in its breadth, is too small. The VSM format of 210 × 297 mm, in its attempts to achieve a balance between the octavo and folio sizes, is not suitable for magazines, books, etc. Furthermore, the exact ratio of 1:1.41

is unimportant; the rounding down to 1:4 is, in practice, adequate for all purposes.

For this reason, we propose to implement series B, which the VSM intended only for supplemental use, by rounding down the ratio of 1:√2 to become a "metric series." We have already tested and employed this series for our own purposes for a long time.

Metric Series	VSM Series B	
1000 × 1400 mm	1000 × 1400 mm	
700 × 1000 ″	700 × 1000 ″	Plans, posters
500 × 700 ″	500 × 700 ″	Plans
350 × 500 ″	350 × 500 ″	Plans, newspapers, tables
250 × 350 ″	250 × 350 ″	Magazines and books (large scale), standard specification sheets, cost estimates, account ledgers, and records
175 × 250 ″	175 × 250 ″	Magazines and books (small scale), letters, reports, brochures, catalogs
125 × 175 ″	125 × 175 ″	Books (paperbacks), notepads, postcards

12
Max Burchartz

Gestaltung der Reklame (Advertising design)

Bochum, June 1924. Translated by Annika Fisher.

Advertising is the handwriting of the entrepreneur! Just as handwriting reveals the strength and ability of its writer, the advertisement reveals these traits in a company. The measure of performance, quality, respectability, energy, and generosity of a company is reflected in the objectivity, clarity, form, and scope of an advertisement. The first condition of success is the high quality of the goods. The second: appropriate sales organization, of which an indispensable factor is good advertisement.

High-quality advertising will be ineffective in the long run with inferior goods. Top-quality goods, however, do not come across with inadequate advertising.

Good advertising:

1. is factual;
2. is clear and concise;
3. makes use of modern methods;
4. packs a formal punch; and
5. is inexpensive.

1. Good advertising is factual. It only makes statements that are true. Trust must be gained and preserved. The advertisement must not raise expectations that do not correspond to facts. Good advertising forcefully and distinctly emphasizes the positive and special features of what is being offered.

2. Good advertising is clear and concise. Modern man is stingy with his time. Who reads long text on hundreds of advertisements and posters? Who listens to long speeches? Show little! Say little! But show or say this little often! Relentless attacks on the same point can break through. Good advertisement takes into account the time of its audience, trusts its own tenacity, is elegant, and renounces idle chatter. Its script is legible and clear; its wording is articulate and unambiguous despite its extreme terseness. A puzzling element (sparingly used) can stimulate great interest. Its solution must be all

the more concise. Even in its representation, good advertising is limited to what is necessary and always emphasizes what is essential, conspicuous, and clearly jumping out. Additional features only distract and obscure. The time of narrative illustrations has passed. Long tales with the secondary intention of serving a purpose outside of themselves contradict the spirit of the time, which demands clarity and economy.

3. Good advertising makes use of modern methods. Who nowadays travels by carriage? Good advertising uses the latest contemporary inventions as new tools of communication. Projections, film, gramophone, and radiotelegraphy provide new possibilities, in addition to the means of typography. The poster, the advertisement, and the printed word are still the essential instruments of advertising. Within typography, new possibilities also arise through the novel use of photographic techniques, such as retouching, the peculiarities of the image, and the combination of differently sized images and perspectival relationships. In the presentation, photography is superior to obsolete handwriting, as it is more factual and economical. Since it is quick to produce, it avoids the overemphasis on individual draftsmanship without losing the expression of uniqueness, which still retains enough leeway through the design. Photography has thus far been rarely employed as a means for artistic composition.

Several techniques and methods (as well as forms)—some not even applied so far—have already proven effective just through their surprising novelty. Modern methods of good advertising place value on the results of scientific, psychological research, and on the development of new aspects of artistic design.

4. Good advertising packs a formal punch. Despite all the diversity of techniques, the means of advertising are always based on visual and vocal effects. In advertising, these effects are bearers of conceptual and verbal communication, figurative depiction, or attention-grabbing formal experimentation. Advertising can be of high artistic quality. Such expression arises from the play of contrasts that characterize the visual and vocal means. The more intensely that contrast is expressed and the more immediate the balance of the whole, the more harmonic is the immediate effect of such objects on our senses. Only by avoiding confusing and ineffective complexity and by avoiding any weakening of contrast can the intensity and impact of the effect be achieved.

Visual design demands the use of strong contrasts, such as black and white, large and small, horizontal and vertical, colorful and achromatic, etc. Especially for a broad view such as required by posters, for example, the use of just a few sharp contrasts can have the most powerful, fascinating, and attention-grabbing results. Designs with different sizes, few colors, photographic representations, and a distinctive logo can produce the simplest and most memorable (geometric) shapes and provide an inexhaustible wealth of compositional possibilities that contain visual contrasts. The greatest vibrancy is attained not through decorative additions, such as little stars or ornamentation, but instead simply through designs that employ the power of proportion and use relationships between the text and images that are essential to its purpose.

A unified, strong impact should not only be required by every single advertisement. The overall organization of a company's advertising activity likewise requires a conscious design. The relationships between the individual operating forces should also be evaluated. Product recommendations, which may be valuable in themselves, can be divergent and not immediately recognizable as appropriate; such advertisements forego the most effective method of advertising: repetition. The individual advertising campaign must be associated with all the other ads for a company through the constant, invariable, recurring, and appropriate application of certain words, signs, and formal characteristics. The largest letters, the logo, or the keyword—preferably all three simultaneously—must always

forcefully express this clear and unified relationship between all the advertising materials for a product as a whole. The novelty of the designs is essential. Formulaic or banal forms of language and artistic design must be avoided.

5. Good advertising is inexpensive. Apart from the fact that the creation of illustrated advertising, as described above, entails a steep decrease in complicated and costly techniques, this approach limits itself to the simplest, and therefore the most effective, methods. The increased success that results from overall professional organization creates greater profits so that many companies can restrict the scope of their previous, conventional advertising without any decrease in impact—and perhaps even see an increase. With high-quality advertising, a small amount is all that is needed. Advertising that conveys quality in every aspect (including the choice of papers, the printing, etc.) will have a greater impact than much more inappropriate, poorly organized advertising. The fees for organizing, designing, and supervising its implementation are hardly anything in relation to the overall costs involved.

Primary Texts on the New Typography

13
Johannes Molzahn

Letterhead
statement, ca. 1925

The rapid, ever-increasing pace of life, the frenzied traffic, the enormous amount of stress every second, the age of cinema and air express—these have not only reshaped our thinking, they have also affected us physically, especially our eyes or "vision", in terms of adaptability and economy. Because the amount it can take in is limited, the eye only absorbs what is essential, what sustains life, the sensation of phenomena, everything that aids the vital instinct to direct our psyche. The fundamental reason for this lies in the will to live in general. In short, the eye takes in only a small fraction of countless optical stimuli, the sum of which is determined by the limit of our capabilities.

Increasingly, production and sales must also demand the creation of advertising according to the same principles that apply to the entire operating process: to achieve the maximum effect with the least expenditure of energy and material resources.

14
Lajos Kassák

Reklám és modern tipográfia (The advertisement and modern typography)

Originally published in *Reklámélet* (Advertising) (August 1928): 1–3. Translation from Lajos Kassák, *The Advertisement and Modern Typography*, ed. Ferenc Csaplár (Budapest: Kassák Museum, 1999), 13–14. Translated by Péter Pásztor.

In order to maintain the unobstructed production of modern industry, which is based on advanced technology and the rational organization of work, we must observe various laws of social justice and co-ordinate commerce properly. An industry which produces without consideration for social organization and commerce as a mediator will easily and periodically surely crash. The balanced state of society primarily depends on a rational solution to the question of production and consumption. Better said, the pace of industrial output should be determined by consumer needs. To ensure that the market does not remain empty and that factories do not overproduce, those who organize production must establish organic cooperation with commerce as a mediator that is acquainted with the demands, economic status, and cultural standards of consumers. To work freely and without embarrassing surprises in the market, commerce requires well-manufactured, quality goods made of good raw materials, and, conversely, to turn out cheap, high-quality goods, producers need open-minded tradesmen who understand the quality of goods and serve the interests of the buying public. It is therefore a question of what ways and means are available to commerce as the mediator to best fulfill its obligations to individuals and society.

The astute tradesman realized long ago that, if he wanted to be an active factor in our lives, he would not only have to scrupulously serve the buyers turning up in his shop, but also to advertise in a well-organized, rational, and ongoing manner.

In the past decade, European commerce has at last taken notice of the American pace. Producers have begun to rationalize their shops, and commerce has begun to make use of the greatest means of influencing the consumer: the modern advertisement. Advertisements appear in hundreds and hundreds of forms before the consumer, and displays published in papers and magazines are among the most important types of advertisement. According to the latest American statistics, eighty per cent of the buying public read advertisements in the papers, trust them and allow themselves to be influenced by them. In Europe, advertisements cannot claim such a powerful effect, nor are European production and consumer markets so consciously organized. The European tradesman still looks down upon the world with haughty elegance; he still has not realized the significance of the paradoxical truth that goods are not bought but sold.

The majority of European tradesmen are only prepared to start an advertising campaign when their businesses are on the brink of bankruptcy, and it is only natural that in this last moment they spend vast sums of money on campaigns that were not thought out and yield little. Even though it is undoubtedly true that advertising, carefully planned and implemented and created with an honest desire that business should be done, brings newer and newer circles of buyers into the market.

But tradesmen must be aware of the psychology of the buying public and must make up their advertisements so as to be sober and objective and thus generally inspire confidence.

Unfortunately, however, the backwardness of European advertising is caused not only by the lack of principle in tradesmen but also by the ineptitude on the part of the creators of advertisements. The tradesman advertising his goods, the designer of street posters and the printer typesetting newspaper displays *have* to be clear about the content and formal essence of advertising.

The good, modern advertisement must:
1) be cheap and easy to reproduce;
2) be factual, truthful, and convincing; and
3) praise the article, but qualify it, and make it familiar to the public.

In the case of posters, pictorial stylization must be *given up*; in newspaper advertisements, typesetters' pseudo-artistic efforts and bravura tricks with characters should be excluded. If typesetters want to contribute constructively to the shaping of advertisements, they must liberate themselves from the various influences of the fine arts, they must concentrate on the given object and its texture. For making advertisements is not a creative but a formative activity. It comes into being for the sake of practical applicability, not for the sake of art. The type used should be surprising and effective, not decorously beautiful. An advertisement *over* decorated with festoons and other graphic flourishes distracts from the object advertised. It might appeal to one's sense of beauty, but it will hardly call attention to the cheapness, quality, and indispensability of the article, which was the raison d'etre of the advertisement in the first place. Just think of the so-called expressionist advertisements which were all the rage not too long ago, with their whimsically scattered characters and crooked rules. The typesetter might well have given vent to his "artistic" ambitions, but the buyer often as not could not make heads or tails of these "works of art," and had no idea what they were supposed to advertise. Who has the patience to figure out these individualistic games of typesetters? The buying public will, by their very nature, never make concessions in either financial questions or issues of taste. To a certain degree, the producer and the tradesman always stand in opposition to them. The tradesman must therefore *give* up his individual posturing, remove his masks, and fill his advertisements with purity and directness. And the makers of advertisements must naturally work with such considerations in mind. The advertisement must set out to conquer the market: it must be decisive in form and content and be quick and elementary in effect.

After America, it was Germany that most realized the fundamental requirements of making advertisements. The work of German advertisement designers ought to receive the greatest possible attention from our craftsmen. The Germans, as always, direct the development of advertising on the basis of scientific observations. Their flourishing industry and commerce clearly demonstrate that they have built on solid foundations and conducted their experiments in the right direction. In textual composition they try as far as possible to confine themselves to slogans and interjections, in their formal expression they remain within the limits of the capabilities of the printing press. They work with straight rules and simple Doric type. Their designs are based on the laws of equilibrium, not symmetry. Their modern decorative materials are simple geometric diagrams, and these insets are meant to achieve not an artistically decorative but an effect of being spotted. One of their most beautiful of such supplemental designs is the Blickfang series.

One can, however, even with this basic material, despoil advertisements by dabbling in art and turn them into kitsch, as with festoons and flourishes. One would be grossly mistaken to think that the unthinking use of these geometrical figures is enough to shape an elementary typography. We now find modern typographical efforts even in Hungary, and we often observe that the Blickfang is used as a decorative element in these works. And it is understandable that certain decision-makers object to the use of this material and tell the typesetter to throw away the completed work because they think it looks more like a merger of blacks than a pure product of the printing press. This is primarily a conservative bias speaking in such managers, but there is often undeniable truth in their objections and criticisms. The incorrect use of compact geometrical forms makes for slipshod and disheveled advertisements, which primarily offend one's aesthetic sensibilities. It is this lack of aesthetic clarity that makes those who commission advertisements uncertain about the economic and cultural significance of modern typography.

But this is all part of the difficulties of a new beginning. If our designers and typesetters grasp and sense the essence of elementary typography, it will be easy to demonstrate to deci-sion-makers, those who commission advertisements, and the buying public that the modern advertisement is not only inexpensive and technically easy to produce but is also one of the most effective mediators between produc-tion and the consumer markets.

15
Jan Tschichold

Was ist und was will die neue Typografie? (What is new typography and what are its aims?)

Introduction to *Eine Stunde Druckgestaltung* (Stuttgart, 1930). Translation from Christopher Burke, *Active Literature: Jan Tschichold and New Typography* (London: Hyphen Press, 2007), 314–16. Translated by Robin Kinross.

Note: An abridged English translation was first published as "New Life in Print," *Commercial Art* (London: July 1930), after which the essay was translated into several other languages.

The endeavors of some young designers, principally from Germany, the Soviet Union, the Netherlands, Czechoslovakia, and also Switzerland and Hungary, are being gathered under the single term of 'New Typography'. The beginnings of these endeavors in Germany reach back to the war period. One can see the existence of New Typography as the outcome of the **personal** work of its originators; it seems to me more correct however to consider them more as exponents of movements of the time and of actual necessity (which does not in any way mean that the creative achievements and the local innovations of the initiators should be devalued).

The movement would never have experienced the spread that it now has, uncontested, in Central Europe, if it had not matched present-day practical necessities. It meets these in such an exceptional way because the program of New Typography demands first of all the unprejudiced adjustment of typography to whatever is the task at hand.

It is necessary to describe briefly the state of typographic development before the war. After the stylistic confusion of the 1880s, the Arts & Crafts movement followed, emanating from England (Morris, 1892); at least in the domain of typography it was predominantly historicist in orientation (imitation of incunables).

Later (around 1900) 'Jugendstil' attempted, without lasting success, to free design work of all historical models. With a misconceived copying of natural forms (Eckmann), finally even with a renewed Biedermeier (Wieynck), Jugendstil ended up as a new historicism.

Historical models were discovered yet again and imitated, albeit with better understanding (German book art, 1911–1914–1920). This more intensive study gave rise to a new adoration of historical form and resulted of course in a limitation of creative freedom, which ended in paralysis. The most important achievement of these years was—against expectations—the rediscovery of old typefaces (Walbaum, Unger, Didot, Bodoni, Garamond, and so on), which have for some time already been rightly preferred to their 'fore runners', in reality their imitators.

Let us look at the principles that were followed in prewar typography. The majestic historical model knew only one scheme of composition: the central axis and axial arrangement, whose clearest case was the title-page. Every kind of typography used this scheme, no matter what the nature of the job was—whether newspapers or brochures, letter headings or advertisements. It was only after the war that a dark secret was revealed: that different tasks with quite different practical requirements could be resolved creatively.

The natural reaction to the stiffness of pre-war typography was New Typography, which brought a loosening of design methods to the task.

For any typographic work one can discern two parts of the job: recognition and fulfillment of **practical demands**—and the **visual** design, which is a matter of **aesthetics**. (It is useless to want to avoid this term.)

In this, typography is quite different from architecture. In very many cases the visual form of a new house can be—and, by the best architects, is—derived completely from the practical demands placed upon it; but in typography, apart from a few exceptions, an aesthetic dimension of the design process is clearly evident. This circumstance puts typography nearer to the domain of 'free' spatial design (painting and graphic art) than to that of architecture. In typographic and free graphics or painting it is always a matter of spatial design. One can understand from this why it is that these new painters—the 'abstractionists'—had to be the discoverers of New Typography. It would be too much of a detour here to add an account of the new painting: one only has to look at the exhibitions of abstract painting to see the obvious connections between this painting and New Typography. This connection is not, as some think—those who have not understood abstract painting either—a formalistic one; rather it is a genetic one. Abstract paintings are '**purpose-free**', designed relations of pure colors and forms, without literary admixtures. Typography means visual (or **aesthetic**) order of **given** elements (= practical demands, type, image, colors, etc.) in a space. The difference between painting and typography is just that in painting the elements are left to free choice and the resulting picture serves no practical purpose. The typographer can do no better than take up an intensive study of spatial design, as one finds it in abstract painting.

The speed of modern communication also compels the most exact calculation of the amount of text, for greater economy of design. Typography had to find forms that were simpler and clearer than centered title-page designs, and at the same time to design these in a way that was visually more stimulating and more varied. In France Guillaume Apollinaire with his *Calligrammes*, in Italy Marinetti with *Les mots en liberté futuristes* (1919), in Germany the Dadaists all gave impulse to the new development of typography. Dadaism is still regarded by many, who haven't taken the trouble to look into its motivation, as pure madness; only a later age will properly value the pioneer work of the circle of Hausmann, Heartfield, Grosz, Hülsenbeck, and others. In any event, the pamphlets and writings of the Dadaists (which date from the war years) are the earliest documents of New Typography in Germany. Around 1922, the movement widened as some abstract painters made typographic experiments. The special number of *Typographische Mitteilungen*, "elementare typographie" (printed in an edition of 28,000 copies), edited by the author in 1925, contributed to the further effect in which these endeavors, brought together for the first time, were made known to the broad mass of compositors. At first the aims of New Typography were strongly attacked from almost all sides, but now, apart from a few ill-tempered people, no-one thinks of disputing the New. New Typography has prevailed.

If one wants to differentiate New Typography from what went before, it appears that the main characteristic is a negative: it is not historicizing. The blame for this negative description is its rival, which was exactly historically oriented. In fact New Typography is not so much anti-historical as un-historical, because it knows no formalistic limitations. The liberation from historical handcuffs brings complete freedom in the choice of means. To enrich typographic design, one can, for example, use all historical and ahistorical types, all kinds of spatial organization, all directions of line. The goal is only design: purposefulness and creative ordering of the visual elements. So limits, such as the demand for unity of type, admissable and forbidden mixtures of types, are not drawn. It is also wrong to propose some tranquility of appearance as the single aim of design—there is also designed **unrest**.

As well as its ahistorical focus, New Typography is characterized by its preference for new technical processes.

Thus:

type	not drawn letters
machine composition	not hand-setting
photography	not drawing
process blocks	not woodcuts
machine-made paper	not hand-made paper
powered presses	not handpresses
etc.	

and also:

standardization	not individualization
cheap books	not private-press editions
active literature	not passive leather-bindings

Through its design methods, New Typography encompasses the whole sphere of printing, not just the more narrow domain of typesetting. So, for example, with photography we have an objective process of graphic reproduction that is open to anyone. Photography is, along with type, another means of visual language.

The working method of New Typography rests on the clear identification of purpose and the best way of fulfilling it.

However beautiful a piece of modern typography may be, it is not 'new' if it sacrifices the purpose of its form for this. Form is a **consequence** of the work and not the realization of some external formal **conception**. This necessary truth goes unrecognized by a whole crowd of quasi-modernists. The nearest possible attainment of purpose is the highest demand of New Typography. Thus the shedding of all decorative additions becomes self-evident. And—this cannot be stressed enough—really good legibility is also part of purpose. Lines of text that are too short or lines that are long and too little leaded are hard to read and thus to be avoided from the outset. The correct application of various new printing processes almost always produces specific forms, which

it should be one of the typographer's tasks to recognize and design with. Good typography is not conceivable without a thorough knowledge of technical conditions.

The number of printed things that concern any individual, and of which he will receive an often considerable part, demands the application of **standardized formats**.

Of the basic repertoire of **types**, the grotesque (sanserif) is closest to New Typography, because it is simply designed and has good legibility. The use of other legible and also historical types—**in a new sense**—is quite possible if the letterform has been **evaluated** against that of other types present, i.e. if the visual tensions between them have been designed. So this is not to demand that **everything** be set in grotesque, even if grotesque may be the most appropriate choice for a large number of printed items. Many applications are available in the different variants of this letterform (light, semi-bold, bold, thin, wide, narrow, spaced, etc.), and in juxtaposition this can result in rich and differentiated contrast. Another kind of contrast comes from using roman types together (Egyptienne, Walbaum, Garamond, italics, etc.), and there can be no objection to making use of this specific effect. (Another very particular and effective letterform is typewriter type.)

Typographic design is the best ordering and correct choice of type sizes, according to their place within the logical structure of the text (this can be heightened or played down). The conscious use of movement (through type, and occasionally a thick or thin rule or aggregation of rules), the visually judged contrast of small and large, thin and thick, narrow and expanded types; grey and colored areas, inclined and horizontal, limited and open groups, and soon, are further means of design. They represent the 'aesthetic' aspect of typographic design. Within definite boundaries, drawn up by practical purpose and logical structure, one can often take very different routes, so that from there on the visual sense of the typographer is decisive. This becomes apparent when several designers are given the same job: as many different solutions follow, each probably with almost the same advantages. Essentially the same means thus encounter an extraordinary number of possibilities of application. These examples also show that modern means do not, as is often thought, entail a flattening of expression—on the contrary, the results are essentially more differentiated and above all more original than the typography of the pre-war years.

Color is another part of the repertoire, like typeface. In a sense, color should be seen alongside the unprinted space—the discovery of which is to be counted among the achievements of the young forces in typography. White space is to be regarded as an active element, not a passive background.

Red is to be preferred among available colors; it is **the** color in making the greatest contrast to normal black.

The clear tones of yellow and blue take their place in the front rank, just because they are clear and simple. Colors are not to be used as decorative, 'beautifying' extras, rather one uses the characteristic psycho-physical properties of each color as means to enhance, or diminish, an effect.

The **image** is produced by photography. The object is in this way reproduced at its most objective. Whether photography may or may not be an 'art' is not of importance here; its connection with type and space **can** be art, because here the criteria are merely those of structural contrast and visual relationships. Many people regard drawn images with distrust; the often false drawings of earlier times are no longer convincing and their individualistic manner is no longer attractive. The wish to present several images simultaneously, juxtaposing and contrasting different things, led to the origination of **photomontage**. Just the same general methods of design apply here as for typography; in conjunction with typography, the aggregate of photographs becomes part of the whole; so it has also to be correctly judged in this connection, to result in a harmonious design. The designed juxtaposition of typography and photography (or photomontage) is termed **typophoto**. A rare, but very rich possibility in photography is the photogram. A photogram is made without a camera, simply by placing an object—somewhat transparent or not—on a light-sensitive surface (paper, film or plate).

    Primary Texts on the New Typography

The extraordinary adaptability of New Typography to any conceivable purpose makes it an essential phenomenon of our time. It is not a matter of fashion; rather it can be used as the foundation of all future work in typography.

Karel Teige (Prague) has summarized the main features of New Typography:

Constructivist typography [the New Typography] means and requires:

1. The liberation from tradition and prejudice: overcoming of archaism and academicism and elimination of any decorativism. Disrespect for academic and traditional rules that cannot be supported on visual grounds, but which are merely rigid forms (Golden Section, unity of type).

2. Selection of types of completely clear legibility and geometrically simple design, understanding for the spirit of types and the use of them in accordance with the nature of the text: contrast in the typographic material for the purpose of greater emphasis of content.

3. Complete fulfilment of the purpose of the job. Differentiation of special needs. Posters, which need to be readable from a distance, pose demands that are different from those of a scientific book, which are different again from poetry.

4. Harmonic balancing of the surface and of the type area according to visually objective principles; comprehensible structure and geometric organization.

5. Exploitation of all possibilities that are offered by past and future technical discoveries; **union of image and type through typophoto**.

6. The closest collaboration of the graphic designer with the people in the printing house is to be desired, just as between an architect and the builders, and between the employer and those carrying out the job; this requires equally **specialization and division of work and the closest contact**.

We have nothing to add to this statement, apart from saying that the Golden Section, like other definite ratios of measurement, is often more memorable than arbitrary relationships, and so should not be completely ruled out.

16
Władysław Strzemiński

Druk funkcjonalny (Functional printing)

From *Grafika: Organ Zwiazku Polskich Artystow Grafikow i Zrzeszenia Kierownikow Zakladow Graficznych* (Graphic Art: Journal of the Union of Polish Graphic Artists and Print Workshop Managers) 3, no. 2 (1933): 37–45.

In the past, the most authoritative model for printing was that of the Renaissance. This form of printing is based upon a softening of tones and accents:

    a) a uniformly gray and pearl-like quality to the printed surface;

    b) ending chapters or even individual pages with a gradually tapering triangle;

    c) uniform intensity of the print tone in type and vignettes (replacing the triangle with straightforward letterpress at the end of the chapter or page);

    d) symmetry of the composition, along the vertical axis;

    e) use of the same typeface throughout to harmonize and ease the overall visual impression.

This form of printing has been going on from the very beginning of Italian Renaissance printing to the present. It was subject to some minor and insignificant modifications during the Baroque period, returned to its original model in Rococo printing, only to develop and flourish as the Romantic style of printing in the first decades of the nineteenth century. Secessionist printing could not overcome these established rules and got lost in an excess of ornamentation. Among all the Secessionist printers, only in Stanislaw Wyspiański (designer of the magazine *Życie* [Life]) do we see a conscious attempt to contrast the printed surface with the white field of unprinted paper and the wavy tangled line of a vignette.

Renaissance printing (and all its offshoots) took as their starting point the approach of the draftsman, both in the form of the letters, which still follow the movement of a pencil or pen (typical of antiquity), and in the draftsmanlike texture of its even gray lines—the letterforms and the compositional structure of rectangles and triangles filled with print. Therefore, this "drafts-

Primary Texts on the New Typography

manlike" printing requires vignettes, inserts, and other graphic ornaments as its necessary complement.

This type of printing, whose age has now passed, should be known as ornamental printing.

It was not until the enormous changes that took place both in economics and in modern life, thus ushering in a new era, that we saw the emergence of a new type of printing, which should be called functional. The nature of Renaissance printing (along with that of its offshoots) resulted from forcing the printed matter into a preconceived format based on drawings. In modern printing, form is a function of content. The form follows the content.

The ultimate aim is not decorative and luxurious printing, but practicality, purposefulness, and readability in everyday printed matter (poster, placard, book cover, advertisement, letterhead, business card, etc.). The sequence of activities in print composition and individual design is now reversed. In the past, the ideal of the typographer was to combine professional knowledge with the skill of an artist. Nowadays, that is not enough. Above all else, the typographer should be educated in literature and literary style (to have an accurate understanding of the meanings and inflections of each word, and the ability to refine the text stylistically).

The precise understanding of the text allows for its division into individual units of meaning. A text that is badly composed (in literary terms) makes the graphic composition opaque and confusing. It should be developed stylistically, moving forward and connecting its individual parts, so that the course of the sentence proceeds clearly in one direction and does not break up into confusing clauses with different meanings. The composition of the printed matter should be equivalent to the literary structure.

As in every interpretation of a literary work, there is not only one single graphic solution to the composition of the printed text. The end result depends on which parts of the text we wish to emphasize and which parts we consider to be secondary or tertiary. When seeking to emphasize different components of a text, therefore, the graphic composition will look different.

Understandably, all kinds of graphic ornaments obscure the clarity of the text, distract the attention of the viewer unnecessarily, and should be completely removed. The greatest economy of readability applies.

After dividing the text into subject or semantic groups, each group should be emphasized by selecting the appropriate typeface and font size. For the sake of clarity, the text should not contain more than five or fewer than three groups of distinct content. If a composition consists of more than five subject groups, it becomes extremely difficult to design the graphic layout.

Modern painting, especially the abstract or nonobjective tendencies, has had a significant impact on the appearance of contemporary print design. Instead of a deeper understanding of the foundations of a given art movement, however, we often see the direct transference of the shapes employed in it. The difference in materials (type and paper instead of paint), the length of individual words and how they are put together, and finally the relationship between the graphic design and the content of the words expressed by this shape—all these factors mean that the resulting effect can never be the same.

The need to separate each subject group within a text graphically creates the system of contrasts that most modern art movements share, although each one approaches this issue from their own point of view. For example, the main purpose of Neoplasticism is the division of the compositional plane and the shared ratio of proportions.

We arrange individual pieces of text based on the contrasting divisions of the printing plane. The sequence of black printing type of various sizes and weights and the contrast of spacing create a peculiar rhythm of elements that cannot be foreseen.

Understandably, the previously unwavering principle that the same typeface must be used throughout an entire piece has to be dropped. This view collapses under pressure from both utilitarian requirements (the functional nature of the individual parts) as well as changes in artistic criteria.

In printed work that was subordinated to a preestablished formal scheme (as in Renaissance printing), there was no need to extract individual parts from the whole but rather the opposite—the even distribution of print within the forms prepared for them.

In functional printing, each piece of text should relate to and should express the content that it contains. Various types and sizes of fonts can be used to bring out its emotional character.

On the other hand, Cubism has stimulated our sensitivity to the values of surface texture. For us designers, the surface of a printed work is not just a printed surface, but the specific density of the ink, achieved by the shape and size of the fonts, and by their thickness and spacing. By contrasting the intensity of the ink in individual groups of text, we can achieve a greater formal tension.

There is also the question of illustration within the text. As with letterpress printing, illustrations involve a certain variety and intensity in the tone or color of the ink. Depending on the character of the illustration, it will consist of some darker or lighter shapes. According to our general system of contrasts, the task is to thoroughly analyze the shapes, marks, and dots from which the illustration is composed, and to find a suitable contrast in the fonts employed in the text captions, both as to the strength of the color impact, and the size and shape of the typeface.

The halftone screen from a photograph is the only form of illustration that can be contrasted appropriately with letterpress printing. The sharp, distinct shapes of the type contrast well with the softly shaded gray tones, so that lettering placed next to the half-

Primary Texts on the New Typography

tone is made clearer. The same is true of process blocks and especially line blocks after hand drawings, which have been given up for reasons of utility, costs, etc. The style of modernity is not the result of mere aesthetics. Its foundation is deeper, and whatever we initiate in one field, it is immediately confirmed in another—sometimes seemingly very far away.

A Note on the Jan Tschichold Collection in the Museum of Modern Art

In the later 1930s, when he was beginning to have doubts about the universal claims that he himself had made for the New Typography ten years earlier, Jan Tschichold considered selling a few items from his collection. Since fleeing to Switzerland in 1933, he and his family had survived on the modest income from the design work he undertook for the publisher Benno Schwabe and some teaching in the Basel Gewerbeschule. He had been able to keep much of the sizable collection of modernist printed material and graphic ephemera that he had patiently assembled during the 1920s and early 1930s through correspondence with designers across Europe. In 1937, however, he sold a cache of sixty-seven posters to the Museum of Modern Art, including seven posters by Gustav Klutsis. MoMA was one of the few museums with a genuine commitment to contemporary design, and the Klutsis works suggest that it was not averse to work with an overt polit-

ical content at this time.[1] In addition, just two years earlier, in 1935, the museum held an exhibition on "European Commercial Printing of Today" that emphasized the central role of Germany in the development of the New Typography and graphic design. As the press release stated, "the exhibition, which will fill the first floor of the Museum, will be limited to commercial typography. Each example shown will be accompanied by a label describing the process, the type and the purpose for which it was designed."

After the war, Tschichold turned to MoMA once again. On April 11, 1950, he wrote to the museum, offering a substantial part of his collection, such as "would fit in a small packing case," for $350.00.[2] A typescript by Tschichold survives under the heading "LIST of an unique collection of examples of BEGINNING AND EARLY DEVELOPMENTS OF THE NEW TYPOGRAPHY from about 1920 until about 1936."

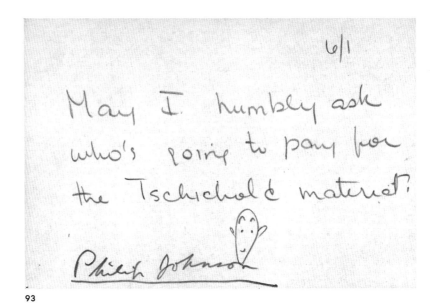

93

This details the range of the material, including books, portfolios, journals, notepaper, advertisements, cards, and other design work by, among others, Theo van Doesburg, Aleksandr Rodchenko, Piet Zwart, Willi Baumeister, Max Burchartz, John Heartfield, El Lissitzky, László Moholy-Nagy, Joost Schmidt, Kurt Schwitters, Władysław Strzemiński, and Ladislav Sutnar. He adds, almost nonchalantly, at the end, "About 60 large posters, very good condition, by Herbert Bayer, Max Bill, G. Kluzis, Dexel, Cassandre, Molzahn, Moholy-Nagy, Tschichold, Karel Teige, Matter, El Lissitzky, Rossmann, and others, from 1926 until 1938."

On May 22, Alfred H. Barr wrote back expressing his interest in the collection and said that he would take it up with his committee. Barr followed up

nine days later, on May 31, writing that, "after considerable difficulties" he was able to offer only $300.00 for the collection, or else $350 if Tschichold would bear the costs of transport to the museum. He continued, "I must make you this offer which is slightly less than you ask because we do not have any funds for this purchase, and I have to raise the money privately." At this point, letters between Tschichold and Barr must have crossed, because Tschichold had already written to Barr on May 30, saying the MoMA offer was "too late," and that he had sold the collection to Jack Gyer of Dawson's Book Shop on South Grand Avenue, Los Angeles. Tschichold added, "Possibly they still could sell the collection to you. It will arrive there shortly." Barr immediately opened discussions with Dawson's Book Shop and, after some prompting by Tschichold, Dawson himself reported that the collection was intact and that they were prepared to sell it to MoMA for the original asking price of $350.00.

On June 1, Philip Johnson, as head of the Department of Architecture and Design, sent a note to Barr with the cryptic question "May I humbly ask who's going to pay for the Tschichold material?," with a caricature of himself looking somewhat quizzical. Whether Johnson was slyly referring to his plan to purchase the collection is unclear, but it seems that Barr was still having difficulty raising the funds. By the end of June, however, the problem was resolved, and Dawson was able to send a receipt for the sale of the "Tschichold collection of books, pamphlets, Ephemera and broadsides, examples of the New Typography" at $350.00. It is only from the MoMA archives that the source of the funds can be identified. It appears that Johnson himself paid for the collection with his own money and donated it to the Department of Architecture and Design. Taken as a whole, this collection numbers several hundred items and includes work by some of the greatest artist-designers from the heroic phase of modernism.

1 In 1937–38, for example, MoMA acquired a group of posters related to the Spanish Civil War. "Drawing parallels with contemporary American design, the Spanish works were displayed in the exhibition *Spanish and U.S. Government Posters*, shown at MoMA at the end of 1938. Contemporary political posters were also exhibited during the Second World War. Yet such explicit political engagement was the exception at the museum, where aesthetic and technical concerns would typically dominate MoMA's presentation of even the most politically radical propaganda art." Juliet Kinchin, "Political Posters," in *Being Modern: MoMA in Paris*, ed. Quentin Bajac (Paris: Fondation Louis Vuitton, 2017), 78–81.

2 Jan Tschichold correspondence file, Department of Architecture and Design, Museum of Modern Art. All quotations in this section are taken from the same file.

Exhibition Checklist

A note on the checklist:
The information provided on the checklist is current at the time of publication; printer and publishing information is given when known. Substrate is paper unless otherwise stated.

Cat. 1 [Figs. 1, 28, 29, 31, 44]
Jan Tschichold (Swiss, born Germany, 1902–1974)
Die neue Typographie (The New Typography), 1928
Publisher: Bildungsverband der deutschen Buchdrucker, Berlin
8 ⅞ × 6 ¼ × ⅝ in. (22.54 × 15.88 × 1.59 cm)
Bard Graduate Center

Cat. 2 [Fig. 18]
Jan Tschichold (Swiss, born Germany, 1902–1974)
Typographische Mitteilungen, Sonderheft: Elementare Typographie (Typographic Studies, Special Issue: Elemental Typography), October 1925
Publisher: Bildungsverband der deutschen Buchdrucker, Berlin
Letterpress
12 ¼ × 9 ¼ in. (31.1 × 23.5 cm)
The Museum of Modern Art, New York, Gift of Suzanne Slesin, 698.2013

Cat. 3 [Fig. 24]
Jan Tschichold (Swiss, born Germany, 1902–1974)
Die Frau ohne Namen (The Woman Without a Name), Phoebus Palast poster, 1927
Printer: Gebrüder Obpacher AG, Munich
Photolithograph
48 ¾ × 34 in. (123.8 × 86.4 cm)
The Museum of Modern Art, New York, Peter Stone Poster Fund, 225.1978

Cat. 4 [Fig. 10]
Theo van Doesburg (born Christian Emil Marie Küpper, Dutch, 1883–1931), possibly with Vilmos Huszár (Dutch, born Hungary, 1884–1960)
De Stijl NB 73/74, 1926
Letterpress
8 ⅝ × 10 ⅞ in. (21.9 × 27.6 cm)
The Museum of Modern Art, New York, Jan Tschichold Collection, Gift of Philip Johnson, 674.1999

Cat. 5 [see Fig. 49]
Kurt Schwitters (German, 1887–1948)
Merz no. 11, *Typoreklame* (Typographic advertising), page 97, 1924

Printer: A. Molling & Comp., Hanover
Letterpress
11 ¾ × 8 ¾ in. (29.8 × 22.2 cm)
The Museum of Modern Art, New York, Jan Tschichold Collection, Gift of Philip Johnson, 912.1999

Cat. 6
Kurt Schwitters (German, 1887–1948)
Merz, 1926–27
Letterpress
11 × 11 1⁄16 in. (27.9 × 28.1 cm)
The Museum of Modern Art, New York, Jan Tschichold Collection, Gift of Philip Johnson, 917.1999

Cat. 7 [Fig. 80]
Kurt Schwitters (German, 1887–1948)
Die neue Gestaltung in der Typographie (The New Design in Typography) brochure, 1930
Letterpress
5 ⅞ × 4 ¼ in. (14.9 × 10.8 cm)
The Museum of Modern Art, New York, Jan Tschichold Collection, Gift of Philip Johnson, 921.1999.2

Cat. 8 [Fig. 4]
El Lissitzky (Russian,
1890–1941)
Pro dva kvadrata (About Two
Squares) by El Lissitzky, 1920
Printer: E. Haberland, Leipzig
Publisher: Skythen, Berlin, 1922
Letterpress
11 × 8 ¾ in. (28 × 22.3 cm)
The Museum of Modern Art,
New York, Jan Tschichold
Collection, Gift of Philip
Johnson, 562.1977

Cat. 9
El Lissitzky (Russian,
1890–1941)
Merz-Matinéen (Merz Mati-
nees) advertisement, 1923
Publisher: Robert Leunis &
Chapman, Hanover
Letterpress
9 × 11 in. (22.9 × 27.9 cm)
The Museum of Modern Art,
New York, Jan Tschichold
Collection, Gift of Philip
Johnson, 561.1977

Cat. 10
El Lissitzky (Russian,
1890–1941)
*Khorosho! Oktyabrskaya
poema* (Good! October Poem)
by Vladimir Mayakovsky, book
cover, 1927
Publisher: Gosudarstvennoe iz-
datel'stvo, Moscow-Leningrad
Letterpress
8 ⅜ × 11 ⅝ in. (21.3 × 29.5 cm)
The Museum of Modern Art,
New York, Jan Tschichold
Collection, Gift of Philip
Johnson, 564.1977

Cat. 11
John Heartfield (born Helmut
Herzfelde, German, 1891–1968)
*Zum Krisen - Parteitag der
SPD* (On the Occasion of the
Crisis - Party Congress of the
SPD), 1931
Publisher: Arbeiter Illustrierte
Zeitung, Berlin
Photolithograph
13 ⅞ × 10 ¼ in. (35.2 × 26 cm)

The Museum of Modern Art,
New York, Jan Tschichold
Collection, Gift of Philip
Johnson, 685.1999

Cat. 12
László Moholy-Nagy
(American, born Hungary,
1895–1946)
*Staatliches Bauhaus Weimar
1919–1923* (State Bauhaus
Weimar …) prospectus, 1923
Publisher: Bauhaus Verlag,
Munich
Letterpress
9 ⅞ × 9 ⅞ in. (25.1 × 25.1 cm)
The Museum of Modern Art,
New York, Jan Tschichold
Collection, Gift of Philip
Johnson, 763.1999

Cat. 13
László Moholy-Nagy
(American, born Hungary,
1895–1946)
Der Direktor des Staatlichen
Bauhauses zu Weimar (The
Director of the State Bauhaus
in Weimar) letterhead, ca.
1923
Letterpress
11 ¼ × 8 ¹⁵⁄₁₆ in. (28.6 × 22.7 cm)
The Museum of Modern Art,
New York, Jan Tschichold
Collection, Gift of Philip
Johnson, 571.1977

Cat. 14 [Figs. 14, 16]
Herbert Bayer (American,
born Austria, 1900–1985)
and László Moholy-Nagy
(American, born Hungary,
1895–1946)
*Staatliches Bauhaus in Weimar
1919–1923* (State Bauhaus in
Weimar …) catalogue, 1923
Publisher: Bauhaus Verlag,
Weimar and Munich
Letterpress and lithography
9 ⅞ × 10 × ⅞ in. (25.1 × 25.5 ×
2.2 cm)
The Museum of Modern Art,
New York, Jan Tschichold
Collection, Gift of Philip
Johnson, 570.1999

Cat. 15
Herbert Bayer (American,
born Austria, 1900–1985)
Der Direktor Bauhaus Dessau,
Hochschule für Gestaltung
(The Director of the Bauhaus
Dessau, School of Design)
letterhead, 1927
Printer: Bauhausdruck, Dessau,
Germany
Letterpress
11 ¹¹⁄₁₆ × 8 ¼ in. (29.7 × 20.9 cm)
The Museum of Modern Art,
New York, Jan Tschichold
Collection, Gift of Philip
Johnson, 545.1977

Cat. 16
John Heartfield (born Helmut
Herzfelde, German, 1891–1968)
Der Sumpf (The Swamp) by
Upton Sinclair, book jacket,
1922
Publisher: Malik Verlag, Berlin
Letterpress
7 ⅜ × 17 ½ in. (18.7 × 44.5 cm)
The Museum of Modern Art,
New York, Jan Tschichold
Collection, Gift of Philip
Johnson, 678.1999

Cat. 17 [Fig. 34]
Aleksandr Rodchenko
(Russian, 1891–1956)
Pro eto (About This) by
Vladimir Mayakovsky, book,
1923
Publisher: Gosudarstvennoe
izdatel'stvo, Moscow
Letterpress
9 ⅛ × 6 in. (23.2 × 15.3 cm)
The Museum of Modern Art,
New York, Jan Tschichold
Collection, Gift of Philip
Johnson, 813.1999

Cat. 18 [Fig. 43]
Filippo Tommaso Marinetti
(Italian, 1876–1944)
"Après la Marne, Joffre visita
le front en auto" (After the
Marne, Joffre Visited the
Front in an Automobile) from
Les mots en liberté futuristes
by F.T. Marinetti, 1919

Publisher: Edizioni Futuriste di Poesia, Milan
Letterpress
10 ³⁄₁₆ × 9 ¼ in. (25.9 × 23.5 cm)
The Museum of Modern Art, New York, Jan Tschichold Collection, Gift of Philip Johnson, 598.1977.3

Cat. 19
Max Burchartz (German, 1887–1961)
Fordern Sie Forkardt-Futter (Ask for Forkardt chucks) advertisement, ca. 1926–28
Letterpress
11 ¹¹⁄₁₆ × 8 ¼ in. (29.7 × 21 cm)
The Museum of Modern Art, New York, Jan Tschichold Collection, Gift of Philip Johnson, 608.1999

Cat. 20
Max Burchartz (German, 1887–1961)
Werbe-Bau (Advertising construction) postcard, 1925–26
Letterpress
2 ¹⁵⁄₁₆ × 4 ⅛ in. (7.5 × 10.5 cm)
The Museum of Modern Art, New York, Jan Tschichold Collection, Gift of Philip Johnson, 603.1999

Cat. 21
László Moholy-Nagy (American, born Hungary, 1895–1946)
Deutsche Messingwerke: Metallprofile für jeden Verwendungszweck (German brass works: metal profiles for every purpose) cover proof, ca. 1930s
Letterpress
14 ½ × 19 ⅞ in. (36.8 × 50.5 cm)
The Museum of Modern Art, New York, Jan Tschichold Collection, Gift of Philip Johnson, 744.1999

Cat. 22 [Fig. 78]
Kurt Schwitters (German, 1887–1948)
6 Punkte bilden die Vorzüge

der Stopfbüchslosen, Rheinhütte Säurepumpen, Weise Söhne, Halle/S (Six points create advantages for ... acid pumps, Weise Sons, Halle/Saale) brochure, ca. 1927
Letterpress
11 ¾ × 8 ¾ in. (29.8 × 22.2 cm)
The Museum of Modern Art, New York, Jan Tschichold Collection, Gift of Philip Johnson, 925.1999

Cat. 23
Johannes Molzahn (German, 1892–1965)
Nema Werkzeugmaschinen-Fabrik (Nema machine tool factory) leaflet, 1925–30
Letterpress
11 ¹¹⁄₁₆ × 8 ⁵⁄₁₆ in. (29.7 × 21.1 cm)
The Museum of Modern Art, New York, Jan Tschichold Collection, Gift of Philip Johnson, 805.1999

Cat. 24 [Fig. 71]
Max Burchartz (German, 1887–1961)
Europas grösste industriekonzerne Besitzen Europas höchste Schornsteine, Erbaut von J. Ferbeck & Cie. (Europe's largest industrial corporations have Europe's highest smokestacks, built ...) advertisement, 1928–30
Printer: Graphische Anstalt der Fried. Krupp A.G., Essen, Germany
Letterpress
11 ¹¹⁄₁₆ × 8 ⁵⁄₁₆ in. (29.7 × 21.1 cm)
The Museum of Modern Art, New York, Jan Tschichold Collection, Gift of Philip Johnson, 610.1999

Cat. 25 [Fig. 66]
Max Burchartz (German, 1887–1961)
Wehag brochure, 1930
Printer: W. Giradet, Essen
Letterpress and gravure
11 5/8 × 8 1/4 in. (29.5 × 21 cm)
The Museum of Modern Art,

New York, Jan Tschichold Collection, Gift of Philip Johnson, 611.1999

Cat. 26
Max Burchartz (German, 1887–1961)
Vierradbremse "Poulet" (Poulet, four-wheel brakes) advertisement, ca. 1925–26
Letterpress
18 × 12 ⅜ in. (45.7 × 31.4 cm)
The Museum of Modern Art, New York, Jan Tschichold Collection, Gift of Philip Johnson, 605.1999

Cat. 27
Designer unknown
Farp-Patent-Index leaflet, ca. 1926
Letterpress
11 ¹¹⁄₁₆ × 8 ⁵⁄₁₆ in. (29.7 × 21.1 cm)
The Museum of Modern Art, New York, Jan Tschichold Collection, Gift of Philip Johnson, 626.1999

Cat. 28
Designer unknown
Bergal-Senkel unübertroffen! (Bergal-Senkel unsurpassed!) advertisement, ca. 1930
Letterpress
11 ¹¹⁄₁₆ × 8 ¼ in. (29.7 × 21 cm)
The Museum of Modern Art, New York, Jan Tschichold Collection, Gift of Philip Johnson, 1125.1999

Cat. 29
Walter Dexel (German, 1890–1973)
Bauten der Technik: Das Licht im Dienste der Werbung, Ausstellung am Adolf-Mittag-See (Building for Technology: Light in the Service of Advertising, Exhibition at ...) poster, 1929
Printer: W. Pfannkuch & Co., Magdeburg, Germany
Lithograph
38 × 23 ½ in. (96.5 × 59.7 cm)
The Museum of Modern Art,

New York, Purchase Fund, Jan Tschichold Collection, 308.1937

Cat. 30 [Fig. 88]
Lajos Kozma (Hungarian, 1884–1948)
Korszerü Vas-ès Fém Portàlok (State of the Art Metal and Iron . . .) *Markus Lajos RT* brochure, ca. 1930
Lithograph
11 ¾ × 8 ¼ in. (29.8 × 21 cm)
Private Collection, New York

Cat. 31
Piet Zwart (Dutch, 1885–1977)
PCH advertisement, 1929
Letterpress
11 ¹¹⁄₁₆ × 16 ⁹⁄₁₆ in. (29.7 × 42.2 cm)
The Museum of Modern Art, New York, Jan Tschichold Collection, Gift of Philip Johnson, 610.1977

Cat. 32
László Moholy-Nagy (American, born Hungary, 1895–1946)
Die neue Linie (The New Line) no. 1, cover, September 1929
Printer: Otto Beyer, Leipzig and Berlin
Letterpress
14 ½ × 10 ⅜ in. (36.8 × 26.4 cm)
The Museum of Modern Art, New York, Jan Tschichold Collection, Gift of Philip Johnson, 772.1999.2

Cat. 33
Gustav Klutsis (Latvian, 1895–1938)
All Union Spartakiada Sporting Event Moscow postcard, 1928
Offset lithograph
5 ¾ × 4 ⅛ in. (14.1 × 10.5 cm)
The Museum of Modern Art, New York, Purchase, 449.1992.2

Cat. 34
Gustav Klutsis (Latvian, 1895–1938)

Budni letayuschih ludei (The everyday life of aviators) by Nikolai Bobrov, book cover, 1928
Publisher: The Moscow Worker, Soviet Union
Line block, halftone relief, and letterpress
15⁄16 × 12 ¼ in. (22.7 × 31.2 cm)
The Museum of Modern Art, New York, Jan Tschichold Collection, Gift of Philip Johnson, 557.1977

Cat. 35
Joost Schmidt (German, 1893–1948)
Dessau: Auf dem Boden alter Kultur – lebendiges Schaffen der Gegenwart (Dessau: On the Ground of Old Culture – Active Creation for the Present) brochure, 1931
Publisher: Gemeinnütziger Verein Dessau
Printer: Bauhausdruck, C. Dünnhaupt, Dessau
Letterpress
9 ¹⁄₁₆ × 9 ¼ in. (23 × 23.5 cm)
The Museum of Modern Art, New York, Jan Tschichold Collection, Gift of Philip Johnson, 901.1999

Cat. 36
Anton Stankowski (German, 1906–1998)
Orion brochure, ca. 1930
Lithograph and letterpress
8 ¼ × 5 ⅞ in. (21 × 14.9 cm)
The Museum of Modern Art, New York, Jan Tschichold Collection, Gift of Philip Johnson, 974.1999

Cat. 37 [Fig. 79]
Herbert Bayer (American, born Austria, 1900–1985)
Werbe Entwurf und Ausführung (Advertising Design and Realization) advertisement, 1928
Printer: Bauhausdruck, Dessau
Letterpress
4 ¼ × 5 ¹³⁄₁₆ in. (10.8 × 14.8 cm)

The Museum of Modern Art, New York, Jan Tschichold Collection Gift of Philip Johnson, 533.1999

Cat. 38
László Moholy-Nagy (American, born Hungary, 1895–1946)
14 Bauhausbücher (14 Bauhaus books) prospectus, 1928
Publisher: Albert Langen Verlag, Munich
Letterpress
5 ¹⁵⁄₁₆ × 8 ⁵⁄₁₆ in. (15.1 × 21.1 cm)
The Museum of Modern Art, New York, Jan Tschichold Collection, Gift of Philip Johnson, 568.1977.1

Cat. 39
Paul (Geert Paul Hendrikus) Schuitema (Dutch, 1897–1973)
Model Z, zoo duidelijk zoo klein, elke streep 5 gram (Model Z, so clear so small, every dash 5 grams), *N.V. Mij. Van Berkel, Rotterdam* leaflet, 1928
Letterpress
8 ¼ × 5 ½ in. (20.9 × 13.9 cm)
The Museum of Modern Art, New York, Jan Tschichold Collection, Gift of Philip Johnson, 585.1977

Cat. 40 [Fig. 86]
Zdeněk Rossmann (Czech, 1905–1984)
Žena doma (Woman at Home) exhibition catalogue, 1929
Printer: Letovice Humana, Prague
Letterpress
9 × 6 in. (23 × 15.3 cm)
The Museum of Modern Art, New York, Jan Tschichold Collection, Gift of Philip Johnson, 858.1999

Cat. 41 [Fig. 65]
Johannes Canis (German, 1895–1977)
Fortschritt-Stuhl (Fortschritt

chair) advertisement, 1928–29
Letterpress
9 ⅞ × 7 ⅞ in. (25.1 × 20 cm)
The Museum of Modern Art,
New York, Jan Tschichold
Collection Gift of Philip
Johnson, 966.1999

Cat. 42 [Fig. 81]
Max Burchartz (German,
1887–1961)
*Internationale Ausstellung
Kunst der Werbung, Essen
1931* (International Exhibition:
Art of Advertising . . .) poster,
1931
Printer: Graphische Anstalt F.
W. Rohden, Essen
Offset lithograph
23 ¼ × 33 in. (59.1 × 83.8 cm)
The Museum of Modern Art,
New York, Purchase, 1961,
174.1991

Cat. 43 [Fig. 39]
Aleksandr Rodchenko
(Russian, 1891–1956)
*Novyi LEF: Zhurnal levogo
fronta iskusstv* (New LEF:
Journal of the Left Front of
the Arts) 6, 1927
Publisher: Gosudarstvennoe
izdatel'stvo, Moscow
Letterpress
9 × 6 ¹⁄₁₆ in. (22.8 × 15.4 cm)
The Museum of Modern Art,
New York, Jan Tschichold
Collection Gift of Philip
Johnson, 820.1999

Cat. 44 [Fig. 74]
Max Burchartz (German,
1887–1961)
*Tanzfestspiele zum 2.
Deutschen tänzerkongress
Essen 1928* (Dance Festival
at the Second German Dance
Congress . . .) poster, 1928
Printer: F. W. Rohden, Essen
Photolithograph
35 ½ × 33 ¼ in. (90.2 × 84.5 cm)
The Museum of Modern Art,
New York, Purchase Fund,
Jan Tschichold Collection,
326.1937

Cat. 45
Paul Schuitema (Geert Paul
Hendrikus, Dutch, 1897–1973)
Nutricia, le lait en poudre
(Nutricia, powdered milk)
advertisement, 1927–28
Letterpress
14 ½ × 11 ¹³⁄₁₆ in. (36.8 × 30.0 cm)
The Museum of Modern Art,
New York, Jan Tschichold
Collection, Gift of Philip
Johnson, 584.1977

Cat. 46
László Moholy-Nagy (Ameri-
can, born Hungary, 1895–1946)
*Bauen in Frankreich, Bauen
in Eisen, Bauen in Eisenbeton*
(Building in France, Building
in Iron, Building in Ferro-
concrete) by Sigfried Giedion,
book cover, 1928
Publisher: Klinkhardt & Bier-
mann Verlag, Leipzig and Berlin
Letterpress
10 ½ × 7 ⅝ in. (26.7 × 19.4 cm)
The Museum of Modern Art,
New York, Jan Tschichold
Collection, Gift of Philip
Johnson, 753.1999

Cat. 47
Aleksandr Rodchenko
(Russian, 1891–1956)
Materializatsia fantastiki (Ma-
terialization of the Fantastic)
by Ilya Erenberg, 1927
Publisher: Kinopechat',
Moscow-Leningrad
Letterpress
6 ⅞ × 5 ³⁄₁₆ in. (17.5 × 13.2 cm)
The Museum of Modern Art,
New York, Jan Tschichold
Collection, Gift of Philip
Johnson, 572.1977

Cat. 48
Anton Stankowski (German,
1906–1998)
*Buchstaben und Schriften BAG
A–Z* (Letters and Fonts BAG
A–Z) catalogue, 1929–34
Printer: Max Dalang, A.G.,
Zurich
Letterpress

5 ¾ × 8 ¼ in. (14.6 × 21 cm)
The Museum of Modern Art,
New York, Jan Tschichold
Collection, Gift of Philip
Johnson, 965.1999

Cat. 49
Designer unknown
*Hafen: Die öffentlichen
Hafenanlagen der Stadt
Magdeburg* (Port: The Public
Port Facilities of the City of
Magdeburg) brochure, ca.
1929–31
Printer: Wohlfeld, Magdeburg
Letterpress
7 × 10 in. (17.8 × 25.4 cm)
The Museum of Modern Art,
New York, Jan Tschichold
Collection, Gift of Philip
Johnson, 1179.1999

Cat. 50
Gustav Klutsis (Latvian,
1895–1938)
*The Development of Trans-
portation is One of the Main
Tasks of the Five-Year Plan*
poster, 1929
Gravure
28 ⅞ × 19 ⅞ in. (73.3 × 50.5 cm)
The Museum of Modern Art,
New York, Purchase fund, Jan
Tschichold Collection, 146.1968

Cat. 51
Sergei Senkin (Russian,
1894–1963) and Gustav Klutsis
(Latvian, 1895–1938)
*May Day: We fight for the Five-
Year Plan, for the Bolshevik
tempo, for the armament of
the USSR, for the International
October* [Revolution] poster,
1931
Lithograph
40 ⅝ × 28 ¾ in. (103.2 × 73 cm)
The Museum of Modern Art,
New York, Purchase Fund, Jan
Tschichold Collection, 358.1937

Cat. 52 [Fig. 53]
Hans Leistikow (German,
1892–1962) and Grete
Leistikow (German, 1893–1989)

Das neue Frankfurt (The New Frankfurt) 3, nos. 7–8, cover, July–August 1929
Printer and publisher: Englert und Schlosser, Frankfurt am Main
Lithograph
10 5/16 × 9 1/2 in. (26.2 × 24.1 cm)
Private Collection, New York

Cat. 53 [Fig. 77]
Johannes Molzahn (German, 1892–1965)
Wohnung und Werkraum (Dwelling and Workplace) poster, 1929
Printer: Druckerei Schenkalowsky, A.G., Breslau
Lithograph
23 5/8 × 33 in. (60 × 83.8 cm)
The Museum of Modern Art, New York, Purchase Fund, Jan Tschichold Collection, 346.1937

Cat. 54
Johannes Molzahn (German, 1892–1965)
Wohnung und Werkraum envelope, 1929
Offset lithograph
9 × 12 3/4 in. (22.9 × 32.4 cm)
The Museum of Modern Art, New York, Jan Tschichold Collection, Gift of Philip Johnson, 796.1999

Cat. 55 [Fig. 76]
Johannes Molzahn (German, 1892–1965)
Wohnung und Werkraum advertisement, 1929
Letterpress on cellophane
2 1/4 × 5 3/4 in. (5.7 × 14.6 cm)
The Museum of Modern Art, New York, Jan Tschichold Collection, Gift of Philip Johnson, 797.1999

Cat. 56
Johannes Molzahn (German, 1892–1965)
Besucht die Werkbundausstellung in Breslau: Wohnung und Werkraum (Visit the

Werkbund Exhibition in Breslau: Dwelling and Workplace) brochure, 1929
Printer: Friedrichdruck, Breslau
Offset photolithograph
8 1/4 × 4 3/8 in. (21 × 11.1 cm)
The Museum of Modern Art, New York, Jan Tschichold Collection, Gift of Philip Johnson, 801.1999

Cat. 57
Johannes Molzahn (German, 1892–1965)
Wohnung und Werkraum letterhead, 1929
Letterpress
11 11/16 × 8 1/4 in. (29.7 × 21 cm)
The Museum of Modern Art, New York, Jan Tschichold Collection Gift of Philip Johnson, 795.1999

Cat. 58
Johannes Molzahn (German, 1892–1965)
Wohnung und Werkraum brochure, 1929
Printer: Friedrichdruck, Breslau
Offset photolithograph
11 3/4 × 8 5/16 in. (29.8 × 21.1 cm)
The Museum of Modern Art, New York, Jan Tschichold Collection, Gift of Philip Johnson, 793.1999

Cat. 59
Herbert Bayer (American, born Austria, 1900–1985)
Tapetenhaus Rühl (Rühl's House of Wallpaper) envelope, 1925–26
Printer: Bauhausdruck, Dessau
Letterpress
4 1/2 × 6 3/8 in. (11.4 × 16.2 cm)
The Museum of Modern Art, New York, Jan Tschichold Collection, Gift of Philip Johnson, 581.1999

Cat. 60
Herbert Bayer (American, born Austria, 1900–1985)
Tapetenhaus Rühl (Rühl's House of Wallpaper)

letterhead, 1925
Printer: Bauhausdruck, Dessau
Letterpress
11 1/4 × 8 1/4 in. (28.6 × 21 cm)
The Museum of Modern Art, New York, Jan Tschichold Collection, Gift of Philip Johnson, 579.1999

Cat. 61 [Fig. 73]
Herbert Bayer (American, born Austria, 1900–1985)
Fagus Schaftmodelle (Fagus shoe lasts) brochure, 1925
Printer: Bauhausdruck, Dessau
Letterpress
5 3/4 × 8 1/4 in. (14.6 × 21)
The Museum of Modern Art, New York, Jan Tschichold Collection, Gift of Philip Johnson, 578.1999

Cat. 62
Joost Schmidt (German, 1893–1948)
YKO Bürobedarf (YKO office supplies), Paul Henss Weimar letterhead, ca. 1924
Printer: Paul Henss Weimar
Letterpress
11 1/4 × 8 7/8 in. (28.6 × 22.5 cm)
The Museum of Modern Art, New York, Jan Tschichold Collection, Gift of Philip Johnson, 896.1999

Cat. 63 [Fig. 70]
Joost Schmidt (German, 1893–1948)
YKO Bürobedarf catalogue, 1924
Letterpress
9 5/8 × 6 7/8 in. (24.4 × 17.4 cm)
The Museum of Modern Art, New York, Jan Tschichold Collection, Gift of Philip Johnson, 895.1999

Cat. 64 [Fig. 5]
Piet Zwart (Dutch, 1885–1977)
Paper: Insulated High Tension Cables, High Ionization Voltage, Low Dielectric Loss NKF. Nederlandsche Kabel-Fabriek Delft (Holland) brochure,

ca. 1925
Letterpress
11 5/8 × 8 1/4 in. (29.6 × 20.9 cm)
The Museum of Modern Art,
New York, Jan Tschichold
Collection, Gift of Philip
Johnson, 615.1977

Cat. 65 [Fig. 69]
Piet Zwart (Dutch, 1885–1977)
N.V. Nederlandsche Kabel-
fabriek Delft, Koperdraad in
Elk Profiel; Netherlands Cable
Works Ltd Delft (Holland),
Copper Wire—Any Shape
brochure, ca. 1928
Letterpress
12 × 8 3/8 in. (30.3 × 21.3 cm)
The Museum of Modern Art,
New York, Jan Tschichold
Collection, Gift of Philip
Johnson, 617.1977

Cat. 66
Piet Zwart (Dutch, 1885–1977)
NKF (Netherlands Cable
Works) brochure, 1928
Printer: N.V. Drukkerij Trio,
The Hague
Lithograph
16 1/2 × 11 3/4 in. (42.0 × 29.8 cm)
The Museum of Modern Art,
Jan Tschichold Collection, Gift
of Philip Johnson, 612.1977

Cat. 67
Typographische Mitteilungen
(Typographic Studies) 27, no. 2,
February 1930
Publisher: Bildungsverband der
deutschen Buchdrucker, Berlin
Letterpress
12 1/4 × 9 1/4 in. (31.1 × 23.5 cm)
Private Collection, New York

Cat. 68
Designer unknown
Nyomdász Évkonyv és
Útikalauz (Printers' Almanac),
1931 and 1933
Publisher: The Hungarian
Printers' Association and
Printers' Relief Society,
Budapest
Each: 5 3/4 × 3 3/4 × 3/8 in.

(14.6 × 9.5 × 1 cm)
Private Collection, New York

Cat. 69
Designer unknown
Szenzációs az SHB Kistmo-
torkerékpár Sachs-Motorral
(The small SHB motorcycle
with the Sachs-engine is sen-
sational), Schweitzer Henrik,
Budapest, advertisement,
ca. 1935
Lithograph
11 5/8 × 8 1/4 in. (29.5 × 21 cm)
Private Collection, New York

Cat. 70
Designer unknown
Pelikan Caoutchouc Kohlenpa-
pier . . . (Pelikan carbon paper)
packaging, after 1928
Offset lithograph
13 7/16 × 8 5/8 in. (34.1 × 21.9 cm)
The Museum of Modern Art,
New York, Jan Tschichold
Collection, Gift of Philip
Johnson, 1223.1999

Cat. 71
Designer unknown
Neue Kunst Fides: Abteilung
für neuzeitliche Wohnung-
skultur (Neue Kunst Fides:
Department of Modern Living)
advertisement, 1926
Letterpress
5 13/16 × 4 3/16 in. (14.8 × 10.6 cm)
The Museum of Modern Art,
New York, Jan Tschichold
Collection, Gift of Philip
Johnson, 604.1977

Cat. 72
El Lissitzky (Russian,
1890–1941)
Siegellack Pelikan (Pelikan
sealing wax) packaging, 1924
Printer: Günther Wagner,
Hannover und Wien
Letterpress
4 3/8 × 13 3/4 in. (11.1 × 34.9 cm)
The Museum of Modern Art,
New York, Jan Tschichold
Collection, Gift of Philip
Johnson, 721.1999

Cat. 73 [Fig. 57]
Walter Dexel (German,
1890–1973)
Neue deutsche Baukunst,
Kunstverein Jena (New German
Architecture, Jena Art Society)
announcement, 1924
Letterpress
5 15/16 × 5 15/16 in. (15.0 × 15.0 cm)
The Museum of Modern Art,
New York, Jan Tschichold
Collection, Gift of Philip
Johnson, 550.1977

Cat. 74 [Fig. 58]
Walter Dexel (German,
1890–1973)
Thüringer Verlagsanstalt und
Druckerei (Thuringian Publish-
ing House and Press) *G.m.b.H.*
Jena calendar, 1927
Printer: Thüringer Verlag-
sanstalt und Druckerei, Jena,
Germany
Letterpress
12 9/16 × 9 3/4 in. (31.9 × 24.8 cm)
The Museum of Modern Art,
New York, Jan Tschichold
Collection, Gift of Philip
Johnson, 652.1999

Cat. 75
Designer unknown (possibly
Georg Trump)
Die neue Baukunst als Aus-
druck moderner Lebensgestal-
tung (The New Architecture
as an Expression of Modern
Life) poster, ca. 1928
Letterpress
13 × 17 1/4 in. (33 × 43.8cm)
The Museum of Modern Art,
New York, Purchase Fund,
Jan Tschichold Collection,
302.1937

Cat. 76
Walter Dexel (German,
1890–1973)
Verwende stets nur Gas . . .
Spart Arbeit Zeit Geld (Use
Only Gas . . . Saves Work Time
Money) poster, 1924
Letterpress
19 × 25 1/2 in. (48.3 × 64.8 cm)

The Museum of Modern Art, New York, Abby Aldrich Rockefeller Purchase Fund, 303.1937

Cat. 77
Georg Trump (German, 1896–1985)
Deutsche Schriften der Schriftgießerei, H. Berthold A.G. Berlin SW 61, Selbaldus-Gotisch, Probe Nr. 281 (German Fonts of the Typefoundry, H. Berthold …) catalogue, 1933–34
Printer: H. Berthold A.G., Berlin
Letterpress
11 11/16 × 8 ¼ in. (29.7 × 21 cm)
The Museum of Modern Art, New York, Jan Tschichold Collection, Gift of Philip Johnson, 1008.1999

Cat. 78
Piet Zwart (Dutch, 1885–1977)
Wij Nu: Experimenteel Tooneel [Vereeniging] (Wij Nu: experimental theater [union]) advertisement, 1925
Letterpress
11 9/16 × 16 ¾ in. (29.3 × 42.6 cm)
The Museum of Modern Art, New York, Jan Tschichold Collection, Gift of Philip Johnson, 609.1977

Cat. 79
Theo H. Ballmer (Swiss, 1902–1965)
Neues Bauen (New Building) poster, 1928
Printer: W. Wasserman, Basel
Lithograph
50 ⅛ × 35 ⅝ in. (127.2 × 90.5 cm)
The Museum of Modern Art, New York, Gift of The Lauder Foundation Leonard and Evelyn Lauder Fund, 253.1980

Cat. 80
Walter Dexel (German, 1890–1973)
Die Form: Zeitschrift für gestaltende Arbeit (The Form: Magazine for Creative Work) 10, no. 5/6, cover, 1934

Publisher: Verlag Hermann Reckendorf, Berlin, for the Deutsche Werkbund
Photolithograph
12 1/16 × 9 3/16 in (30.6 × 23.3 cm)
Private Collection, New York

Cat. 81
Piet Zwart (Dutch, 1885–1977)
Internationale Tentoonstelling Op Filmgebied (International Film Festival) poster, 1928
Photolithograph
42 ½ × 30 ⅝ in. (107.9 × 77.7 cm)
The Museum of Modern Art, New York, Acquired by exchange, 205.1968

Cat. 82 [Fig. 59]
Walter Dexel (German, 1890–1973)
Die Sport Ausstellung (The Sport Exhibition) poster, 1929
Printer: W. Pfannkuch & Co., Magdeburg
Lithograph
33 ⅛ × 23 ½ in. (84.1 × 59.7 cm)
The Museum of Modern Art, New York, Purchase Fund, Jan Tschichold Collection, 339.1937

Cat. 83
Max Burchartz (German, 1887–1961) and Johannes Canis (German, 1895–1977)
Fort mit dem Kronleuchter, Werbeblatt 2 (Away with the Chandelier), bulletin 2, 1925
Publisher: Werbebau, Bochum, Germany
Letterpress
11 ⅝ × 8 ¼ in. (29.5 × 21 cm)
The Museum of Modern Art, New York, Jan Tschichold Collection, Gift of Philip Johnson, 623.1999

Cat. 84
Karel Teige (Czech, 1900–1951)
S lodí jež dováží čaj a kávu, Poesie (With the Ship that Brings Tea and Coffee, Poetry) by Konstantin Biebl, book cover, 1928
Publisher: Odeon, Prague

Letterpress
7 ⅞ x 5 ⅛ in. (20.0 x 13.0 cm)
The Museum of Modern Art, New York, Jan Tschichold Collection, Gift of Philip Johnson, 601.1977

Cat. 85
Zdeněk Rossmann (Czech, 1905–1984)
Graficke schema pro konstrukci pisma (Graphic Scheme for Type Production) teaching aid, 1934
Letterpress
11 11/16 × 8 3/16 in. (29.6 × 20.8 cm)
The Museum of Modern Art, New York, Jan Tschichold Collection, Gift of Philip Johnson, 867.1999

Cat. 86
László Moholy-Nagy (American, born Hungary, 1895–1946)
Bauhaus Bücher 5: Piet Mondrian: Neue Gestaltung - Neoplastizismus - Nieuwe Beelding (Bauhaus Books 5, Piet Mondrian: Neoplasticism), 1925
Publisher: Albert Langen Verlag, Munich
Letterpress
9 5/16 × 15 in. (23.7 × 38.1 cm)
The Museum of Modern Art, New York, Jan Tschichold Collection, Gift of Philip Johnson, 569.1977

Cat. 87
Willi Baumeister (German, 1889–1955)
Akademischer Verlag Dr. Fr. Wedekind u. Co. Stuttgart letterhead, 1927
Letterpress
11 1/2 × 8 1/4 in. (29.2 × 21 cm)
The Museum of Modern Art, New York, Elaine Lustig Cohen Collection, Gift of Lawrence Benenson and the Committee on Architecture and Design Funds, 1124.2015.1

Cat. 88
Friedrich Vordemberge-Gildewart (Dutch, born Germany, 1899–1962)
Die Abstrakten Hannover: Ortsgruppe der Internationalen Vereinigung der Expressionisten Futuristen Kubisten und Konstruktivisten (The Abstract Hanover: Local Branch of the International Association of Expressionists Futurists Cubists and Constructivists) letterhead, 1927
Letterpress
11 ⅝ × 8 ⁵⁄₁₆ in. (29.5 × 21.0 cm)
The Museum of Modern Art, New York, Jan Tschichold Collection, Gift of Philip Johnson, 597.1977

Cat. 89 [Fig. 52]
Willi Baumeister (German, 1889–1955)
Wie wohnen? Die Wohnung (How should we live? The Dwelling) *Deutscher Werkbund Ausstellung . . . Stuttgart* poster, 1927
Lithograph
44 ¾ × 32 ⅜ in. (113.7 × 82.2 cm)
The Museum of Modern Art, Gift of Philip Johnson, 364.1950

Cat. 90 [see Fig. 56]
Johannes Molzahn (German, 1892–1965)
Postanschrift: Johs. Molzahn Magdeburg Sternstr. 24 letterhead, 1925–30
Printer: Faber'sche Buchdruckerei, Magdeburg
Letterpress
11 ⅝ × 8 ¼ in. (29.5 × 21 cm)
The Museum of Modern Art, New York, Jan Tschichold Collection, Gift of Philip Johnson, 799 .1999

Cat. 91
Joost Schmidt (German, 1893–1948)
Offset: Buch und Werbekunst, Bauhaus-Heft (Offset: Book and Advertising Art, Bauhaus issue) 2, no. 7, cover, 1926
Publisher: Offset-Verlag, Leipzig
Lithograph
12 ½ × 9 ¾ × 2 ¾ in. (31.75 × 24.77 × 5.08 cm)
Bard Graduate Center

Cat. 92
Designer unknown
Typographische Mitteilungen (Typographic Studies) 28, no. 7 cover, July 1931
Publisher: Bildungsverband der deutschen Buchdrucker, Berlin
Letterpress
12 ¼ × 9 ¼ in. (31.1 × 23.5 cm)
Private Collection, New York

Cat. 93
Jan Tschichold (Swiss, born Germany, 1902–1974)
Thomas Morus Utopia (Utopia by Thomas More), 1920
Calligraphy on handmade paper
10 × 7 in. (25.4 × 17.78 cm)
Collection of Jerry Kelly

Cat. 94 [Fig. 8]
Jan Tschichold (Swiss, born Germany, 1902–1974)
An die Freude, Fünftes Palatino-Buch (Ode to Joy, Fifth Palatino Book) by Friedrich Schiller, 1919
Publisher: Karl Schnabel, Berlin
Calligraphy, transferred by photolithography
9 ½ × 8 in. (24.1 × 20.3 cm)
Collection of Jerry Kelly

Cat. 95
Jan Tschichold (Swiss, born Germany, 1902–1974)
"noch eine neue schrift: beitrag zur frage der ökonomie der schrift" (Another new font: Contribution to the question of the economics of fonts) by Jan Tschichold in *Typographische Mitteilungen* (Typographic Studies) 27, no. 3,

unpaginated supplement, March 1930
Publisher: Bildungsverband der deutschen Buchdrucker, Berlin
Lithograph
12 ¼ × 9 ¼ in. (31.1 × 23.5 cm)
Private Collection, New York

Cat. 96
Designer unknown
"Über die Kritik der Neuen Satzgestaltung: Konstruktivismus und Elementare Typographie" (About the Critique of the New Layout: Constructivism and Elemental Typography) in *Typographische Mitteilungen* (Typographic Studies) 23, no. 8, 214–15, August 1926
Publisher: Bildungsverband der deutschen Buchdrucker, Berlin
Letterpress
12 ¼ × 9 ¼ in. (31.1 × 23.5 cm)
Private Collection, New York

Cat. 97
Jan Tschichold (Swiss, born Germany, 1902–1974)
Das Fahrten und Abenteuerbuch (Book of Travels and Adventures) by Colin Ross, 1930
Publisher: Verlag der Büchergilde Gutenberg, Berlin
9 ¹⁵⁄₁₆ × 6 ¾ × ⅝ in. (24 × 17.3 × 1.5 cm)
Private Collection, New York

Cat. 98
Jan Tschichold (Swiss, born Germany, 1902–1974)
Buster Keaton in: "Der General" Phoebus Palast poster, 1927
Printer: F. Bruckmann A.G., Munich
Offset lithograph
47 × 33 in. (119.4 × 83.8 cm)
The Museum of Modern Art, New York, Gift of the designer, 291.1938

Cat. 99
Jan Tschichold (Swiss, born Germany, 1902–1974)

Edith Tschichold letterhead,
1920s
Letterpress
11 ⅝ × 8 ¼ in. (29.5 × 21 cm)
The Museum of Modern Art,
New York, Elaine Lustig Cohen
Collection, Gift of Lawrence
Benenson and the Committee
on Architecture and Design
Funds, 1377.2015

Cat. 100
Jan Tschichold (Swiss, born
Germany, 1902–1974)
*Phoebus-Palast: Musikalische
und Filmdarbietungen von
Rang; Programm* (Phoebus-
Palast: Music and Film Perfor-
mances by rank; program), 1927
Letterpress
12 ³⁄₁₆ × 9 ³⁄₁₆ in. (31.0 × 23.5 cm)
The Museum of Modern Art,
New York, Jan Tschichold
Collection, Gift of Philip
Johnson, 602.1977

Cat. 101 [Fig. 23]
Jan Tschichold (Swiss, born
Germany, 1902–1974)
Die Hose (The Trousers),
Phoebus Palast poster, 1926
Printer: F. Bruckmann A.G.,
Munich
Offset lithograph
47 × 33 in. (119.3 × 83.8 cm)
The Museum of Modern
Art, New York, Gift of Armin
Hofmann, 1284.1968

Cat. 102 [Fig. 21]
Jan Tschichold (Swiss, born
Germany, 1902–1974)
Nina Chmelowa letterhead,
1924
Letterpress
10 ¼ × 7 ⅞ in. (26 × 20 cm)
The Museum of Modern Art,
New York. Elaine Lustig Cohen
Collection, Gift of Lawrence
Benenson and the Committee
on Architecture and Design
Funds, 1380.2015

Cat. 103
Jan Tschichold (Swiss, born
Germany, 1902–1974)
*König Lear, Macbeth, Timon
von Athen; Shakespeares dra-
matische Werke*, Vol. 2, 1943
Publisher: Birkhauser Verlag,
Basel, Switzerland
7 ⅝ × 4 ¾ in. (19.5 × 12.0 cm)
Private Collection, New York

Cat. 104
Jan Tschichold (Swiss, born
Germany, 1902–1974)
*Die romanischen Glasgemälde
des Strassburger Münsters*
(The Romanesque Glass
Paintings of the Strasbourg
Minster) by Fridtjof Zschokke,
1942
Publisher: Benno Schwabe,
Basel
12 ¾ × 9 in. (32.5 × 23 cm)
Private Collection, New York

Cat. 105
Jan Tschichold (Swiss, born
Germany, 1902–1974)
Selection of Penguin books,
1947–49
Publisher: Penguin Books Ltd.,
Harmondsworth, Middlesex,
Great Britain
Dimensions variable
Private Collection, New York

Cat. 106
Jan Tschichold (Swiss, born
Germany, 1902–1974)
Penguin Composition Rules,
1947
Publisher: Penguin Books Ltd.,
Harmondsworth, Middlesex
11 × 6 in. (27.9 × 15.2 cm)
Collection of Jerry Kelly

Cat. 107
Jan Tschichold (Swiss, born
Germany, 1902–1974)
Penguins Progress, no. 8, 1949
Printer: King and Hutchings
Ltd., Uxbridge, Middlesex
7 × 4 ½ in. (17.8 × 11.4 cm)
Private Collection, New York

Bibliography

Writings by Jan Tschichold
Tschichold was a prolific author of books and articles, generally treating subjects related to printing and graphic design but occasionally touching on other matters as well as the events of his life. While essential as primary sources, his various memoirs and autobiographical writings are sometimes contradictory, especially toward the later stages of his career, when he tended to revise his earlier assessments. For a compilation of his publications and bibliography, see *Schriften 1925–1974*, 2 vols. (Berlin: Brinkman and Bose), 1991–92.

With regard to the main themes of this book, there are two key publications:

"elementare typographie." Special issue, *Typographische Mitteilungen* 22, no. 10 (October 1925): 191–214. Facsimile, Mainz: Hermann Schmidt, 1986.
Die neue Typographie: Ein Handbuch für zeit-gemäss Schaffende. Berlin: Bildungsverband der Deutschen Buchdrucker. 1928. Reprint, Berlin: Brinkman and Bose, 1987. Translated by Ruari McLean as *The New Typography: A Handbook for Modern Designers.* Berkeley: University of California Press, 1995.

Four secondary books written by Tschichold in this period are discussed in the text:

Foto-Auge / Oeil et photo / Photo-eye. Stuttgart: Wedekind, 1929.

Eine Stunde Druckgestaltung: Grundbegriffe der neuen Typografie in Bildbeispielen für Setzer, Werbefachleute, Drucksachenverbraucher und Bibliofilen. Stuttgart: Wedekind, 1930.
Schriftschreiben für Setzer. Frankfurt: Klimsch, 1931.
Typografische Entwurfstechnik. Stuttgart: Wedekind, 1932.

Tschichold's papers and manuscripts are spread throughout several collections in Europe and the Unites States, as are the papers of his friends, collaborators, and contemporary designers. Of these collections, I was able to consult the following:

Jan and Edith Tschichold Papers, Getty Research Institute, Special Collections, Acc. no. 930030.
Ruari McLean Collection, National Library of Scotland, Manuscripts Division, Acc. no. 12125, and Printed Books, Dept. 362 (uncatalogued). McLean worked with Tschichold and maintained a correspondence with him for many years, although the bulk of this material is more relevant to Tschichold's impact on British design.
Other holdings of Tschichold material are listed in Christopher Burke, *Active Literature: Jan Tschichold and New Typography.* London: Hyphen Press, 2007.

Note: Other sources are cited with full publication information in the notes.

Further Readings

Andel, Jaroslav. *Avant-Garde Page Design 1900–1950.* New York: Delano Greenidge, 2002.

Anikst, M., ed. *Soviet Commercial Design of the Twenties.* New York: Abbeville, 1987.

Bartram, Alan. *Bauhaus, Modernism and the Illustrated Book.* London: British Library, 2004.

Baumler, S., ed. *Die Kunst zu Werben: Das Jahrhundert der Reklame.* Munich: Münchner Stadtmuseum, 1996.

Benjamin, Walter. *Illuminations.* London: Fontana, 1973.

——. *One Way Street and Other Writings.* London: Penguin, 2009.

Benson, Timothy, O., ed. *Between Worlds: A Sourcebook of Central European Avant-Gardes, 1910–1930.* Cambridge, MA: MIT Press, 2002.

——. *Central European Avant-Gardes: Exchange and Transformation 1910–1930.* Los Angeles: LACMA, 2002.

Bergdoll, Barry, and Leah Dickerman, eds. *The Bauhaus: Workshops of Modernity.* New York: MoMA, 2009.

Bierut, Michael, William Drenttal, Steven Heller, and D. K. Holland, eds. *Looking Closer: Critical Writings on Graphic Design.* New York: Allworth, 1994.

——. *Looking Closer 3: Classic Writings on Graphic Design.* New York: Allworth, 1999.

Blackwell, Lewis. *Twentieth Century Type.* London: Laurence King, 1992.

Blauvelt, A., ed. "New Perspectives: Critical Histories of Graphic Design." *Visible Language* 28, no. 3 (Spring 1994), no. 4 (Fall 1994), and 29, no. 1 (Winter 1995).

Botar, Oliver. *Sensing the Future: Moholy-Nagy, Media and the Arts.* Zurich: Lars Muller, 2014.

Breuer, Gerda, ed. *Max Burchartz, 1887–1961: Künstler, Typograf, Pädagoge.* Berlin: Jovis, 2010.

——. *Poster Collection: The Magic of Things.* Zurich: Lars Muller, 2012.

Brooker, Peter, et al., eds. *The Oxford Critical and Cultural History of Modernist Magazines,* vol. 3: *Europe 1880–1940.* Oxford: Oxford University Press, 2017.

Broos, Kees, and Paul Hefting. *Dutch Graphic Design: A Century.* Cambridge, MA: MIT Press, 1993.

Buddensieg, Tilman, ed. *Berlin 1900–1933: Architecture and Design.* New York: Cooper-Hewitt Museum, 1987.

Burckhardt, Lucius. *The Werkbund: History and Ideology, 1907–1933.* Woodbury, NY: Barron's, 1980.

Bury, Stephen. *Breaking the Rules: The Printed Face of the European Avant Garde, 1990–1937.* London: British Library, 2007.

Carter, Sebastian. *Twentieth Century Type Designers.* 2nd ed. London: Lund Humphries, 1995.

Chanzit, Gwen. *Herbert Bayer: Collection and Archive at the Denver Museum.* Seattle: University of Washington Press, 1988.

Cohen, Arthur A. *Herbert Bayer: The Complete Work.* Cambridge, MA: MIT Press, 1984.

Constantine, Mildred. *Word and Image: Posters from the Collection of the Museum of Modern Art.* New York: MoMA, 1968.

Csaplár, Ferenc. *Lajos Kassák: The Advertisement and Modern Typography.* Budapest: Kassák Museum, 1999.

Dexel, Walter. *Werkverzeichnis der Druckgrafik von 1915–1971.* Köln: Buchhandlung W. König, 1971.

Dluhosch, Eric, and Rostislav Švácha, eds. *Karel Teige 1900–1951: L'Enfant Terrible of the Czech Modernist Avant-Garde.* Cambridge, MA: MIT Press, 1999.

Doubleday, Richard. *Jan Tschichold Designer: The Penguin Years.* New Castle, DE: Oak Knoll, 2006.

Dreyfus, John. *Into Print: Selected Writings on Printing History, Typography and Book Production.* Boston: Godine, 1995.

Drucker, Johanna. *The Visible Word: Experimental Typography and Modern Art 1909–1923.* Chicago: University of Chicago Press, 1996.

Eisele, Petra. *Futura: The Typeface.* London: Laurence King, 2017.

Eskilson, Stephen. *Graphic Design: A New History.* 2nd ed. New Haven, CT: Yale University Press, 2012.

Etlin, R., ed., *Art, Culture, and Media under the Third Reich.* Chicago: University of Chicago Press, 2002.

Evans, David. *John Heartfield: AIZ / VI 1930-38.* New York: Kent, 1992.

Evans, David, and Sylvia Gohl. *Photomontage: A Political Weapon.* London: Fraser, 1986.

Fernandez, Horacio. *Fotografía Pública: Photography in Print 1919-1939.* Madrid: Museo Nacional Centro d'Arte Reina Sofia, 1999.

Fleischmann, Gerd, ed. *Bauhaus: Drucksachen, Typografie, Reklame.* Dusseldorf: Marzona, 1984.

Bibliography

Forty, Adrian. *Objects of Desire: Design and Society since 1750*. London: Thames and Hudson, 1986.

Goodman, S. T., and Jens Hoffmann. *The Power of Pictures: Early Soviet Photography, Early Soviet Film*. New Haven, CT: Yale University Press, 2015.

The Great Utopia: The Russian and Soviet Avant-Garde 1915–1932. New York: Guggenheim Museum, 1992.

Greenhalgh, Paul, ed. *Modernism in Design*. London: Reaktion, 1990.

Gropius, Walter, ed. *Bauhaus 1919–1928*. New York: MoMA, 1938.

Grosskinsky, Manfred, and Birgit Sander, *Willi Baumeister 1889–1955: Die Frankfurter Jahre 1928–1933*. Frankfurt a. M.: Museum Giersch, 2005.

Guffey, Elizabeth. *Posters: A Global History*. London: Reaktion, 2015.

Heller, Steven. *Iron Fists: Branding the 20th Century Totalitarian State*. New York: Phaidon, 2007.

———. *Merz to Émigré and Beyond: Avant-Garde Magazine Design of the Twentieth Century*. London: Phaidon, 2003.

Heller, Steven, and Philip Meggs, eds. *Texts on Type: Critical Writings on Typography*. New York: Allworth, 2001.

Herf, J. *Reactionary Modernism: Technology, Culture and Politics in Weimar and the Third Reich*. Cambridge: Cambridge University Press, 1986.

Heskett, John. *German Design 1870–1918*. New York: Taplinger, 1986.

Hochuli, Jost. *Tschichold in St. Gallen: Jan Tschicholds Arbeitsbibliothek in der Kantonsbibliothek Vadiana St. Gallen*. VGS St. Gallen: Wallstein Verlag, 2016.

Holstein, Jürgen. *Blickfang: Bucheinbände und Schutzumschläge Berliner Verlage 1919–1933*. Berlin: Holstein Verlag, 2005.

Jackman, Jarrell, and Carla Borden, eds. *The Muses Flee Hitler: Cultural Transfer and Adaptation 1930–1945*. Washington, DC: Smithsonian Institution, 1983.

Jobling, Paul, and David Crowley. *Graphic Design: Reproduction and Representation since 1800*. Manchester, UK: Manchester University Press, 1996.

Kaplan, Wendy, ed. *Designing Modernity: The Arts of Reform and Persuasion 1885–1945*. New York: Thames and Hudson, 1995.

Kermer, Wolfgang. *Willi Baumeister: Typographie und Reklamegestaltung*. Stuttgart: Edition Cantz, 1989.

Khan-Magomedov, Selim. *Rodchenko: The Complete Work*. London: Thames and Hudson, 1986.

Kostelanetz, Richard, ed. *Moholy-Nagy: An Anthology*. New York: Praeger, 1970.

Lampe, Angela. *Chagall, Lissitzky, Malevich: The Russian Avant-Garde in Vitebsk, 1918–1922*. New York: The Jewish Museum, 2018.

Lavin, Maud. *Cut with the Kitchen Knife: The Weimar Photomontages of Hannah Höch*. New Haven, CT: Yale University Press, 1993.

Le Coultre, Martijn, and Alston Purvis. *Jan Tschichold: Posters of the Avantgarde*. Basel: Birkhauser, 2007.

Lebeck, Robert, and Bodo von Dewitz. *Kiosk: A History of Photojournalism*. Gottingen: Seidl, 2001.

Lissitzky-Küppers, Sophie. *El Lissitzky: Life, Letters, Texts*. Greenwich, CT: New York Graphic Society, 1968.

Lodder, Christina. *Russian Constructivism*. New Haven, CT: Yale University Press, 1983.

Lupton, Ellen, and Elaine Lustig Cohen. *Letters from the Avant Garde*. New York: Princeton Architectural Press, 1997.

Lupton, Ellen, and J. Abbot Miller. *Design Writing Research: Writing on Graphic Design*. New York: Allworth, 1996.

Margolin, Victor. *The Struggle for Utopia: Rodchenko, Lissitzky, Moholy-Nagy*. Chicago: University of Chicago Press, 1997.

McLean, Ruari. *Jan Tschichold: A Life in Typography*. New York: Princeton Architectural Press, 1997.

———. *Jan Tschichold: Typographer*. London: Lund Humphries, 1975.

———. *Typographers on Type: An Illustrated Anthology from William Morris to the Present Day*. London: Lund Humphries, 1995.

Molzahn, Johannes. *Das druckgraphische Werk*. Duisburg: Wilhelm-Lehmbruck-Museum, 1977.

Moran, James. *The Double Crown Club: A History of Fifty Years*. London: Westerham, 1974.

———. *Printing in the 20th Century: A Penrose Anthology*. London: Northwood, 1974.

———. *Printing Presses: History and Development from the Fifteenth Century to Modern Times*. London: Faber, 1973.

Neue Sachlichkeit and German Realism of the Twenties. London: Arts Council, 1978.

Nisbet, Peter, ed. *El Lissitzky, 1890–1941*. Cambridge, MA: Harvard Art Museums, 1987.

Pachnicke, Peter, and Klaus Honnef. *John Heart-field*. New York: Abrams, 1992.

Pavitt, Jane. *Brand New*. London: Victoria & Albert Museum, 2000.

Perloff, Nancy, and Brian Reed, eds. *Situating El Lissitzky: Vitebsk, Berlin, Moscow*. Los Angeles: Getty Research Institute, 2003.

Peto, James, and Donna Loveday. *Modern Britain, 1929–1939*. London: Design Museum, 1999.

Public Photographic Spaces: Exhibitions of Propaganda, from "Pressa" to "The Family of Man," 1928–55. Barcelona: Museu d'Art Contemporani, 2008.

Purvis, Alston. *Dutch Graphic Design 1918–1945*. New York: Van Nostrand Reinhold, 1992.

Rainey, Lawrence, Christine Poggi, and Laura Wittman, eds. *Futurism: An Anthology*. New Haven, CT: Yale University Press, 2009.

Rattemeyer, Volker, et al. *Typographie kann unter Umständen Kunst sein*. 3 vols. Wiesbaden: Das Museum, 1990.

Rosenfeld, A., ed. *Defining Russian Graphic Arts from Diaghilev to Stalin 1898–1934*. New Brunswick, NJ: Rutgers University Press, 1999.

Rothschild, Deborah, ed. *Graphic Design in the Mechanical Age: Selections from the Merrill C. Berman Collection*. New Haven, CT: Yale University Press, 1998.

Rowell, Margit, Deborah Wye, and Jared Ash. *The Russian Avant-Garde Book 1910–1934*. New York: MoMA, 2002.

Schmoller, Hans. *Two Titans: Mardersteig and Tschichold, a Study in Contrasts*. New York: Typophiles, 1990.

Schwartz, Frederic J. *Blind Spots: Critical Theory and the History of Art in Twentieth-Century Germany*. New Haven, CT: Yale University Press, 2005.

Sobieszek, R. *The Art of Persuasion: A History of Advertising Photography*. New York: Abrams, 1988.

Spencer, Herbert, ed. *The Liberated Page*. San Francisco: Chronicle Books, 1987.

——. *Pioneers of Modern Typography*. London: Lund Humphries, 1969.

Spielmann, Heinz. *Willi Baumeister: Werkkatalog der Druckgraphik*. Ostfildern-Ruit: Hatje Cantz, 2005.

Strauss, Monica J. *Captured Glance: The Avant-Garde and Advertising in the Twenties*. New York: Helen Serger / La Boetie, 1987.

Teitelbaum, Matthew. *Montage and Modern Life 1919–1942*. Cambridge, MA: MIT Press, 1992.

Timmers, Margaret, ed. *The Power of the Poster*. London: Victoria & Albert Museum, 1998.

Tupitsyn, Margarita. *El Lissitzky: Beyond the Abstract Cabinet*. New Haven, CT: Yale University Press, 1999.

——. *Rodchenko and Popova: Defining Constructivism*. London: Tate, 2009.

Twyman, Michael. *A History of Chromolithography: Printed Colour for All*. London: British Library, 2013.

——. *Printing 1770–1970: An Illustrated History of Its Development and Uses in England*. London: British Library, 1970.

Vitt, Walter, ed. *Schöne Tag im Hause Dexel: Das Gästebuch*. Cologne: Galerie Stolz, 1990.

White, Michael. *De Stijl and Dutch Modernism*. Manchester, UK: Manchester University Press, 2003.

Wilk, Christopher, ed. *Modernism: Designing a New World, 1914–1939*. London: Victoria & Albert Museum, 2006.

Willett, John. *Art and Politics in the Weimar Period: The New Sobriety, 1917–1933*. London: Pantheon, 1978.

——. *The Weimar Years: A Culture Cut Short*. London: Thames and Hudson, 1984.

Witkowski, Matthew. *Foto: Modernity in Central Europe, 1918–1945*. Washington, DC: National Gallery, 2007.

Wöbkemeier, Ruth. *Walter Dexel: Bild, Zeichen, Raum*. Bremen: Kunsthalle Bremen, 1990.

——. ed. *Walter Dexel 1890–1973: Werkverzeichnis: Gemälde, Hinterglasbilder, Gouachen, Aquarelle, Collagen, Ölstudien, Entwürfe zu Bühnenbildern*. Heidelberg: Edition Braus, 1995.

Woodham, Jonathan. *Twentieth Century Design*. Oxford: Oxford University Press, 1997.

Zolotkinkina, I. *Posters of the Revolutionary Era*. St. Petersburg: State Museum of Russia, 2017.

Index

A

ABC (Swiss journal), 32, 62, 66, 104, 134, 158n28, 199

advertising and typography, 104, 121–34, 147, 150–51, 175; American model of, 133–34, 141, 166, 181; British disapproval of, 180; Burchartz on, 126, 214–16; Ehrlich on, 183; Kassák on, 132–34, 218–21; Molzahn on, 217

Agha, Mehemed Fehmy, 184

Akzidenz Grotesk, 58

Albers, Josef, 75

Aldus, 13

Altman, Natan, 32, 35

Antiqua, xiv, xv, 57, 186n8, 200

Apollinaire, Guillaume, 15n11, 63, 224

Arntz, Gerd, 138, 140

Arp, Hans, 22, 90, 98

Arts and Crafts movement, 20, 25, 52, 80, 179, 222

asymmetry, 54, 80, 81, 82, 100–101, 110, 167

Atatürk, Mustafa Kemal, xiii

B

Ball, Hugo, 90

Barr, Alfred H., 184

Bauer Type Foundry, xiv, 37, 59, 151, 184

Bauhaus, 13–14, 15n17, 25–28, 83n18-19, 83n24, 110, 157, 167; closing of, 164; Der Ring neue Werbegestalter and, 153–54; graphic design limitations of, 113–14, 159n50; MoMA exhibition of, 185; 1923 exhibition of, 6, 25, 27–28, 30, 88; revival of, 186n12; U.S. reputation of, 159n47

Bauhausbuch series, 94, 156–57

Baumberger, Otto, 32, 156, 167

Baumeister, Willi, 13, 48, 105–9, 159n30; *Das neue Frankfurt* and, 111 *Die Wohnung* exhibition and, 107–8, 109, 144; "Neue Typographie," 106–7, 202–5; on symmetry, 202

Bayer, Herbert, 5, 13, 28, 30, 32, 56, 63, 68, 76, 153, 154; Fagus design, 141–42; Foto-Auge and, 70; Nazis and, 166; in the US, 185; Werbe Entwurf und Ausführung and, 148, 149

Behne, Adolf, 49, 111

Behrendt, Walter Curt, 85n76

Behrens, Peter, 135

Bembo, 13, 179

Benjamin, Walter, 85n66, 87

Benscheidt, Karl, 141

Berlage, Hendrik Petrus, 8

Berlewi, Henryk, 168

Biermann, Aenne, 71

Bildungsverband der Deutschen Buchdrucker, 49

Bill, Max, 13, 15n15, 79, 156; later career of, 167, 186n12

Bismarck, Otto von, 57

blackletter (Gothic), xiv, 57, 165, 186n8, 200

Block group, 168; Blok (journal), 168, 169

Bosselt, Rudolf, 116

Brecht, Bertolt, 14n2, 21

Breuer, Marcel, 1

Brodovitch, Alexey, 184

Buchkunstbewegung, 20, 82n7

Bugra (*Internationale Ausstellung für Buchgewerbe und Graphik*), 20, 82n8

Bukharin, Nikolai, xiii

Burchartz, Max, 5, 22, 32, 45, 48, 76, 105, 113, 135, 165; advertising design and, 123–32; dance festival poster of, 86, 142–43; *Das Lichtbild* exhibition and, 155; *Foto-Auge* and, 70; *Gestaltung der Reklame*, 59, 125–26, 199, 214–16; *Kunst der Werbung* exhibition and, 149–50, 151; photography and, 126; statistics design and, 138–39

C
Canis, Johannes, 124, 128–29
Chmelowa, Nina, 40
Communist Party of Germany (KPD), 67, 78
Composing Room, The, 185, 187n42
Congress of Constructivists and Dadaists, 22, 123
Congress of the Union of International Progressive Artists, 22
Constructivism, 3, 6, 8, 22, 24, 28, 91–92, 100, 105, 123–24, 203; in Poland, 168; technological limitations in, 158n18; Tschichold and, 34–35, 53, 68, 79, 104, 227
corporate and event identity, xiv, 12, 135–50, 161n80
Crawford, William, 159n60
Cubism, 53, 230
curriculum development in graphic design, 108–21, 159nn47–48; in the 1950s, 168
Cyliax, Walter, 156, 167
Czechoslovakia, New Typography in, 12, 66, 80, 171–75, 184

D
Dada, 11, 15n11, 22, 53, 63, 82n13, 90–91, 98, 100, 224
Dalang, Max, 166
Dana, John, 181
Deffke, Wilhelm, 116, 165
Delitsch, Hermann, 17, 82n2
De Stijl, 22, 34, 53, 98–99, 121, 123, 230
Deutsche Werkbund (DWB), 37, 68, 144
Deutschland-Ausstellung, 166
Dexel, Walter, 13, 36, 45, 48, 105, 111, 116–20, 165, 186n5; corporate identity projects of, 136, 143; "Was ist neue Typographie?," 59, 206–9
Domela, César, 48, 152; *Fotomontage* exhibition and, 155–56
Double Crown Club, 80, 180
Dyrynk, Karel, 172

E
Ehmke, Fritz, 134
Ehrenburg, Ilya, 24, 92
Ehrlich, Frederic, 182–83
Ekran (Czech journal), 172–73
Entartete Kunst (Degenerate Art) exhibition, 165
Erbar, xiv, 57, 151, 181
Erbar, Jakob, xiv

Erste russische Kunstausstellung, 22
expressionism, 21–22, 30
Egység (Hungarian journal), 24

F
Fagus (shoe-last factory), 141–42
Feininger, Lyonel, 30, 83n18
Film und Foto exhibition (FiFo), 4, 68–70, 144, 147, 155
Fischer, Alfred, 149
Fleischmann, Gerd, 159n50
Fleuron: A Journal of Typography, 80–81
Form, Die, 85n76, 106, 134, 161n79
Fraktur, xiv–xv, 58, 75, 186n8, 203; Hitler's dislike of, xiv, 186n8
Frenzel, Hermann Karl, 134
Frutiger, Adrian, 168
Futura, xiv, 37, 38, 57–59, 61, 84n64, 151
Futurism, 11, 63, 88–90, 189; Pessoa on, 157n6

G
G (journal), 104, 121, 158n28, 199
Gabo, Naum, 22
Gebrauchsgraphik, 66, 134
Gefesselter Blick, 68, 85n82, 155–57, 167
German cultural identity and typography, xiii–xiv, 18, 57
Giedion, Sigfried, 110, 174
Giesecke, Albert, 36, 84n36
Gill, Eric, 179–80
Goebbels, Joseph, 164
Gothic script. *See* blackletter
Goudy, Frederic, 180–81
Graeff, Werner, 121, 152, 160n57
Graphis (Swiss journal), 168, 186n14
Graphische Berufsschule, 37, 39, 77
Grimm, Jacob, 55, 204
Gropius, Walter, 30, 35, 57, 110; Bauhaus and, 26, 27–28, 83n19, 94, 114, 185; Fagus and, 141
Gutenberg, Johannes, 52, 47, 196

H
halftone process, 96, 158nn21–22, 230–31
Hausmann, Raoul, 98
Havinden, Ashley, 160n77
Heartfield, John, 70, 144, 152
Helvetica, 168
Hepworth, Barbara, 80
Hertwig, Max, 121, 134
Hitler, Adolf, xiv, 77, 164, 186n8
Hofmann, Armin, 167
Hoffmann, Eduard, 168
Hoffmann, Hermann, 38, 186n9
Hungary, New Typography in, 24, 36, 66, 175–76
Huszar, Vilmos, 98

I

Insel Verlag, 20
International Typographic Style ("Swiss Style"), 167–68, 185
Isotype (International System of Typographic Picture Education), 139
Itten, Johannes, 28

J

Janus-Presse, 20, 82n7
Johnson, Philip, 184
Johnston, Edward, 18

K

Kabel, 57, 181
Kalivoda, František, 80, 172, 174–75
Karl Schnabel Verlag, 19–20, 82n6
Kassák, Lajos, 5, 6, 48, 53, 132, 152; "Reklám és modern tipográfia," 132–34
Kauffer, Edward McKnight, 80
Kaufmann, Edgar, Jr., 184
Keller, Ernst, 167
kineticism, 95
Klee, Paul, 30
Klinger, Julius, 121
Klutsis, Gustav, 6, 155
Knapp, Alfred, 160n76
Kner, Imre, 175
Koch, Rudolf, 18, 20–21, 82n9, 109
Koch-Otte, Benita, 28
Kozma, Lajos, 175–76
Kracauer, Siegfried, 14n2, 22, 87
Kunst der Werbung (exhibition), 149–50

L

Lane, Allen, 12
Larisch, Rudolf von, 17–18, 82n2
Le Corbusier, 1, 60, 106
Léger, Fernand, 106
Leistikow, Hans, 70, 152–53; and Grete, 110–11, 159n41, 163
letterheads, 40–41, 62–63
Lichtbild, Das (exhibition), 155, 161n98
Lissitzky, El, 3, 6–8, 14, 22, 24, 34, 40, 48, 53, 63, 68, 83n33, 110, 114, 155, 198; on advertising, 122–23, 130; on "America," 133; background of, 15n7; at FiFo, 70; Electro-Library concept of, 32, 95, 158n19, 190; *Merz* and, 100, 102; photography and, 59; Pressa and, 144–45; on Tschichold's "elementare typographie," 35;
PUBLICATIONS: *About Two Squares*, 8–9, 30, 32; "Topographie der Typographie," 7, 31–32, 54, 95, 100, 102, 190; "Typographische Tatsachen," 96–97, 193–94;

Veshch/Gegenstand/Objet (with Ehrenburg), 24, 30, 82n16, 92
Lissitzky-Küppers, Sophie, 6–7
Lonberg-Holm, Knud, 185
Loos, Adolf, 54–55, 204
lowercase proposals: by Baumeister, 204; by Dexel, 206; by Roh, 57, 210; by Tschichold, 55–57, 200–201
Ludwig & Mayer foundry, xiv, 151
Lukács, Georg, 14n2, 22
Lund Humphries Ltd, 80
Luther, Martin, 57

M

MA, 66–67, 132, 158n10, 175
Malevich, Kazimir, 8, 53, 100, 168
Mallarmé, Stéphane, 90, 157n5, 189
Marinetti, Filippo Tommaso, 15n11, 53, 89–90, 224; 224; "Rivoluzione tipografica," 54, 157n3, 189
Matter, Herbert, 79, 185
May, Ernst, 60, 109–11, 153, 159n39; May Brigade, 163
Mayakovsky, Vladimir, 63–65
Meisterschule für Deutschlands Buchdrucke, 39–40, 77
McMurtrie, Douglas C., 181
Merz (journal), 7, 11, 32, 54, 95, 99–103, 134; origin of name, 98; on typographic advertising, 123
Meyer, Adolf, 27–28, 141
Michel, Robert, 48, 136, 151–52
Midcentury Modern style, 185
Miedinger, Max, 168
Moholy, Lucia, 6–7, 14n6, 22
Moholy-Nagy, László, 3, 6, 8, 13, 22, 24, 34, 35, 45, 53, 68, 83n17, 154, 164; background of, 92–93, 158nn10–11; Bauhaus and, 28–30, 32; in *Gefesselter Blick*, 156–57; photography and, 59, 70–71, 93–94, 192; *Telehor* dedicated to, 174–75
PUBLICATIONS: "Die neue Typographie," 6, 14, 28–29, 31, 54, 59, 88, 92, 191–92; *Malerei, Photographie, Film*, 93–95; "Produktion—Reproduktion," 157n2; "Typophoto," 32, 59, 94–95, 195–97; *Von Material zu Architektur*, 158n13
Molnár, Farkas, 32, 176, 177
Molzahn, Johannes, 13, 32, 45, 49, 105, 152; on advertising, 134; corporate identity projects of, 141, 143, 146; later career of, 165; "Letterhead statement," 217; Magdeburg activities of, 114–18, 147; "Nicht mehr lesen! Sehen!," 147
Mondrian, Piet, 17, 53, 100
Monotype Corporation, 179

Morison, Stanley, 80, 179, 180
Morris, William, 18, 130, 160n68, 180
Muche, Georg, 27–28
Müller-Brockmann, Josef, 167, 186n14
Museum of Modern Art (MoMA), 184–85

N
Nazism, 12, 77–78; purge of graphic designers by, 164–65, 186n3
Nederlandsche Kabelfabriek, 8, 136
Neoplasticism. See De Stijl
Netherlands, New Typography in the, 3, 6, 12, 36, 66, 98, 154, 176–78. See also De Stijl
Neue Grafik (Swiss journal), 168, 186n14
Neurath, Otto, 138, 140
New Frankfurt, 87, 109–10, 159n39; *Das neue Frankfurt* (journal), 110–11, 153, 159n40
New Objectivity, 3, 14n2, 87, 126
New Photography, 72, 87, 126–27, 136
"New Typography" term, 3, 6, 13, 88
New Vision, 94, 158n13
Nicholson, Ben, 80
Novembergruppe, 105

O
ornaments, 34, 54, 167, 175, 201, 205, 227
orthography reform, 55–57
Orwell, George, 138

P
painting, graphic designers' view of, 105, 158n29, 223
paper sizing, 62, 74; DIN standards for, 62, 74, 85n72, 138, 201; "Normalisierung der Papierformate," 62, 211–13
pedagogy. *See* curriculum development in graphic design
Penguin Books, 12–13, 64
Pessoa, Fernando, 90, 157n6
Philobiblon, 30–31
Phoebus-Palast, 40–44, 84n38
photography and typography, 59–60, 68–72, 93, 95–96, 130, 144; Burchartz on, 126; Moholy-Nagy on, 192, 196–97; Tschichold on, 226
photomontage, 42–44, 59, 61, 110, 226; Czech examples of, 172–73; *Fotomontage* exhibition, 155–56, 161n99; Lissitzky and, 70–71, 155; Moholy-Nagy and, 94; Schuitema and, 176, 178
poetry and typography, 90, 97, 99, 157n5
Poland, New Typography in, 12, 168–71
politics and typography, xii–xv, 36, 57–58, 165
Porstmann, Walter, 56–57, 200–201
Praesens (Polish journal), 169–70
Pressa (exhibition), 144

R
Rabelais, François, 194
Rasch, Heinz and Bodo, 85n82, 155–56
Ray, Man, 53
Read, Herbert, 80
Reidemeister, Marie, 138
Reimann School, 120–21, 165
Renger-Patzsch, Albert, 126–27
Renner, Paul, xiv, 37–39, 57, 76, 77, 109, 111, 159nn37–38, 165
Richter, Hans, 22, 158n28
Rietveld, Gerrit, 99
Ring neue Werbegestalter, Der, 4, 8, 11, 48–49, 68, 85n82, 121, 150–56; exhibitions by, 154–55; final years of, 164
Rodchenko, Aleksandr, 6, 34, 53, 63–64, 65, 72–73, 91–92, 155
Rogers, Bruce, 181
Roh, Franz, 57, 77; *Foto-Auge* and Fototek series (with Tschichold), 70–72, 147; "Warum 4 Alphabete," 57, 210
Rossman, Zdeněk, 48, 80, 172–73
Ruge, Willi, 69–70

S
sanserif forms, xiv, xv, 13, 34, 42, 57–58, 75, 81, 110, 168, 179; Baumeister on, 107, 203–4; postwar adoption of, 167–68; Tschichold on, 225
Schlemmer, Oskar, 105, 111, 114
Schmidt, Joost, 136–37, 153
Schuitema, Paul, 48, 136, 152, 154, 176
Schwabe, Benno, 78
Schwitters, Helma, 152
Schwitters, Kurt, 3–4, 8, 11, 14, 22, 45, 53–54, 98–100; Merz term by, 98; Merz-Werbe studio, 147–4; Nazi ridicule of, 165 Ring founding by, 48–49, 151–54, 161n92. *See also Merz* PUBLICATIONS: *Die neue Gestaltung in der Typographie* (brochure), 148, 150, 151; "Thesen über Typographie," 32, 102–4, 198–99; "Ursonate," 11
Seitz, Joseph, 49
Siemsen, Hans, 122
Simon, Oliver, 80, 180
Soupault, Philippe, 99
Soviet Union: avant-garde movements in, 3, 8, 22, 24, 34–35; language reform in, xiii
Stalin, Joseph, xiii
Stam, Mart, 32, 60
standardization, 56, 60, 62–64, 138
statistics and typography, 138–40
Stepanova, Varvara, 34, 91–92
Strzemiński, Władysław, 6, 48, 168–71; "Druk funkcjonalny," 171, 228–31; Tschichold and, 169–70

Suprematism, 8, 34, 53n
Sutnar, Ladislav, 6, 48, 80, 172, 185

T
Taeuber-Arp, Sophie, 22
Tatlin, Vladimir, 53, 100
Taut, Bruno, 60, 114, 116
Taut, Max, 49
Teige, Karel, 5, 6, 48, 152, 154, 172, 227
Telehor (Czech journal), 162, 173–74
Tér és Forma (Hungarian journal), 175–76, 177
Tiemann, Walter, 20, 67
Times New Roman, 179
Trump, Georg, 40, 48, 76, 152; City typeface, 181; later career of, 165–66
Tschichold, Edith, 6–7, 12, 14n6, 15n2, 37, 40, 78
Tschichold, Jan: background of, xii, 2, 17–20, 105; book design and, 12–13, 63–64, 167; British influence on, 80, 180, 187n26; design collection of, 5, 11, 12, 14nn3–4, 40, 48, 66, 72–73, 79, 140, 186n10; on exhibitions, 144; film posters by, 41–47; letterheads and stationery by, 40–41, 48; on Lang's *Metropolis*, 84n40; lowercase preference of, 55–57, 200–201; name changes by, xii, 3, 30–31, 40, 82n1; Nazi arrest of, xiv, 12, 78, 164; Penguin Books career, 12–13, 64, 167; photography and, 59–60; political views of, xii, 12, 36–38, 68, 78; Ring membership of, 8, 48, 152; standardization preference of, 57, 62, 138, 201, 225; statistics display and, 140; Swiss exile of, 78–80, 166, 171; teaching career of, 11, 39–40, 77–78
PUBLICATIONS: *Die Konstruktivisten*, 79; *Die neue Typographie* (book), xii, 2–3, 11–12, 45, 49–68, 73–74, 84n42, 128, 150–51, 155–56, 172, 182; "Die neue Typographie" (lecture), 39; "Die neue Typographie" (manifesto), 31–32; *Eine Stunde Druckgestaltung*, 74; "elementare typographie," 11–12, 32, 34–38, 45, 53, 54, 59, 66, 113, 153, 161n95, 166, 172, 200–201; *Foto-Auge* and Fototek series (with Roh), 70–72, 147; *Schriftschreiben für setzer*, 74, 77; *Typografische Entwurfstechnik*, 74–75, 77; "Was ist und was will die neue Typografie?," 59, 74, 222–27; "Wo stehen wir heute?," 85n89
Tschichold, Peter, 12, 77
Typographische Mitteilungen, 11, 31–36, 66, 83n26, 134, 224; New Typography survey by, 75–76, 164
Tzara, Tristan, 22, 53, 90–91, 98, 99

U
Üecht Gruppe, 106
Uitz, Béla, 24
Ultra Modern, 181, 183
United Kingdom, New Typography in, 80, 160n77, 179–80, 187n27
United States, New Typography in, 180–85. *See also* advertising and typography
Univers, 168
Updike, Daniel Berkeley, 180

V
van de Velde, Henry, 25, 83n18
van Doesburg, Theo, 22, 27, 53, 66, 82n13, 98, 99, 114, 121, 123, 152; Lissitzky on, 158n29; Ring membership and, 152, 161n94; teaching career of, 160n55
Vordemberge-Gildewart, Friedrich, 48, 152

W
Werkman, H. N., 178, 186n22
Wichert, Fritz, 108–10
Wiertz, Jupp, 134
Wieynck, Heinrich, 20, 66–67, 222
Wilhelm-Kästner, Kurt, 149
Wohnung, Die (exhibition), 107–8, 109, 144
Wohnung und Werkraum (exhibition), 146, 147
Wolpe, Berthold, 82n9
Worringer, Wilhelm, 82n10
Wright, Frank Lloyd, 110

Y
Young, Edward, 13

Z
Zdanevitch, Ilia, 90–91, 100
Zwart, Piet, 5, 6, 8, 10, 48, 136–37, 152, 177–78; *Foto-Auge* and, 70